.95

W9-BAM-520

EGO, HUNGER

AND AGGRESSION

EGO, HUNGER
AND AGGRESSION

THE BEGINNING
OF GESTALT THERAPY

BY F. S. Perls

Vintage Books
A Division of Random House
New York

Copyright © 1969, 1947 by F. S. Perls

All rights reserved under International and Pan-American Copyright Conventions. Published in the United States by Random
House, Inc., New York, and simultaneously in Canada by Random House of Canada Limited, Toronto. Originally published
in Great Britain by Allen & Unwin Ltd., London.

Library of Congress Catalog Card Number: 68-28547
Manufactured in the United States of America

To the Memory of

MAX WERTHEIMER

For today's reader, *Ego, Hunger, and Aggression* represents the transition from orthodox psychoanalysis to the Gestalt approach. It contains many ideas which even now—after twenty years—have not found their way into modern psychiatry.

The concepts of here-and-now reality, the organism-as-a-whole, and the dominance of the most urgent need are being accepted. However, the significance of aggression as a biological force, the relation of aggression to assimilation, the symbolic nature of the Ego, the phobic attitude in neurosis, the organism-environment unity are far from being understood.

In the last decade the awareness theory has been widely accepted, and is practiced under the names of sensitivity training and T-groups. The significance of spontaneous non-verbal expression (such as movements of the hands and eyes, posture, voice, etc.) has been recognized. In the therapeutic setting, the emphasis begins to shift from the phobic (so-called objective) couch situation to the encounter of a human therapist with, not a case, but another human being.

These are good beginnings, but there is still much to do. The probability that individual and long-range therapy might both be obsolete has not yet dawned upon the vast majority of therapists and patients. True enough, groups and workshops find increasing acceptance, but more for their economic feasibility than for their efficacy. Yet the individual session should be the exception rather than the rule. Perhaps this sounds as heretical as a proposal I made some time ago: Dealing with behavior out of the here-and-now is a waste of time.

Great strides have been made since Freud's monumental discoveries. To note a few important ones: Sullivan's emphasis on the self-esteem; Berne's concept of game playing; Roger's of feed-back; and, especially, Reich's bringing down to earth the psychology of resistances. The development from symptom to character to existential therapy to the arrival of humanistic psychology is most promising.

Since I wrote the manuscript for *Gestalt Therapy,* I have developed many new ideas. Most important, I have finally succeeded in breaking through the impasse, the point of status quo at which the average therapy seems to get caught. Without adequate perspective, a therapist is lost from the beginning. The use of the best technique or the most ingenious concept will not prevent the patient from counterbalancing the efforts of the therapist. This freezes the therapy and prevents true maturation.

Ego, Hunger, and Aggression will facilitate the acquisition of this perspective. As perspective is based upon polarities and centering, the first chapter, although not easy to read, is important. As for the rest, much of its historical material is now obsolete, but the significance of misplaced aggression is as valid today as it was when I wrote this book. A return of the power of aggression from the destruction of cities and people to assimilation and growth...a consummation devoutly to be wished... Bloody unlikely.

Frederick S. Perls
1969

INTENTION

"Psycho-analysis is founded securely upon the observations of the facts of mental life; and for that reason its superstructure is still incomplete and subject to constant alteration."—Sigm. Freud.

The aim of this book is to examine some psychological and psychopathological reactions of the human organism within its environment.

The central conception is the theory that the organism is striving for the maintenance of a balance which is continuously disturbed by its needs, and regained through their gratification or elimination.

Difficulties arising between the individual and society will result in the production of delinquency and neurosis. Neurosis is characterized by many forms of avoidance, mainly the avoidance of contact.

The relations which exist between individual and society, and between social groups, cannot be understood without considering the problem of aggression.

In the present war there is no other word more used or more despised than "aggression." A great number of books have been published which not only condemn aggression but attempt to find a remedy for it, but neither the analysis nor the meaning of aggression have been sufficiently clarified. Even Rauschning stops short of the biological foundation of aggression. On the other hand the remedies prescribed for the cure of aggression are always the same old ineffective repressive agents: idealism and religion.

We have not learnt anything about the dynamic of aggression in spite of Freud's warning that repressed energies not only do not disappear but may even become more dangerous and more effective if driven underground.

When I set out to examine the nature of aggression I became more and more convinced that there was no such energy as aggression, but that aggression was a biological function which in our time had turned into an instrument of collective insanity.

Whereas by the use of the new intellectual tools *holism* (field conception) and *semantics* (the meaning of meaning) our theoretical outlook can now be tremendously improved, I am afraid that with regard to collective aggression I am not in a position to offer a practical remedy.

Instead of looking at neurosis and aggression from a purely psychologistic point of view, the holistic-semantic approach is made which reveals a number of shortcomings even in the best developed of the psychological methods: namely, psycho-analysis.

Psycho-analysis stresses the importance of the Unconscious and the sex instinct, of the past and of causality, of associations, transference and

7

repressions, but it either under-estimates or else neglects the functions of the Ego and of the hunger instinct, of the present and of purposiveness, of concentration, spontaneous reactions and retroflection.

After the gaps have been filled in, and dubious psycho-analytical terms such as libido, death-instinct and others examined, the larger scope of the new concept will be demonstrated in the second part dealing with mental assimilation and the paranoid character.

The third part is designed to give detailed instructions for a therapeutic technique resulting from the changed theoretical outlook. As avoidance is assumed to be the central symptom of nervous disorders, I have replaced the method of free associations or flight of ideas by that antidote of avoidance—concentration.

CONTENTS

PART ONE

HOLISM AND
PSYCHO-ANALYSIS

I

DIFFERENTIAL THINKING

The urge to know all about oneself and one's fellow-men has prompted young intellectuals of all times to turn to the great philosophers for information about the human personality. Some achieved a satisfactory outlook, but many remained dissatisfied and disappointed. They either found very little realism in academic philosophy and psychology, or they felt inferior and stupid, apparently unable to grasp such complicated philosophical and scientific concepts.

For a long period of my own life I belonged to those who, though interested, could not derive any benefit from the study of academic philosophy and psychology, until I came across the writings of Sigmund Freud, who was then still completely outside academic science, and S. Friedlaender's philosophy of "Creative Indifference."

Freud showed that man has created Philosophy, Culture and Religion and that, to solve the riddles of our existence, we have to take our bearings from man and not from any outside agent, as all religions and many philosophers have maintained. The interdependence of observer and observed facts, as postulated by present-day science, has been fully confirmed by Freud's findings. Consequently his system, too, should not be considered without including himself as the creator.

There is hardly a sphere of human activity where Freud's research was not creative, or at least stimulating. To bring order into the relations of the many observed facts, he developed a number of theories which together formed the first system of a genuinely *structural* psychology. Since the time when Freud built his system upon the basis of inadequate material on the one hand, and certain personal complexes on the other, we have gained so much new scientific insight that we can make the attempt to reinforce the structure of the psycho-analytical system where its incompleteness and even faultiness is most obvious:

(a) In the treatment of psychological facts as if they existed isolated from the organism.

(b) In the use of the linear association-psychology as the basis for a four-dimensional system.

(c) In the neglect of the phenomenon of differentiation.

In this revision of psycho-analysis I intend:

(a) To replace the psychological by an organismic concept (I.8).
(b) To replace association-psychology by gestalt-psychology (I.2).
(c) To apply differential thinking, based upon S. Friedlaender's "Creative Indifference."

Differential thinking shows a resemblance to the dialectical theories, but without their metaphysical implications. It therefore has the advantage of saving heated discussions on the subject (as many readers will have acquired either an enthusiasm for, or an idiosyncrasy against the dialectical method and philosophy) without sacrificing the valuable nucleus contained in the dialectical way of thinking.

The dialectical method can be misused, and often has been misused: sometimes one may even feel inclined to agree with Kant's remarks to the effect that dialectic is an *ars sophistica disputatoria*, idle talk (Geschwaetzigkeit)—an attitude, however, which did not prevent him from applying dialectical thinking himself.

A great deal has to be said against Hegel's dialectical idealism as a philosophical attempt to replace God by other metaphysical concepts. Marx's transposition of the dialectical method of materialism is progress, but not a solution. His mixture of scientific research with wishful thinking has likewise not achieved dialectical realism.

My intention is to draw a clear distinction between dialectics as a philosophical concept, and the usefulness of certain rules as found and applied in Hegel's and Marx's philosophy. These rules coincide approximately with what we might call "differential thinking." Personally, I am of the opinion that in many cases this method is an appropriate means of arriving at new scientific insight, leading to results where other intellectual methods, e.g. that of thinking in terms of cause and effect, fail.

Many a reader will be reluctant to follow a rather theoretical discussion as an introduction to a book dealing with problems of practical psychology. But he needs the acquaintance with certain basic concepts pervading the whole of this book. Although the practical value of these ideas will become apparent only through following up their repeated application, he should at least right from the beginning know their gross structure. This method has a further advantage: previously it was accepted that the scientist observes a number of facts, and draws conclusions from them. We have, however, now come to appreciate that everybody's observations are dictated by specific interests, by preconceived ideas and by an—often unconscious—attitude which collects and selects facts accordingly. In other words: there is no such thing as objective science, and, as every writer has some subjective viewpoint, every book must depend upon the mentality of the writer. In psychology more than in any other science observer and observed facts are inseparable. The most conclusive orientation should be obtained if we could find a point from which the observer could gain the most comprehensive and undistorted view. I believe that such a viewpoint has been found by S. Friedlaender.

In his book *Creative Indifference*, Friedlaender brings forward the theory that every event is related to a zero-point from which a differentiation into opposites takes place. These *opposites* show *in their specific context* a great affinity to each other. By remaining alert in the centre, we can acquire a creative ability of seeing both sides of an occurrence and completing an incomplete half. By avoiding a one-sided outlook we gain a much deeper insight into the structure and function of the organism.

We might gain a preliminary orientation from the following example: Looking at a group of six living beings: an imbecile (i), an average "normal" citizen (n), an outstanding statesman (s), a tortoise (t), a cat (c) and a race horse (r), it strikes us immediately that they sort themselves out into two groups—human beings and animals, and that of the infinite number of characteristics of living beings each group has a specific quality: (i), (n) and (s) show varying degrees of intelligence; (t), (c) and (r) varying degrees of velocity—they "differ" from each other in intelligence or speed. If we sort them out further we can easily establish an order: n's I.Q. (Intelligence Quotient) will be found to be larger than i's and s's larger than n's, just as c's speed is greater than that of t, and r's greater than c's $(s > n > i; r > c > t)$.

We can now choose more animals and human beings—each a little different from the next in the selected characteristics, we can measure the differences, we can even with the help of the differential calculus fill in the gaps, but finally we come to a point where the ways of mathematics and psychology seem to part.

The mathematical language does not know "slow" and "quick," only "slower" and "quicker," but in psychology we operate with terms like "slow," "quick," "stupid," or "intelligent." Such terms are conceived from a "normal" point of view, which is "in"-different to all those events which do not impress us as being out of the ordinary. We are indifferent to everything which is "not differentiated" from our subjective point of view. The interest evoked in us is "naught."

This "naught" has a two-fold significance, that of a *beginning* and that of a *centre*. In the counting of primitive tribes and children naught is the beginning of the *row*, 0, 1, 2, 3, etc.—in arithmetic it is the middle of a plus/minus *system*, it is a zero-point with two branches stretching in the plus and minus direction. If we apply the two functions of naught to our examples, we can either make two rows or two systems. If we assume that (i) has an I.Q. of 50, (n) of 100, and (s) of 150 we can construct a row: 0, 50, 100, 150. This is an order of increasing intelligence. If, however, we accept an I.Q. of 100 as normal, then we have a plus/minus system: —50, 0, +50, in which the numbers indicate the degree of differentiation from the zero (centre)-point.

Actually there are many systems in our organism centred around the zero-point of normality, health, indifference, etc. Each of these systems differentiates into two opposites like plus/minus, clever/stupid, quick/slow, etc.

Perhaps the most obvious example from the psychological sphere is the pleasure/pain system. Its zero-point is—as will be shown later—the balance of the organism. Any disturbance of this balance is experienced as painful, the return to it as pleasant.

The physician is well acquainted with the metabolic zero-point (basic metabolic rate) which, though arrived at by a complicated formula, has the practical aspect of normal $= 0$. The deviations (increased or decreased metabolism) are expressed in relation to the zero-point.

Differential thinking—the insight into the working of such systems—provides us with a mental precision tool which is neither extremely difficult to grasp nor to handle. I shall restrict the discussion to those three points which are indispensable for the understanding of this book: opposites, pre-difference (zero-point) and degree of differentiation.

* * *

The three figures Nos. 1a, 1b and 1c may be helpful in clarifying my conception of differential thinking, in so far as it concerns my contentions here.

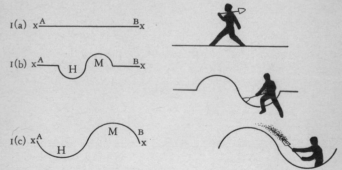

FIGURE 1a

Let A–B represent the surface of a piece of ground. We take any point as the zero-point, the point from which differentiation starts.

FIGURE 1b

We have differentiated parts of the ground into a hole (H) and its corresponding mound (M). Differentiation is gradual and proceeds simultaneously (in time) and in exactly the same degree to either side (in space). Every spadeful of soil produces a deficit in the ground which is heaped as a surplus upon the hillock (polarization).

FIGURE 1C

Differentiation is finished. The entire level has been changed into two opposites, hole and mound.

Thinking in opposites is the quintessence of dialectics. Opposites *within the same context* are more closely related to each other than to any other conception. In the field of colour one thinks of white in connection with black, rather than with green or pink. Day and night, warm and cold, in fact thousands of such opposites are coupled in everyday language. We can even go so far as to say that neither "day" nor "warm" would exist either in fact or in words, if they were not contrasted by their opposites "night" and "cold." Instead of awareness, sterile indifference would prevail. In the terminology of psycho-analysis we find wish-fulfilment/ wish-frustration; sadism/masochism; conscious/unconscious; reality-principle/pleasure-principle, and so on.[1]

Freud has seen and recorded as "one of our most surprising discoveries" that an element in the manifest or remembered dream which admits of an opposite may stand for itself, for its opposite or for both together.

He also draws our attention to the fact that in the oldest languages known to us, opposites such as light—dark, big—small were expressed by the same root words (the so-called antithetical sense of primal words). When spoken, these were differentiated into their two different meanings by intonation and accompanying gestures, and, when written, were differentiated by the addition of a determinative, i.e. a picture or sign which was not meant to be expressed orally by sounds.

For our two words "high" and "deep," the Latin has only one: "*altus*," which simply means extending in the vertical plane; the situation or the context determines whether we translate this word by "high" or "deep."

---

[1] Roget, in his *Thesaurus*, appreciated how much the world of words exists in opposites:

"For the purpose of exhibiting with greater distinction the relations between words expressing opposite and correlative ideas, I have, whenever the subject admitted of such an arrangement, placed them in two parallel columns on the same page, so that each group of expression may be readily contrasted with those which occupy the adjacent column, and constitute their antithesis."

And further, indicating that the opposites are dictated not by words but by their context:

"It often happens that the same word has several correlative terms, according to the different relations in which it is considered. Thus, to the word 'giving' are opposed both 'receiving' and 'taking': the former correlation having reference to the persons concerned in the transfer, while the latter relates to the mode of transfer. 'Old' has for opposites both 'new' and 'young' according to its application to things or living beings. 'Attack' and 'defence' are correlative terms, as are also 'attack' and 'resistance.' 'Resistance' again has for its correlative 'submission.' 'Truth' in the abstract is opposed to 'error,' but the opposite to truth communicated is falsehood," etc.

Similarly the Latin "*sacer*" means "taboo," which in translation is usually transcribed as either "sacred" or "accursed."

Thinking in opposites is deeply rooted in the human organism. Differentiation into opposites is an essential quality of our mentality and of life itself. It is not difficult to acquire the art of polarization, provided that one keeps the point of pre-difference in mind. Otherwise mistakes will occur, leading to arbitrary and wrong dualisms. For the religious person "Heaven and Hell" are correct antipodes, but "God and the World" are not. In psycho-analysis we find love and hatred as proper opposites, but sex- and death-instinct as incorrect poles.

Opposites come into existence by differentiation of "something not differentiated," for which I suggest the term "pre-different." The point whence the differentiation starts is usually called zero-point.[1]

The zero-point is either given by the two opposites—as in the case of a magnet—or is determined more or less arbitrarily. In measuring temperatures, for instance, science has accepted the temperature of melting ice as zero-point: the Fahrenheit thermometer, still in common use in many parts of the world, chooses as zero-point a temperature corresponding to 17.8 of the Celsius scale. For medical purposes one could introduce a thermometer with the normal body temperature as zero-point. Usually we differentiate between warm and cold according to the awareness of our organism. On leaving a hot bath we perceive as cold the temperature of a room which we would describe as pleasantly warm after a cold bath.

The situation, the "field," is a decisive factor in the choice of the zero-point. If Chamberlain on his return from Munich had been greeted with the chorus, "Down with the guttersnipe Hitler!" there would probably have been an outcry, a protest at having thus insulted the head of a friendly state, whereas two years later these words became the British slogan.

---

[1] Most cosmogenic myths and philosophies try to explain the coming into being of the universe by assuming a primeval stage of complete non-differentiation. This pre-different state is the Chinese Wu Gi, which is symbolized by a simple circle O, and denotes the non-beginning, a conception similar to the Biblical *tahu wawohu* (Chaos before the creation).

The Tai Gi by a symbol expresses the progressive differentiation into opposites and corresponds in its meaning to the Biblical story of Creation.

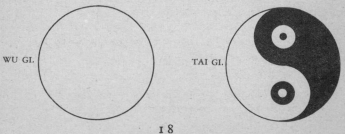

WU GI.   TAI GI.

Hitler was as much a guttersnipe in 1938 as in 1940, but the emotional zero-point of the British had changed considerably.

S. Friedlaender differentiates between the uninterested detachment—the "I-don't-care" attitude—and "creative indifference." Creative indifference is full of interest, extending towards both sides of the differentiation. It is by no means identical with an absolute zero-point, but will always have an aspect of balance. One may cite as examples from the medical sphere the amount of thyroxine in the human organism, or the pH quotient: the opposites (the deviations from the zero-point) being Grave's disease or myxoedema, and acidosis or alkalinosis, respectively.[1]

It has to be emphasized that the two (or more) branches of a differentiation develop simultaneously, and that, generally, the extension is equal on both sides. In a magnet the intensity of the attracting energy of both poles increases and decreases equally with the distance of the poles from the zero-point. The amount of differentiation, though often neglected as being "only a matter of degree," is of great importance. Beneficial drug and deadly poison, though opposite in their effect, are distinguished only by degree. Quantity is transformed into quality. With lowered tension pain turns into pleasure, and vice versa, through mere changes in degree.

Here is an example of "thinking in opposites" which may serve to show the advantage of this form of thinking. Let us assume you have suffered a disappointment. Probably you will be inclined to blame persons or circumstances. If you polarize "disappointment" you will find as its opposite: "fulfilled expectation." You thereby gain a new aspect—the knowledge that there exists a functional connection between your disappointments and your expectations: great expectation—great disappoint-

[1] Roget's remarks to this theme are: "In many cases two ideas which are completely opposed to each other admit of an intermediate or neutral idea equi-distant from both: all these being expressible by corresponding definite terms. Thus in the following examples the words in the first and third columns, which express opposite ideas, admit of the intermediate sense with reference to the former:

Identity	Difference	Contrariety
Beginning	Middle	End
Past	Present	Future

In other cases the intermediate word is simply the negative of each of two opposite positions, as for example:

| Convexity | Flatness | Concavity |
| Desire | Indifference | Aversion |

Sometimes the intermediate word is the proper standard with which each of the extremes is compared, as in the case of

| Insufficiency | Sufficiency | Redundance |

For here the middle term, sufficiency, is equally opposed, on the one hand, to insufficiency, and, on the other, to redundance."

ment; little expectation—little disappointment; no expectation—no disappointment.[1]

The words "differentiation" and "progress" are often used almost as synonyms. The highly differentiated members of a well organized society are called specialists. If they were eliminated the proper functioning of the whole organization would be seriously impeded. The development of an embryo is a differentiation into diverse kinds of cells and tissues with correspondingly different functions. If highly complicated cells in the finished organism are destroyed a *regression* to the production of less differentiated cells takes place (e.g. scars). If a person with insufficiently developed ego-functions encounters problems in life too difficult for solution, those problems are avoided and there is no progress to new differentiations and developments, but sometimes a retrogression involving parts of previous development. Such a regression, however, seldom reverts to a truly infantile level.

K. Goldstein has demonstrated this regression in soldiers with lesions of the brain. In such cases, not only do those parts of the personality which correspond to the injured part of the brain cease to function properly, but the whole personality retrogresses to a more primitive state. Whilst we are able to perform very complicated intellectual stunts like isolating words from their meaning, making statements like "The snow is black," such an assertion is impossible for people with certain lesions of the brain; like children they will contradict: "But that is not true, the snow is white."

* * *

In this book I intend making full use of the above demonstrated differential thinking. On the other hand I intend to be as careful as possible with the application of the law of cause and effect. Not only have recent scientific discoveries[2] thrown doubt upon the universal value of this law as the only one being capable of explaining events, but also has the indiscriminate, nearly obsessional, search for "causes" has become a stumbling block rather than a help in science as well as in everyday life. Most people take as satisfactory answers to their "why?":

Rationalization (he killed him *because* his honour demanded it);
Justification (he killed him *because* he had offended him);
Compliance (he was executed *because* the law provided the death penalty for his crime);
Excuse (he killed him by chance *because* the trigger went off);

[1] A comparatively recent attempt to polarize opposites in order to form a new theory of the universe has been made by A. S. Eddington. Here the differentiation is called bifurcation and the poles are the symmetrical (space, time and gravitation) and the anti-symmetrical (electro-magnetic) fields.

[2] Planck's quantum theory and Heisenberg and S. Nordinger's "principle of uncertainty" arising from the disorderly behaviour of the quantum energies.

Identity (he arrived late at the office *because* he missed the bus);

Purpose (he went to town *because* he wanted to do some shopping).

It is preferable and productive of excellent results to forgo causal explanations of events and to restrict oneself to a *description* of them—to ask "how?" instead of "why?" Modern science has realized more and more that all relevant questions can be answered by exact and detailed description.

Causal explanation, furthermore, applies only to isolated strings of events. In reality we find over-determination (Freud) or coincidence—many causes of greater or lesser significance converging into the specific event.

A man has been killed by a tile falling from the roof of a house—what is the cause of his death?

There are innumerable causes. The time he passed the dangerous spot; the storm that loosened the tile; the carelessness of the builder; the height of the house; the material of the tile; the thickness of the victim's skull; the fact that he did not see the falling tile, etc., *ad infinitum*.

In psycho-analysis (my own field of observation) one is often inclined to say "Eureka" whenever one believes one has found the "cause"; subsequently one is bound to be disappointed when the expected change in the patient's condition does not take place.

D'Alembert, Mach, Avenarius and others substituted the conception of function (if "a" changes, "b" changes) for that of causality. Mach even went so far as to call causality a clumsy conception: "A dose of cause results in a dose of effect: it is a kind of pharmaceutic weltan-schauung."

The conception of function covers the coincidences both of an event and of its prime mover—its dynamic. *In this book where I use the word "energy" I mean an aspect of a function.* Energy is immanent in the event. It is, to use a definition by F. Mauthner, "the relation between cause and effect," but should by no means be considered as a force inseparable from the event and yet in some magic way causing it.

Greek philosophy used the expression ἐνέργεια (ἐν ἔργῳ) simply as meaning action, activity, almost synonymous with πρᾶξις. Later, however, it assumed more and more the meaning of a force by which events were created. The physicist J. P. Joule (1818–89) speaks of energies which God bestowed upon matter.

This theological conception of energies as something working behind events, causing them in some inexplicable way, is purely magical. Life and death, wars and epidemics, lightning and rain, earthquakes and floods made men assume that these phenomena were produced by "energies," "causes," for instance by "gods." These god-energies were conceived according to human pattern. In the Mosaic religion they became simplified to a single god, Jehovah, who was theoretically meant to represent an energy without an image.

Such an energy, however, was too undifferentiated. It was a screen energy which, by explaining everything, explained nothing. Therefore new gods were created and, in order to distinguish them from the supernatural god-energies of ancient times, they were called powers of nature (e.g. gravitation, electricity).

An interesting example of the "return of the repressed" is found in Freud's work. Here the denial of God is followed up by the dominating power of the Libido, and later "Life" is conceived as a conflict between Eros and Thanatos, between the gods of love and death.

If we decide that causal thinking is too arbitrary and if we take our bearings rather from differential and functional thinking, we may try to attain an orientation in the manifold functions and energies constituting our existence.

Science has revealed that two energies, magnetism and electricity (which were previously considered as two distinct forces), have a number of functions in common. They were consequently brought under one heading: electro-magnetism.

On the other hand, contrary to this simplification, new complications have arisen. Thus it is assumed that dead, inorganic matter contains tremendous amounts of energy within its atoms: that gigantic joining forces keep together the particles of an atom. Millions of volts are applied to disjoin these particles and to set free the joining functions, and it is *in these joining and dis-joining processes that we encounter a law which, I am convinced, can be generally applied.*

Every change in the substance of the world occurs in space and time. Every change means that particles of the world are either drawing closer together or moving away from each other. $\Pi \acute{a} \nu \tau a \ \dot{\rho} \epsilon \tilde{\iota}$: Everything is in a state of flux—even the density of the same substance changes with differences of pressure, gravitation and temperature.

A simple and obvious example is provided by the function of magnetic iron. One side of the magnet attracts, the other side repels magnetized iron particles, and the larger the distance from the zero-point (the point of indifference) the greater are these forces.

As a rule, however, the joining and disjoining functions work simultaneously, and it is often difficult to isolate the opposites.

The joining functions in chemistry are expressed by the word affinity. In electrolysis the disjoining function of the electrical current is obvious. The destructive tendencies of lightning or of x-rays are as well known as the attraction which characterizes gravitation.

Heat is essentially a disjoining function. The atmospheric pressure, being a function of the gravitation of the earth, holds water together in a liquid form. If we either diminish this pressure (e.g. in a vacuum, or by high altitude) or if we apply heat, we overcome the joining force of the pressure.[1]

In this book I shall use the symbol ¶ for the joining function or energy, and ‡ for its opposite.

I would like to put forward a scheme which, though vague, may give an approximate idea of the distribution of the two opposing functions in human relationships.

AFFECTION	¶	¶	¶	¶
SEXUAL ACTIVITY	¶	¶	¶	‡
SADISM	¶	¶	‡	‡
AGGRESSION	¶	‡	‡	‡
DEFENCE (destruction)	‡	‡	‡	‡

Affection is the tendency to make friendly contact, to join oneself to the person towards whom one feels, or from whom one desires, tenderness. There exists a permanent wish to be in touch with the beloved or with anything belonging to him or her whose uninterrupted presence is desired.

The opposite of affection is defence, which (as a tendency to destroy) is directed against any disturbing factor, whatever this may be.

It has to be emphasized that destruction and annihilation are by no means identical. *Annihilation* means making a thing disappear, making "nil" out of "something," whilst destruction, as the word denotes, means making the "structure" only disappear. In a thing destroyed the material itself remains, though changed in its physical or even chemical condition. The disturber may be a mosquito buzzing around us, or an impulse within ourselves which we condemn, or a child's fidgeting which we dislike, regarding it as naughtiness. Anything of this nature may make us irritable, and in all these cases we wish to annihilate the disturbing factor, but we are satisfied to apply destruction, for real annihilation is never possible. A pseudo-annihilation is performed—as we shall see later—with the help of certain psychological conjuring tricks, such as forgetting, projecting, scotomizing, or by repression or flight from the issue.

Between these two extremes I have put sadism as a mixture of ¶ and ‡. The sadist loves his object and, at the same time, wants to hurt it. A milder form of sadism is teasing, its veiled hostility being easily recognized by the teased subject.

In sexual activity the presence of the ¶ is obvious. The ‡, e.g. the overcoming of resistance, is less easily recognized. But this may be so predominant that many people lose interest in any sexual activity if the partner yields too easily. It is even more difficult to realize that, in sexual

[1] The apparent paradoxical use of heat for welding and soldering—for the purpose of joining metals—is easily explained. The heat melts, disjoins the molecules; the joining takes place after the cooling.

activity, heat acts as the ‡ factor. Just as heat loosens up the contact between molecules, so in sex-life a warming up must take place before the ¶ comes into play. A person unable to melt, remaining cold (frigid) and not radiating any warmth (which is the natural means of inducing response in the partner) will probably replace this essential radiation by alcohol or bribery (e.g. flattery or presents).

There remains only aggression to be considered. In aggression the attempts to contact the hostile object are an expression of the ¶. We find in literature, for instance, many examples of how people overcome great difficulties to track down and wreak vengeance on the "villain of the piece"; and vice versa: The Big Bad Wolf takes great pains to get hold of Little Red Riding Hood.

II

PSYCHOLOGICAL APPROACH

Patient: "Yes, Doctor, I have suffered from this before."
Doctor: "Have you had treatment?"
Patient: "Yes, I saw Dr. X about it."
Doctor: "And what did he prescribe?"
Patient: "He gave me little white pills. . . ."

I wonder if there exists a general practitioner who has never received a similarly vague answer, when asking for details of previous treatment. "Little white pills" denote nothing at all; they may stand for hundreds of entirely different medicines; they are a *screen expression*.

We often come across such screen expressions which have no precise referent and which conceal instead of reveal. People speaking of nervousness may mean anxiety, irritability, annoyance, sexual tension, embarrassment and so forth. . . .

"Thinking" is one of the most common screen words, covering such heterogeneous mental processes as planning, remembering, imagining, subvocal talking and so on.

In endeavouring to clarify our minds we should avoid screen expressions, and use, instead, words expressing the precise meaning which we wish to convey. In lieu of "I thought of my childhood," "I thought you were cross," "I thought about this accident," we should say explicitly: "I remembered my childhood," "I was afraid (imagined) you were cross," "I reviewed this accident." Such language is closer to reality, expresses far more distinctly what kind of mental action is meant.

In the mental action of thinking, the use of words is involved to such a degree that we feel tempted to define thinking as subvocal, or silent talking.

This would imply that thinking is always done in words; but, for example, a chess player, in thinking, uses words to a much lesser extent than he uses visualization of the combinations of the pieces.

In other words, subvocal talking is just one form, though a very frequent form of thinking.

We may discern the opposites: vocal and subvocal talking. Their pre-differential stage can be observed in children and aborigines as mumbling, muttering and whispering, and a regression to that stage may occur in excited, aged or insane persons.

Other aspects of thinking can be found as opposites of believing and guessing. Thinking is the "means whereby" we not only anticipate the future, but also fictitiously return to the past (remembering), build pictures of our own (fantasizing) and play all sorts of intellectual games on the chess board of logic (philosophizing).

Thinking is action in homoeopathic doses; it is a "time" and energy-saving device. When we need a pair of shoes, much time will be saved by planning, imagining or visualizing beforehand what kind of shoes we like and where we shall probably find them. In short: we anticipate action.

The energy thus saved develops further: we fuse different sensoric experiences into "objects", label them and operate these "word"-symbols *as if* they were the objects themselves. Here we cannot go into the details of the higher forms of thinking: the categorical (sometimes called "abstract") thinking. Categorical thinking is a pigeon-holing of different related objects and abstractions, facilitating human orientation within, and handling of, the environment. Loss of categorical thinking means limitation of orientation and action. (K. Goldstein).

We meet here with another application of the law that quantity changes into quality. By decreasing the intensity of action, while maintaining the original incentive, action turns into thinking. If this is the case, we should be able to find the zero-point, the stage of pre-difference of thinking and acting. Kœhler's experiments with apes prove that such a zero-point exists. (*Intelligenz-prüfungen an Anthropoiden*, 1917.) One experiment in particular shows a situation where thinking and action are not yet properly differentiated. It serves further as an introduction to the following discussion of "field" psychology.

One of the animals tries to seize a fruit lying on the ground out of reach. He has access to a number of bamboo sticks, which are hollow and can be fitted into each other. At first the animal tries vainly to reach the fruit with one of the sticks. Then he tries others, but finds they are not long enough. At last he seems to visualize a longer stick; by experimenting, he succeeds in putting two sticks together and finally manages to reach the fruit.

It is not difficult to realize that the ape has created a tool. The combination of two sticks in itself is not a tool: it only becomes a tool in this specific situation on being used by this specific animal. It is not a tool (a thing with "adequate functions") for a dog, nor is it a tool even for the ape if the fruit is in a box. It is a tool only in a specific "field," only if determined by the holism of the situation described.

The "field" conception stands in direct opposition to that of traditional science, which has always seen reality as a conglomeration of isolated parts—as a world made up of innumerable bits and pieces.

Even our mind consists, according to this concept, of a great number of single elements. This theory is called association psychology and is based on the assumption that in our minds one idea is attached to another as if by a string, and that one idea after another will break surface if, and when, the string is pulled.

Actually, associations are mental particles, artificially isolated from more comprehensive items which we may call spheres, situations, contexts, categories and such like names. Associations are by no means simply hooked together. On the contrary: rather complicated mental operations are involved. If, for example, I associate "saucer" with "cup," I evoke the picture or category of crockery. From this I select a saucer. Associating "tea" with "cup" means completing an incomplete situation: in this case filling the cup and probably indicating that I am thirsty. With "black" I would associate "white" if I were interested in colours, and "death" if I interpreted black as a part of the mourning context.

No one can escape the impression that associations have something strange and artificial in their make-up. Punning, for instance, is based upon a superficial acoustic similarity very remote from factual content: it is the use of words, isolated from their referents.

Freud used the association psychology and, in spite of this handicap, made amazing discoveries, intuitively seeing a number of "gestalten" behind the associations. The value of associations lies not in the associations themselves, but in the existence of specific spheres of which they form a part. Jung's association-scheme serves as a means to stir up a context which is emotionally charged, for instance, with embarrassment or confusion. Freud's findings include "wholes," such as the Super-ego and the Unconscious, as well as "holoids"—complexes, patterns of repetition, dreams; but, though he broke with the pure isolationist outlook, he overlooked the omnipresence of spheres and recognized mainly such as had a pathological significance. If it were not for Freud, association psychology would rest where it belongs: in the fossil department of some museum of science.

Its place has been taken by the *Gestalt* psychology, developed mainly by W. Köhler and M. Wertheimer, who maintain that there is primarily a comprehensive formation—which they call "gestalt" (figure formation) —and that the isolated bits and pieces are *secondary* formations. Wertheimer formulates the Gestalt theory in this way: "There are wholes, the behaviour of which is not determined by that of their individual elements, but where the part-processes are themselves determined by the intrinsic nature of the whole. It is the hope of gestalt theory to determine the nature of such wholes." Since the word "gestalt" has a specific scientific meaning for which a corresponding English word does not exist, the German expression has largely been retained. R. H. Thouless (in G. F. Stout, *A Manual of Psychology*, London, 1938) suggests replacing the customary term *gestalt psychology* by the more appropriate *field theory of psychology* based upon the "theory of relativity."

I will demonstrate on my typewriter two simple examples of how identical "things" have a different meaning according to the gestalt in which they appear:

A	B
3	2
2	1
soldier	Order
2	1
3	2

The vertical rows consist of the numbers three, two, one, two, three; and two, one, nought, one, two; but no one would read the horizontal rows as "so-one-dier" and "nought-rder." Whether the sign 1 and 0 indicate letters or numerals is determined by their context, by the gestalt of which they form a part. The category of the letters and the category of the numerals overlap each other incidentally, and while the signs are identical in form, they are different in meaning.

That a spoken word is a gestalt, a unity of sounds, can easily be understood. Only when this gestalt is not clear—when, for example, we do not catch the name of a person on the telephone—we ask that the word be spelt—cut up into single letters. This ruling applies to the printed word as well. Errors in reading will show a distinct relation between the read and printed gestalt.

A white object seen against a dark (grey or black) background appears as white, whereas the same object against a green background may appear as red, and against a red background as green, etc.

Another instructive example is that of a musical theme. When a melody is transposed into another key every single note is changed, yet the "whole" remains the same.

A set of chessmen in their box cannot hold one's interest for long, as it consists of 32 *independent pieces*, but the pieces in the game, their *interdependency* and the permanently changing situation, keep the players fascinated. In the box the chessmen represent the isolationist outlook—in the chess "field" the "holistic" conception.

Holism (ὅλος — whole) is the term coined by Field-Marshal Smuts (*Holism and Evolution*, 1926) for an attitude which realizes that the world consists "*per se*" not only of atoms, but of structures which have a meaning different from the sum of their parts. The changing merely of the position of a single piece in a game of chess might mean all the difference between winning and losing.

The difference between the isolationist and the holistic outlook is about the same as between a freckled and a sun-tanned skin.

Whilst the study of Gestalt-psychology requires extensive scientific and detailed experimental work, the careful reading of Smuts's book is highly recommended as being within the scope of many people. It gives a most comprehensive survey of the importance of wholes, in Biology as well as in many other branches of science. Personally I agree with what one could call "structural holism" as a specific expression of the ¶; and I welcome, too, the distinction between wholes and holoids: if an army is an aggressive-defensive whole, then the battalions, squadrons, etc., are holoids; if the human personality is a whole, we can call complexes and patterns of repetition holoids. There is present, however, the danger of deification in Smuts's concept, and I am not inclined to follow him in what I would call idealistic or even theological Holism.

By keeping our eye on the context or field or whole in which a phenomenon is embedded, we avoid many misunderstandings which, as a result of an isolationist outlook, can occur in science even more often than in everyday life. Thus it is usually deemed sufficient to define a word in order to make the reader or listener understand its meaning. The same word, however, may belong to different spheres or contexts and may have a different meaning in each context.

We have seen this with the signs 1 and 0, and with screen words like "think." A sentence, a speech, or a letter away from its context may give a completely distorted meaning.

We also have to bear in mind that thinking in opposites holds good only in their specific sphere or context, just as definitions depend on specific situations. The following scheme serves to illustrate this, and may, at the same time, give us further insight into the problem of differentiation. It gives a few uses of the word "actor" contrasted with its opposites.

An Actor is a	In contrast to	Belonging to the sphere of	Examples of Pre-difference
1. Stage employee	his director	Social Order	Charlie Chaplin
2. Performer	a spectator	Performance	Hamlet, 3. 2
3. Male	an actress	Sex	Actor on Greek stage
4. Impersonator	the author	Literature	Shakespeare
5. Professional	a private person	Personal status	Amateur
6. Play-acting person	a person behaving naturally	Expression	Playing child

The first three columns need no explanation, but as it may be more difficult to understand the examples of pre-difference, a few explanatory remarks may be added.

(1) That Charlie Chaplin is, at the same time, both the chief actor and the director of his films is known to all. In a penny-gaff the difference between the director and his employees may not be distinct, but in a Broadway Theatre the director may not even know some of his actors.

(2) I am referring to the scene of the stage within the stage, where the actor who plays the role of Hamlet watches a performance.

In any dialogue an oscillation of function takes place: the same person who, at one moment, is the performer or speaker may, at the next moment, be the spectator or the listener.

More differentiated still (and showing a certain split of the personality) is the situation of a person rehearsing in front of a mirror before appearing in public or before going to meet someone he desires to impress. The pathological phenomenon of self-consciousness belongs to this sphere. A differentiation into performer and spectator has occurred: a conflict exists between being in the limelight and watching the onlookers.

(3) In many theatres (e.g. the Greek, Japanese, Shakespearean) the actors were exclusively male.

(4) The case of Shakespeare is well known. If he had not succeeded as an author, he would probably have remained exclusively an actor.

(5) The professional actor is the result of a rather advanced development of the scenic art. We find a convincing example of the state of pre-difference in the clowns in *A Midsummer-Night's Dream*.

(6) A child when playing the role of a lion *is* a lion, and it may be so absorbed in its play that it becomes angry if called back to everyday life.

Thus, by having the "field," the context, we can determine the opposites and, by having the opposites, we can determine the specific field. This insight will be of great assistance in the approach to the structure and behaviour of the organism within its environment.

III

THE ORGANISM AND ITS BALANCE

A medical student, at the very beginning of his studies, is faced with thousands of *isolated* facts. Consider only the study of anatomy: herein the student's education, instead of following, proceeds exactly contrary to the development of medical science, which progressed by differentiation: from the general to the particular; from the comprehensive to the detail; from the wholes to the part-processes.

I suggest that a complete reversal of educational methods in such matters might be of great advantage to the medical student. In the observation of complete situations (simple cases) his still fresh curiosity would enable him to build up islands of knowledge by studying anatomical, physiological and pathological details in connection with the living organism. Instead of the customary teaching of isolated facts by individual teachers, a more holistic approach to the human organism should be elaborated by professorial team work. By dealing directly with his patient, the student would face the human personality, whereas under the present system he studies first the dead body, then the mechanical functions of the living organism, and at last he sips a drop of knowledge of the "soul."

Isolated treatment of the different aspects of the human personality only supports thinking in terms of magic, and bolsters up the belief that body and soul are isolated items, joined together in some mysterious way.

Man is a living organism, and certain of his aspects are called body, mind and soul. If we define the body as the *sum* of cells, the mind as the *sum* of perceptions and thoughts, and the soul as the *sum* of emotions, and even if we add "structural integration" (or existence of these sum totals as wholes) to each of the three terms, we still realize how artificial and out of accordance with reality such definitions and divisions are. The superstition that they are different parts, which can be put together or taken apart, is an inheritance from times when man (horrified and reluctant to accept death as such) created the fantasy of spirits and ghosts which live for ever, and slip in and out of the body.

God can—according to such fantasy—breathe into a piece of clay and bring it to life. In the Indian reincarnation the supposed soul can slip from one organism into another, from an elephant into a tiger, from a tiger into a cockroach, and in the next life into a human being, until all conditions of an unattainable standard of ethics would eventually be fulfilled and the soul could find rest in nirvana. Even in our European civilization there are many who believe in ghosts and spirits, and who provide occultists, tea-cup readers and such-like gentry with a welcome opportunity of making a living. And do not millions believe in a life hereafter, because it is comforting to think that the dead are not dead?

Applying this body-soul conception to mechanical things might help to show its absurdity. If you love your motor car, are thrilled with her smooth running, with the beauty of her lines, you might have a feeling that she had a soul. But who could possibly believe that her soul could suddenly leave her body to enjoy itself in a Heaven for motor cars (or suffer torture in a Hell for misbehaved vehicles), whilst the corpse of the car rots and rusts on a motor car graveyard?

You could object: the motor car is something man-made, something artificial. But who cares to talk about the immortal soul of an octopus or a dog—things man has certainly not managed to produce? There were people like the late Conan Doyle, however, who were convinced that a Heaven existed for dogs as well as for man. All this may sound cynical and blasphemous, but all I have done is to carry to its ultimate conclusion the conception of such an artificial split of the organism into body and soul.

A compromise between this isolationist conception of the organism[1] and the holistic one is the theory of psycho-physical parallelism, which maintains that physical and psychological functions work apart from, though parallel to each other. The main fault of this theory is that it does not reveal anything about the connection between the two strata. Is it that the body, a kind of mirror, apes the soul (and vice versa), both thus performing the same functions simultaneously? Are the functions of body and soul merely coincidences, or are they identities?

It seems to me that the parallelists try to combine two opposing *weltanschauungen*: the materialistic and the idealistic. The materialistic outlook on life proclaims the concrete substance as the basis of being. This "cause" produces soul and mind. Thoughts are a kind of excretion of the brain matter, love a product of sexual hormones. The opposite, the idealistic (or spiritual) conception says: The idea creates the things. The best known example of this *weltanschauung* is the creation of the world by gods. The parallelist glues these two conceptions together without achieving a productive integration of structure.

All these hypotheses are more or less dualistic—are really attempts to find connections between body and soul. But all these theories, even Leibniz's "pre-established harmony," lead one astray, for they are based on an artificial split which has no existence in reality. They mean to re-

[1] *Isoliert stückhafte Betrachtungsweise*, Ternus.

establish a unity which never has ceased to be. Body and soul are identical *"in re,"* though not *"in verbo"*; the words "body" and "soul" denote two aspects of the same thing.

Melancholia, for instance, shows (among others) two symptoms: a thickening of the bile juices ("melancholia" means black gall) and a deep sadness. The man who believes in organic foundation will say: "Because the gall of this person flows thickly, he feels sad." The psychologist maintains: "The depressing experiences and mood of the patient thickens the flow of his gall." Both symptoms, however, are not linked as cause and effect—they are two manifestations of one occurrence.

If the coronary artery of a heart is hardened, excitement leads to, amongst other prominent symptoms, attacks of anxiety. On the other hand an attack of anxiety on a person with a healthy heart is identical with certain physiological changes in the function of the heart and breathing apparatus. An anxiety attack without breathing difficulties, quickening of the pulse and similar symptoms does not exist.

No emotion, like rage, sadness, shame or disgust occurs without its physiological as well as psychological components coming into play.

The ease with which fundamental mistakes are made, can be gauged by a law formulated by the psycho-analyst W. Stekel, who maintains that a neurotic person experiences sensations instead of emotions, e.g. burning of the face instead of shame, heart-pounding instead of anxiety. But these sensations are integral parts of the corresponding emotions. The neurotic does not experience sensations *instead* of emotions, but at the expense or even to the exclusion of the consciousness of the emotional component; having partly lost the "feel of himself" (the senso-motoric awareness) he experiences an incomplete situation—a scotoma (blind spot) for the psychological manifestation of the emotion.

Since in this book we are not so much concerned with a universal holistic conception, as with a specific organismic one, our approach differs from that of Smuts. Instead of his matter, life and mind aspects, we are choosing the aspects of body, soul and mind. To realize—at least in theory—the identity of body and soul is not very difficult. The issue becomes somewhat more complicated, if we take the mind into consideration. Here a differentiation into opposites has taken place. If you are shivering, certain phenomena in the skin, muscles, etc., occur. Simultaneously with these sensations the mind registers: "I am shivering"; or thinks of the opposite: "I want to feel warm, I do not want to shiver." (This protest, this resistance, is a biological phenomenon, and should not be confused with the psycho-analytical conception of resistance.) If the mind always merely accepted the situation, there would be no need of the mind's existence at all. The statement "I am shivering" might be of exhibitionistic or scientific interest, but it would be of no biological value. If, however, this statement were not a mere statement, but an

emotional expression, a cry for help: "I am shivering—give me warmth!"
then it would express the urge for its opposite.

Experiments with animals of low order demonstrate that animals react
principally alike with or without a brain. The only difference is that the
brainless animal reacts slower than the animal with brains. We can interpret this as "the brain providing the organism with improved signals
for its needs." These signals have a sign opposite to the organismic
requirements as the following example will demonstrate: Mr. Brown
goes for a stroll on a very hot day. He perspires and loses a certain
amount of water. If we call the total amount of liquid required by the
balanced organism W and the lost part X, then he is left with the amount
of W—X, a state which he experiences as thirst, as a desire to restore the
organismic balance of water, as an urge to incorporate into his system
the amount of X. This X appears in his mind (which, protesting against
the —X, thinks of its opposite) as the vision of a bubbling stream, a jug
of water or a pub. The —X in the body/soul system appears as X in his
mind.

In other words: W—X exists in the "body" as a deficiency (dehydra-
tion), in the "soul" as a sensation (thirst) and in the "mind" as the complementary image. If the amount X of real water is added to the organism,
the thirst is nullified, quenched, and the balance W restored, the *image*
of X in the mind disappearing together with the arrival of the *real* X in
the body/soul system. Thirst, or for that matter every type of hunger,
represents a deficiency or a minus in the balance of the organism. The
reverse of this situation is: plus in the body/soul and minus in the mind.
The simplest example of such a plus (or surplus, as it may be called) is
the waste matter. Faeces and urine represent a surplus of food assimilation.
This plus of material creates in the human being the image of its minus:
the place where to get rid of this surplus. In the first example the disappearance of the minus restores the organismic water balance. Defaecation, urination or the discharge of secretions (e.g. of the sex-glands) and
of emotions achieve likewise the organismic balance.

Thus the plus and minus functions of metabolism represent the working
of the basic tendency of every organism to strive for balance. In the
working of the organism, some happening tends to disturb its balance
at every moment, and simultaneously a counter-tendency arises to regain
it. According to the intensity of this tendency we call it a desire, an urge,
a need, a want, a passion, and, if its effective realization is regularly
repeated, we call it a habit. From these urges we abstract the existence
of instincts. This is an intellectual conclusion from observations of behaviour, urges and physiological symptoms. As long as we remain conscious
of the fact that the term "instinct" is only a convenient word symbol
for certain complex occurrences in the organism, we may use it. But if
we regard an instinct as a reality, we make the dangerous mistake of

conceiving it as *"prima causa,"* and of falling into a new trap of deification —a trap which not even Freud escaped.

Attempts have often been made to enumerate and classify instincts. Any classification which does not consider the organismic balance, however, must needs be arbitrary, a product of the specific interests of the classifying scientist.

To be entirely exact, one has to recognize hundreds of instincts and to realize that instincts are not absolute, but relative, depending on the requirements of the respective organism. Consider the case of a pregnant woman: the child growing within her requires calcium, and she experiences a calcium-need. If her calcium minus becomes intense enough, the realization of the counter-tendency may develop to such an "instinctive" greed for this mineral, that cases are known in which such a woman will lick the plaster from the walls. Under ordinary circumstances, however, there would be no awareness of this calcium "instinct," as there would usually be enough calcium in the daily food to prevent the development of a calcium minus.

The same situation may apply to the instincts for vitamins or for common salt. These needs are usually not realized, as the substances in question are present in ordinary food. Science can speak of a balanced diet only if all the different kinds of hunger instincts are satisfied.[1]

The deficiencies in the human organism are not exclusively of a biological nature. Civilization particularly has created in man a number of added needs—some imaginary ones, and some real needs of secondary importance.

An instance of secondary needs is the use of certain habit-forming drugs (e.g. morphia) which brings about a real need in the human organism. According to Ehrlich's side-chains theory, the system of a morphinist is overflooded with incomplete molecules, which produce a genuine need for their completion. The morphine hunger has become a genuine, though pathological instinct. That morphinism has indeed become an instinct, is also suggested by the fact that "will power" never succeeds in curing this habit.

The morbidity of such an instinct is obvious, for we observe it mainly in such individuals as appear distinctly different from the majority, whereas

---

[1] An interesting expression of the salt instinct is the sign for NaCl which symbolizes in the writing of an African tribe the importance of, and the greed for it:

From all directions hands are outstretched for the mineral so badly needed.

in collective habits it is less conspicuous. The organism of an obese stock-broker, who has his office on the 40th floor, has changed to such a degree as to develop in the man an "elevator instinct"—indeed, he is incapable of getting to his office unless elevated.

As imaginary needs we can put down hobbies, fashions, gambling, and other things not vital for the organism, but nevertheless consuming intensive interest. From here it is but a step to the (pathological) obsessions and phobias such as senseless counting, making sure several times that a door is locked; being unable to cross a street, or to stay in a closed room.

We cannot enumerate all the different instincts of the organism, but we can arrange them under two headings, according to the main functions of self-preservation and species-preservation. Self-preservation is secured by gratification of the alimentary needs and by self-defence, while the sexual "instincts" take care of species-preservation.

Freud's classification of instincts requires a re-orientation from the organismic point of view. With his Eros/Thanatos theory I shall deal later on. At this stage I have only to contradict his original classification (which he himself did not esteem very highly, regarding it merely as a provisional hypothesis). His distinction between ego instincts and sex instincts is obviously a dualistic conception intended to provide a suitable theoretical background for his observations of the neurotic conflict; but the relationship between ego and sex instinct does not differ intrinsically from the relation between ego and hunger instinct. The ego is neither an instinct, nor has it instincts; it is an organismic function, as I shall show in a later chapter.

The following dream of a soldier in the War of 1914–1918, provides us with a simple illustration of the experience of minuses and pluses in the organism. The following is a summary of his statement:

"It was in the beginning of 1918, in France. Our company was billeted in an old factory building. To reach the 'public convenience,' we had to cross a large courtyard covered with ice and snow, and soldiers of another unit were on guard to prevent us from spoiling the beautiful snow in the yard by using it as a lavatory. The food supplied to us in 1918 was inadequate in every respect. I was sleeping in the top one of two super-imposed beds. I dreamt that I had just arrived in my home town on leave. I was walking from the station towards the suburb where my parents live. My mother had written to me that I should have plum dumplings—my favourite dish—when I came home on leave, and I was looking forward to many helpings of this delicacy. I felt an urgent need to urinate, and entered a public lavatory, where I proceeded to relieve myself. I walked on. . . . This ended my dream, and all of a sudden, my comrade in the lower bed woke up and voiced in flowery language his resentment at my having urinated on him."

36

Incomplete Situation.	*Compensation by dream.*
MINUS	PLUS
Bad Food	Tasty dumplings
Absence of familiar surroundings	At home
SURPLUS	MINUS
Urine	Receptacle
Long cold walk to the urinal	No distant walk

IV

REALITY

No organism is self-sufficient. It requires the world for the gratification of its needs. To consider an organism by itself amounts to looking upon it as an artificially isolated unit, whereas there is always an inter-dependency of the organism and its environment. The organism is a part of the world, but it can also experience the world as something apart from itself—as something as real as itself.

Through the ages few problems have occupied philosophers more than that of reality. There are two main schools of thought: The one maintains that the world exists only through perception, the other assumes a world existing independently of perception. Everybody remembers the story of the man who kicked the philosopher's shin, and tried to make it clear to him that the pain only existed in his, the philosopher's, perception.

But the problem is not as simple as all that. Its solution is simpler and more complicated at the same time. In this book I am not inclined to deal with philosophical questions more than is absolutely necessary for the solution of our problems, and I am certainly not willing to take part in any mere verbal quarrel. What I have to point out is: if the man had not had the impulse to kick, the philosopher would not have become aware of the existence of his shin. We can even go a step further and say: the tools of perception evolve in the service of our interests; therefore the problem should be: does the world exist *per se*, or does it exist only as far as our interests are involved?

For our purpose we assume that there is an objective world from which the individual creates his subjective world: parts of the absolute world are selected according to our interests, but this selection is limited by the range of our tools of perception, and by social and neurotic inhibitions. Later we shall make the acquaintance of another, a pseudo-world, which plays an enormous part in our life and civilization, and which has become a reality of its own—the world of projections.

The whole problem of the world's existence has boiled down to the question: how much of it exists for the individual?

The outer circle may represent the world *per se*.

Next comes a circle indicating our indirect knowledge of the world, a knowledge which we acquire with the tools of our intellect (books, teaching) and of refined means of perception (e.g. telescope and microscope). We realize the existence of this part of the world best by the uncanny experience with the Galton whistle which gives a sound above the range of the human ear. If you blow this whistle the trained dog will stop in the middle of his run although you yourself do not hear a sound. This whistle lies just beyond the next circle which includes our—rather stable—means of perception. Opposed to the stability of the senses is the instability of our interests (following circle) which affects the great variance of our observations and contacts. The subjective world is further narrowed

down by the loss of senses (blindness, anaesthesia, etc.), and by social and neurotic inhibitions.

In order to illustrate in some detail the inter-dependency of the objective and subjective worlds, the following scheme is submitted showing one and the same object in relation to a number of people. A corn-field is chosen as the object.

Farmer	←		→	Agronomist
Pilot	←	— Corn-field —	→	Merchant
Painter	←		→	Couple of lovers

We try to approach the objective world by means of definitions, and we may, approximately, define "corn-field" as a piece of ground on which a cereal is cultivated.

Is this so-called *objective reality* necessarily identical with the *subjective realities* of all the persons given in the scheme? Certainly not. A merchant, looking at the corn-field, will estimate the gain he may derive from handling the sale of the crop, while a couple of lovers, choosing the corn-field as a place in which to withdraw from the world, do not care at all about its monetary value. A painter may grow enthusiastic about its slowly moving harmonies of light and shade, but to the pilot, who is about to make a forced landing, the movement of the corn serves only as a wind indicator. To an agronomist, wind direction or colour harmonies are of no importance, as he considers the chemical composition of the soil. The nearest to the objective reality which we defined above is the subjective reality of the farmer, who cultivated the field and grew the corn.

Things may seem to have become more complicated than before. Out of one reality six emerge; but common to these six is the specific interest which is the characteristic of subjective realities.

That the sphere of interest is the decisive factor in the creation of the subjective reality can be easily demonstrated by choosing alternatives in every one of the above cases. We can replace the corn-field by something else lying within the specific sphere of interest. The connection between the pilot and the corn-field is not the association "wind direction," but the sphere corresponding to the pilot's needs, i.e. his minus situation, which we discussed in the previous chapter. Thus the pilot might use the smoke of a chimney as a wind indicator. The merchant might choose, as an alternative, the buying of poultry, the painter a brook, the lovers a haystack, the farmer cattle rearing and the agronomist a potato field.

The six people have six different spheres of interest. They are interested in such objects of the outer world as are apt to gratify their different needs, and only by *co-incidence* is the corn-field the object common to their different spheres of interest.

We may even go so far as to say that the reality which matters is the reality of interests—the *internal* and not the *external* reality. We realize this best by the absurdity to which an exchange of alternatives would lead if we were to neglect the specific interests. A pilot who would try to get information about the wind direction from a haystack, a merchant who would buy up brooks, lovers who would hide in the smoke of a chimney. . . .

SPECIFIC INTERESTS ARE DICTATED BY SPECIFIC NEEDS.

Thus inserting the specific needs in our scheme we see that in every case the corn-field represents the plus, the means of gratification for the different minuses.

Farmer wants to make a living	←		→	Agronomist looks for scientific data
Pilot needs a landing place	←	Corn-field	→	Merchant wants to make money
Painter searches for subject	←		→	Couple of lovers wish to be by themselves

The relationship between the organism's need and the reality corresponds to the relationship between body/soul and mind. The image in the mind disappears (as we have seen), as soon as the need of the organism is gratified. Exactly the same happens to our subjective realities: they disappear once they are required no further.

After the landing, the pilot is no longer vitally interested in the cornfield, nor is the painter who has finished his picture.

A man whose "hobby" is solving cross-word puzzles may worry for hours, but as soon as he has solved the problem, the puzzle loses its fascination and becomes just a piece of paper. The situation has been completed. The interest in the puzzle has been gratified and *thereby* nullified; it recedes into the background, leaving the foreground free for other activities.

When driving through a town, one does not, under ordinary circumstances, notice the existence of a single letter-box. The situation, however, changes when you have to post a letter. Then, out of an indifferently viewed background, a letter-box will jump into prominence, becoming a subjective reality—in other words, a figure (gestalt) against an indifferent background.[1]

Here is another example: Mr. Y has bought a motor car, for example a Chevrolet. As long as his pride in it prevails, he will find that this particular make will stand out from the multitude of the motor vehicles on the road.

These two examples should suffice to show that we do not perceive the whole of our surroundings at the same time. We do not look at the world as though our eyes were the lenses of a photographic camera. We select objects according to our interests, and these objects appear as prominent figures against a dim background. When taking photographic pictures we endeavour to overcome the optical differences between the human eye and the camera by intentionally producing a figure-background effect. Close-ups on the screen often show the hero as a clear foreground figure against a hazy background.[2]

Freud came close to the solution of the figure-background problem of the "gestalt" psychology. He tried to solve the problem by assuming that objects (real ones as well as images) can be charged with psychological energies, and that every psychological process is accompanied by a change in "cathexis."[3] This theory, though useful as a working hypothesis, has a number of disadvantages:

[1] If one forgets to post the letter, this may not necessarily be due to a repression or resistance. It may, rather, be due to the fact that an interest in posting the letter is not intense enough to produce the figure-background phenomenon.

[2] Under pathological conditions we can observe the lack of figure-background formation in man. This state is known as "de-personalization," and occurs after shock and extraordinary emotional stress, after the loss of someone very dear and, to a lesser degree, during a certain stage of intoxication. The world is then perceived as something rigid, emotionally dull, and, at the same time, optically clear-cut. The resemblance to the working of the inanimate photographic lens is obvious.

[3] Cathexis (Besetzung), meaning the addition of energy which in some mystical way is projected or injected into an object of reality or imagination.

To Freud, cathexis mainly means libidinal cathexis.

The idea of cathexis has been derived from the pseudopodia of the amoeba, which are used to incorporate food. It has been transferred without sufficient justification from the alimentary to the sexual sphere, with the result that alimentary functions in psycho-analytical theory have become mixed up with sexual processes.

*   *   *

The relationship between organism and "mind" corresponds to the relationship between organism and reality in three ways.

(1) Both mind and reality are complements of an organismic need.
(2) They function according to the figure-background principle.
(3) Once gratification has been obtained, both the image and the real object disappear from our consciousness.

There are, of course, differences between reality and image, between perception and visualization, otherwise we should take the image as the reality (hallucination).[1]

Originally, perceptions and visualizations are not differentiated but identical. One can experience this in dreams. In a vivid dream one is actually within the situation, which one experiences as though it were a reality. When awake, very few people are capable of recalling and re-living a dream with all its original intensity. They recall its material alone, and only now and then may they produce some emotion experienced during the dream.

The identity of perception and visualization in the dream—its hallucinatory character—manifests itself by the disappointment or relief experienced when one becomes aware of the fact that the dream was "just a dream."[2]

---

[1] Hallucinations occur not only in insanity, but also in normal people who are in a state of high tension, e.g. hunger or fear.

[2] Jaentsch has furnished the proof of the pre-differential state of visualization and perception. He called this state "eidetic" and has shown that it is usually present in children, and is retained by a number of people in adult life. These people can use their eidetic faculties with great success, for instance in examinations. They simply read in their mind the required passages of the textbook they have read in reality—perhaps without even understanding its contents. Such a good "memory" is in itself not necessarily a sign of intelligence. Many people with an eidetic memory are stupid, although others, like Goethe, found it to be of great assistance in providing their minds with an enormous number of recollections when required. Later I shall give some advice as to how to improve this biological memory.

V

THE ANSWER OF THE ORGANISM

If the existence of the subjective world depends upon our instincts, how, on the other hand, can gestalt-psychology maintain that the organism "answers to" situations? It looks like a reversal of what we have found so far.

Is the organism the primary factor and is the world created by its needs? Or is there primarily a world to which the organism responds? Both views are correct *in toto*. They are by no means contradictions: actions and reactions are interwoven.

Before approaching this problem we have to see what is meant by the words "answer to." We are accustomed to apply the word "answer" in the sense of giving a *verbal* reply to a question. Yet nodding or shaking of the head are also accepted as answers, though they are not verbal. By widening this notion we can call "answer" any reaction, any response to an action. The re-action, the response is a sequence, something secondary to something that has happened primarily.

The *sequence* reality-answer, stands in contrast to the *simultaneousness* of the instinct/reality situation. The internal hunger-tension and the appetizing look of food appear and disappear simultaneously, while a child's reaction upon the nurse's demand takes place as a sequence to it. Again we have to be careful not to presume a causality and not to say that an answer is *determined* by a question. The only exceptions would be those cases in which exactly the same reaction stereotypically follows an action. In such cases we speak for instance of a "reflex," thereby indicating that decisions are without influence upon the sequence action/reaction.

As I have said before, the answer is not confined to words. We may answer a situation with all kinds of emotions—with anxiety, fear, enthusiasm, disgust, with activity, crying, flight, attack or many other reactions.

Just one illustration taken from everyday life: A number of people witness a car accident. Most of them will react either with interest (*interesse = to be among*) or flight, or with either genuine or pretended indifference. The interested people will answer the situation with ¶. They will be drawn to the spot of the accident, and being sensibly active, they will call the ambulance or render assistance; or they may stand around being curious or making a nuisance of themselves. Others will produce associations, e.g. how an aunt met with a similar accident; or they will

43

deliver sermons about the danger of speed or of driving under the influence of liquor. The attitude opposite to that of this group is that of avoidance (‡). One person may faint; others may run away maintaining they cannot stand the sight of blood and mutilated bodies. Others, again, may say that they must not watch the accident, as they are afraid it might prey on their minds and cause them to have an accident themselves. Pretended indifference is the answer of a man who feels groggy, but wants to put up a brave show, and only in genuine indifference is there no answer, as no disturbance of the personality has occurred.

The next step to be considered is this: Not only do we select our world, but we may also be selected by other people as objects of their interests. They may make demands upon us; our answers may either be in the affirmative (we may comply with their wishes) or in the negative (we may be on the defensive, or refuse their demands).

The civilization we have created is full of claims. There are conventions, laws, engagements, distances to overcome, economic difficulties, and a whole host of obligations with which we have to comply. They are a collective reality, and a very powerful reality at that, objective in their effect, even if not in their sense.

And, as though this were not enough, man has created an additional world, which for most people is also a reality. This (imaginary) reality is built up of projections, its chief example being religion.

If we now return to our corn-field example, we can insert the "answer of the organism" to the situation, and arrive at the following amplification:

Person	Corn-field Situation	Answer
Pilot	wind indicator	landing
Farmer	livelihood	harvesting
Painter	landscape	painting
Couple of lovers	secret place	hiding
Agronomist	soil	collecting material
Merchant	merchandise	offering money

We have now completed the cycle of the inter-dependency of organism and environment. We have found:

(1) The organism at rest.
(2) The disturbing factor, which may be
    (a) An external disturber—a demand made upon us, or any interference that puts us on the defensive.
    (b) An internal disturbance—a need which has gathered enough momentum to strive for gratification and which requires
(3) The creation of an image or reality (plus-minus function and figure-background phenomena).

(4) The answer to the situation aiming at
(5) A decrease of tension—achievement of gratification or compliance with the demands resulting in
(6) The return of the organismic balance.

An example of the internal disturbance cycle might be:

(1) I am dozing on a couch.
(2) The wish to read something interesting penetrates my consciousness.
(3) I remember a certain book-shop.
(4) I go there and buy a book.
(5) I am reading.
(6) I have had enough. I set the book aside.

An external disturbance cycle might be:

(1) I am lying on a couch.
(2) A fly is crawling over my face.
(3) I become aware of the disturber.
(4) I get annoyed and fetch a swatter.
(5) I kill the fly.
(6) I go back to the couch.

Basically, the external cycle is not different from the internal. Here, too, an instinct (for instance, self-preservation) is the prime mover. In certain situations I might not notice the fly at all. Then, of course, it would not act as a disturber and the whole circle need not exist.

This circle leads to the grasping of one of the most important phenomena, of the fact of organismic self-regulation which, as W. Reich has pointed out, is very different from the regulation of instincts by morals or self-control. Moral regulation must lead to the accumulation of unfinished situations in our system and to interruption of the organismic circle. This interruption is achieved by means of muscular contraction and the production of anaesthesia. A person who has lost the "feel" of himself, who, for instance, has deadened his palate, cannot feel whether he is hungry or not. Therefore, he cannot expect his "self-regulation" (appetite) to function properly, and he will stimulate his palate artificially.

We may contrast such violations of the principle of healthy self-regulation with normal functions. In sex life, for instance, the production of hormones by the glands leads to an organismic surplus, the increased sexual tension creates an image, or selects in reality an object suitable for gratification of its needs for a restoration of the organismic balance.

It is somewhat more difficult to realize the principle of self-regulation if we come to less manifest functions; but, being a general principle, it applies to every system, every organ, tissue, and to every single cell.

Without self-regulation they would either atrophy or hypertrophy (for instance degeneration or cancer). It is also difficult to demonstrate the exact moment of balance in breathing, as there is a permanent need for oxygen, and the production of carbondioxide is continuing uninterruptedly. Here self-regulation is carried out by the pH concentration. Yawning and sighing are symptoms of self-regulation. In anxiety self-regulation is not working properly.

The restoration of the organismic balance is by no means always as easy and simple as might appear from what has just been said. Often, more or less powerful resistances have to be overcome, which may extend from geographical obstacles to monetary difficulties and social taboos.

* * *

The principle governing our relations with the outer world is the same as the intra-organismic principle of striving for equilibrium. We call the achievement of being in harmony with the outer world adjustment. This adjustment may range from primitive biological functions to far-reaching changes in the world by a single individual.

Generally, the capacity for adjustment is very limited. We can adjust ourselves within a few minutes to the temperature of the water when taking a cool or warm bath, but the difference between the temperature of the body and the water must not go beyond certain limits, otherwise the result would be injurious—would result in burns or shock. Some people, however, have trained their capacity for adjustment so far as to be able to jump into ice-cold water, or even to walk on glowing embers.

If we focus our eyes for a few minutes on some bright colour, the brightness of the colour will disappear. Bright red, for instance, will become dullish red approaching grey. If, then, we look against an indifferent background, we will notice the complementary colour, in this case green, appearing in front of our eyes. This green is the complementary activity of the organism towards adjustment; it is the minus to the plus red.

Often we may not need to adjust ourselves to our environment, but may be able to adjust the environment to our needs and wishes. Air-conditioning or central heating are examples to be contrasted with acclimatization.

We call the adjustment of our environment to our needs an alloplastic (modelling the other) behaviour, the self-adjustment an autoplastic behaviour. The alloplastic activity of a bird changes its environment by building nests or migrating into a warmer climate; the alloplastic character in man produces an urge to organize, to take command, or to invent and discover things. The counterpart, the autoplastic character, is exemplified by the chameleon, and, in human beings, by the power of adaptation and pliability.

Alloplastic and autoplastic behaviour is tragically interwoven in mankind, especially in industrialized countries where the environment changes so rapidly that the human organism cannot keep pace with it.

The result of this is an enormous wear and tear on the human organism which hardly ever has time to restore its balance sufficiently, a theme which has been extensively treated by F. M. Alexander in his book, *Man's Supreme Inheritance,* and also by other writers.

VI

DEFENCE

If there were no sex instinct for propagation, the hunger instinct—the satisfaction of which necessitates the eating of animals and plants—could be satisfied for a while. But as no new supply would be forthcoming, life on earth would soon cease.

On the other hand, were there no instinct of self-preservation, no hunger, but only sex instinct, within a few years flora and fauna would overcrowd this globe to such an extent that no animal would be able to move and no room would be left for the growth of new plants. Thus it seems that conditions of life on this earth are well balanced: multiplication of flora and fauna provides enough food, and their consumption prevents overcrowding. This balance is not the outcome of a mystic Providence but a natural law. Would either side overbalance, life on this planet would cease to exist.

The organisms, however, object to being eaten up and develop mechanic and dynamic defences. Any attack, any aggression aiming at our partial or total destruction is experienced as danger. In the struggle for survival the means for attack and defence develop on related, but different lines. The attacker develops all his means to get at the victim (‡‡‡¶), the defender to render the attacks impotent (‡‡‡).

The aggressor does not aim at annihilation of his object. He wants to get hold of something but he finds a resistance. He then proceeds to destroy the resistance, leaving intact as much as possible of the substance valuable to him. This applies to nations as it does to human individuals and to animals. The Nazis carefully avoided the destruction of the "Skoda Works" when they broke up the Czecho-Slovakian state. The business man who eliminates a competitor takes great care that the competitor's clientele remains intact. The tiger does not kill for the sake of annihilation but for food.

Danger, whether it be an external (attack) or an internal one,[1] is realized by the eyes, ears, skin, in short, by whichever sensoric organs we establish

---

[1] In addition to external danger, we experience (mostly imagine) dangers within ourselves whenever we are hostile to some part of ourselves. An intense emotion may imperil the ideal of being an unmoved he-man; sex-impulses mean danger to the pious virgin, etc. etc.; wherever and whenever such a danger arises we mobilize protective resources.

contact with the enemy. Originally the point of contact and observation was the skin, that biological boundary between the organism and the world. Later the outposts of defence, on the watch for the approach of the enemy, stretched themselves further and further afield. Instead of waiting for epidermic contact, ears, eyes and nose and, lately, technical instruments (periscope, radio-locator, etc.) signal the danger, and the organism goes on the defensive and applies its means of resistance.

The organism lives essentially centrifugally, actively. Every defence involves a tremendous amount of activity sometimes including extensive preparations.

The means of defence are of mechanic or dynamic nature. The mechanical defences are frozen, petrified, accumulated activities like shells or concrete fortifications: the dynamic means of defence are of a motoric (e.g. flight) and secretoric (octopus ink, snake poison) or of sensoric (scouting) nature. Thus the defender is as active as the aggressor, the organismic tendency of living centrifugally being maintained, as in nearly every other function.

Reflexes (in phylogenetics) and conditioned reflexes (in ontogenetics) are the outcome of previous conscious activity. They are a time and concentration saving device. As the organization of a personality functions according to the figure-background principle, the mind, being unable to deal with several tasks at once, is free to attend to the most important one, whilst the lower (the reflex) centres—being well trained—don't need to be looked after. This automatism leads to the still widespread notion that the recipient nerves are different in their direction from those of the motoric and secretoric nerves. To regard only the motoric and secretoric nerves as centrifugal is an inheritance from the mechanical age which assumed that, for instance, the rays of light travelled actively through the wires of the optic nerves and stimulated the organism to some reaction. This theory is still the basis of neurological teaching. It assumes that one part of the nervous system is afferent and the other efferent, and that both are part of a reflex "arc" (figure 1). Another conception sees in them two prongs of a fork (figure 2).

FIG. I   FIG. II

Goethe, the neurologist Goldstein, and the philosopher Marcuse emphasize the centrifugal tendency of the senso-motoric system. Goldstein maintains that the senso- as well as the motoric system tend from the brain towards the periphery.

The British Admiralty did not perceive in a passive way, in the sense of the reflex arc, the whereabouts of the *Bismarck*. It sent out the eyes of the Fleet, the reconnaissance planes.

Wireless sets are installed to pick up wireless messages. We buy newspapers to learn what happens in the world and we select and read what interests us.

As soon as we regard the use of the senses as an activity similar to the use of feelers by an insect, and not as a passivity, as something that happens to us, we realize that the new conception has a wider scope than the old one, and does away with auxiliary theories. If a worm crawled because its sensoric nerves were stimulated by contact with the ground, it would not stop until completely exhausted, as it would have to crawl on and on, forced by the automatic impulses the motoric nerves receive from the sensoric ones. To reconcile theory and observation the scientist has to install additional nerves which inhibit the reflex arc, providing the worm with a free will to inhibit. By assuming that the organism lives centrifugally we eliminate this contradiction. The worm crawls by its sensoric and motoric activities in a biological "field" towards the "end gains" of its instincts.

When walking through a forest at night we change hearing into listening; we sharpen our eyes and turn them in all directions as advance guards against possible danger. The sensoric activity in striving to gratify our needs is the same as that occurring in defence. A hungry child does not just see a bread-roll in the baker's shop. It looks, it *stares* at it. The sight of the bread does not evoke as a reflex the child's hunger. On the contrary, the hunger produces the effect of both being on the look-out for food and of moving towards it. A well-fed fashionable lady does not even *see* the same bread-roll, it does not exist, it is not a "figure" for her.

The fact that the Ego concentrates only on one thing at a time shows one great disadvantage: the organism can be taken by surprise—can be caught unawares.[1]

A compensation of this disadvantage is the use of an armour (shells, etc., in lower animals, character-armour in human beings, houses and fortresses in society). Even the most fortified castle, however, cannot be hermetically sealed: it must have doors and other openings—elastic communications with the world.

To guard such openings the human mind has developed a censor, a

[1] When telling a joke we make use of this weakness in our organization by keeping the attention fixed in one direction and jumping at the listener unexpectedly from another, thus producing a slight shock. We feel lost, stupid, if we don't see the point, but once the meaning of the joke is seen, the holistic balance is restored. This restoration occurs in a similar way with an "anti" shock. The solution jumps into consciousness with an experience of surprise, accompanied by exclamations like "Oh, gee!" "Got it," etc. If the joke is stale, or the solution anticipated, we are uninterested or bored.

moral watchdog. This censor—directed *inwards*—played a great part in Freud's earlier theory. We must, however, not forget that the censor's task is directed *outwards* as well. The censor in a country like Nazi Germany prohibits the entry of unwanted news by jamming radio stations and arresting the entry of adverse newspapers. The censoring instance in our mind tends to stop unwanted material from gaining awareness: thoughts, feelings and sensations from inside: knowledge from outside. The censor's aim is to admit only such material as he considers good and to exclude all bad thoughts, wishes and so on.

What is the meaning of this "good" and "bad"?

VII

GOOD AND BAD

Although gestalt psychology has assisted us greatly in the understanding of our subjective individual worlds, there is one factor which needs further examination: the factor of evaluation. Were it correct that the world exists only according to our needs, then objects would either exist for us or they would not. The average teacher is, for instance, more interested in those pupils who learn easily and give no trouble. There are teachers who, at least occasionally, take no notice of the difficult pupils, treating these at times as if they were non-existent. As a general rule, however, the teachers distinguish their students as good or bad pupils.

This evaluation makes it necessary for us to consider a new aspect of our lives. Thinking in terms of "good" and "bad," appraisement, ethics, morals, or whatever you like to call the evaluations, plays an important part in the human mind and is neither explained by the figure-background phenomenon nor by holism, although a certain relationship exists between "feeling good or bad," and complete and incomplete wholes.

In the name of "good" and "bad," wars are fought, people punished or educated, friendships formed or broken. Dramatic plays usually contain one person—the hero—who is painted white, with invisible wings, and his counterpart, the villain, black, with horns. Heaven and hell. High honours and prison. Sweets and whippings. Praise and condemnation. Virtue and vice. Good and bad; good and bad, good and bad . . . like the unending rumble of a train this "good and bad" never ceases to permeate human thoughts and actions.

Four ingredients, so it appears to me, come together to mix the cocktail of ethics: differentiation, frustration, the figure-background phenomenon and the law that quantity changes into quality.

*   *   *

As an example for the demonstration of differentiation we selected the hole and the mound being created from a level. Let us consider two people who have brought about such a differentiation, a city engineer and the owner of a coal mine. The city engineer has to dig trenches along a street to lay a cable. His interest will mainly be in the correctness of his trenches, and the mound will be a nuisance to him and still more of a nuisance to the traffic.

The owner of a coal mine, on the contrary, is interested in the mound—in the big mountain of coal heaped up and waiting to be sold. To him the hole in the ground, the shaft from which the coal was taken, is a nuisance, as laws exist which demand from him care and caution that no accidents should happen.

Thus we see that the mound and the hole have a different interest and different valuation for these two men. Their likes and dislikes go in opposite directions, their likes being identical with their interests, and their dislikes identical with the demands made upon them. Their attitude itself is similar. Both men feel likes and dislikes with a faint tinge of good and bad. They might curse or bless, but the engineer would not call—as a child might do—the disturbing heap of soil "naughty." He has already learned to differentiate his attitude towards *objects* and *behaviour*, while for the small child all things are animated and "behave" instead of having qualities. We speak of a good or bad apple, approving or disapproving of its quality, but when we apply this evaluation to behaviour we start to moralize.

This moralism—the discrimination between good and bad—comes into existence in early childhood. Psycho-analysis maintains that there is a period in the child's life called the ambivalent stage—the period of double evaluation—and a post-ambivalent stage, in which the youngster achieves an objectivity not previously possessed, enabling him to weigh up the good and bad qualities of a character. Further development (beyond thinking in terms of "good" and "bad") may result in an attitude of "interested" detachment.

What figure-background formations lead to ambivalence?

A child cannot conceive its mother as an individual, or even approach any sort of complete knowledge, or understanding, of her. Only those parts of the world which we need become "figure," standing out clearly from the surrounding chaos. Consequently only those aspects of the mother which it requires exist for the child. For the suckling, as Freud has pointed out, the world exists only as something fleshy, yielding milk. This "something" is later called the breast of the mother. As development proceeds, and as the further requirements of the child become apparent, more and more aspects of the mother come into realization and thus into existence for the child.

Two situations may now arise: the mother either meets the requirements of the child, or else she does not. In the first case (e.g. breast feeding) the child becomes satisfied. It feels "good" and the image of the mother (confined to the feeling, smelling and seeing of the breast) disappears into the background until the returning hunger renews it (organismic self-regulation).

The second situation, opposed to the former in every respect, arises when the needs of the child are not fulfilled. The child suffers a frustration, the tension of the urge increases, and the organism produces energies, the "means" to achieve the "end": satisfaction. The child becomes very agitated, starts crying or flies into a rage. If this intensified activity leads to ultimate satisfaction there is no harm done to the child: on the contrary, it will have developed some energy and means of expression. If, however, the frustration persists beyond the suspense which the child is able to endure, it feels very "bad." The image of the mother, as far as the child conceives it, does not completely recede into the background, but becomes isolated, impregnated (not with libido, but) with anger, and subject to memory. The child has suffered a trauma, which will recur every time a real frustration occurs.

Thus the child (and the human organism in general) experiences two opposite reactions, according to the gratification or the frustration of its requirements. It feels "good" if satisfied, "bad" if frustrated.

Yet somehow our theory does not completely fit the facts: if an instinct is gratified we find that the desired object disappears into oblivion. We take the good things in life for granted. The greatest luxury, once it has become a matter of course (and so long as it is not experienced as the gratification of a real need) does not contribute to our happiness. On the other hand, the ungratified child experiences a trauma: the desired object becomes a "thing" subject to memory.

Against the two facts, however, stands another—the fact that we also remember good things.

Let us consider the details of the following scheme:

	Gratification	Temporary frustration	Frustration
Satisfaction	Immediate	Postponed	Overdue
Memory	Nil	Pleasant	Unpleasant
Influence on personality	Inertia	Work	Trauma
Pleasure/pain principle	Pleasure	"Reality"	Pain
Reaction	Indifferent	Good	Bad

For the explanation of this scheme, let us consider oxygen hunger.[1]

[1] I have intentionally refrained from applying here the example of the breast-fed baby. Firstly, it is too early to discuss the supposed libidinal kathexis here: secondly, the satisfied happy suckling, as we see it, is a product of our civilization. The young animal sucks whenever it wants to, and with primitive peoples it is the habit of the mother to carry the baby around and to suckle it as often as it wants food. (Weinland observed a female kangaroo, cub in pouch, which was still being suckled by its mother.) In our civilization, however, we institute meals, and, if possible, even timed meals, for breast-feeding. Thus when the child gets his breast-meal he attains a two-fold gratification: he regains contact with the mother (the conscious gratification, i.e. the hanging-on-bite) and achieves the postponed gratification of his hunger (second column). Therefore, the question to be decided is whether the baby's happiness is of natural or of social origin (due to the termination of the temporary frustration).

Ordinarily we take our breathing for granted. We are not aware of it and are indifferent to it. Let us assume that we are in a room with a number of people and that the air gradually becomes stuffy, but so imperceptibly that the stuffiness does not transgress the threshold of our consciousness, and our organism has no difficulty in adjusting itself. If, after a while, we go into the open, we immediately notice the difference and feel how good the air is. Returning to the room we become aware of its stuffiness. After that we will be able to recall and compare the experiences of the pure and the polluted air (pleasure-pain principle).

The traumatic effect of repressions or frustrations in childhood led people to the premature conclusion that a child should not suffer deprivations during its upbringing. Children reared in conformity with this conclusion are, however, not less nervous. They show typical signs of a neurotic character, are unable to stand frustrations, and are so spoilt that even a slight delay in gratification produces a trauma. If they do not immediately get what they want they use the technique of crying which they have mastered to perfection. Such children very easily feel bad, and regard their mother (as will be shown presently) as the "bad" mother— the witch.

From this we learn that a child should be brought up on the lines of what Freud calls the "reality principle," the principle which says "yes" to the gratification, but demands that the child be able to endure the suspense of postponement.[1] It should be prepared to do some work in exchange for the gratification, and this should be something more than a mumbled "thank you."

Immediate gratification does not produce a memory. The "good" mother is not experienced as such if she meets all the child's demands immediately, but only if she does so after a delay, after suspense. The good mother, represented in fairy tales by the good fairy, always fulfils extraordinary wishes.

If I have put the pleasure principle into the first column I have done so because theoretically it belongs there: but in the normal course of immediate gratification (without conscious tension) this pleasure will be so slight as to pass almost unnoticed.

As to the social aspect of the pleasure-pain principle, it may well be that people of the privileged classes experience less pain than those of the working classes: but as their life can be compared with that of a spoilt child (fulfilment of their genuine needs is easily granted) and they do not

---

[1] In spite of his kathexis-theory, it seems that Freud regarded reality as something absolute. He did not emphasize sufficiently its dependency upon our individual interests and upon the social structure. This does not diminish the value of what he meant by the reality-principle, which might better be called "delaying" principle in order to emphasize the time factor, and thus contrast it with the shortcut of impatient and greedy behaviour.

experience tension or suspense (the relief of which means happiness) they often create this tension artificially, e.g. by gambling or taking drugs. The gain or loss of money, the frustration and gratification connected with taking drugs creates for them the sensations of pain and pseudo-pleasure. This absence of happiness is very real, although to those of the poorer classes their lives seem glamorous and romantic. A dinner which to a stockbroker might be nothing but a boring duty, endangering his liver, might to his clerk symbolize a feast to be remembered for years. But this experience would only be wonderful as an isolated event. If the clerk entered the privileged classes he would soon take those things just as much for granted and find life as dull as his former employer does (biological self-regulation).

I hope I have made clear one point—for real gratification a certain amount of tension is necessary. When this tension grows too high, then (according to a law of dialectics) quantity changes into quality, pleasure changes into pain, hugging into crushing, kissing into biting, stroking into striking. When the process is reversed and the high tension is lowered, then the unpleasantness changes into pleasantness. This is the state which we call happiness.

*   *   *

Having rectified our first observation about feeling "good" and "bad" (according to gratification and frustration) we must see how it is that we so seldom experience the feeling of "good" or "bad" as reactions. What makes a child say "Mother is bad" instead of "I feel bad"? In order to understand this we have to consider the process of projection, which plays a large part in our mental make-up, and the importance of which cannot be over-estimated.

In a cinema, we have a white screen in front of us: at the rear is a machine called the projector, through which strips of celluloid, called films, run. We seldom see these films and when we are enjoying a performance we certainly do not think of those strips of celluloid. What we see and enjoy is the projected film—the picture which is projected on the screen. The same thing happens when a child or an adult projects. The child, unable to distinguish between its reactions and their originator, does not experience the feeling of good or bad itself: it rather experiences the mother as being good or bad. With this projection two phenomena come into existence: ambivalence and ethics.

We have seen that all extreme behaviour, good or bad, can and will be remembered. Whenever the mother impresses the child strongly with "good" or "bad" deeds, the child remembers them. They don't remain as isolated entities in the child's memory but will form comprehensive wholes, according to their affinities. Instead of a chaotic mass of memories, the child gets two "groups" of memories: pictures of the good mother on the one hand, and of the bad mother on the other. These two groups will crystalize into images: the good mother (the fairy) and the bad mother (the witch). When the good mother emerges into the foreground the witch will recede completely into the background, and vice versa.

Sometimes both mothers are present, and the child is thrown into a conflict by its ambivalent feelings. Being unable to endure this conflict and to accept the mother as she is, it will be torn between love and hate, and will be thrown into utter confusion (like Buridan's donkey or Professor Pavlov's double-conditioned dog).

Ambivalent attitudes are, of course, not confined to the child. Nobody can get beyond them, except in certain spheres and at certain times where rational aspects have replaced the emotional ones. The psycho-analytical idea of a post-ambivalent stage is an unattainable ideal, which, even in the strictly objective world of science, can only be achieved to a certain degree. Often enough scientists of high standing have become abusive when their beloved theories are doubted. Objectivity is an abstraction which can be faintly guessed by working from a great number of opinions, calculations and deductions, but you and I, as human beings, are not "beyond good and bad" (Nietzsche) be it that we moralize or judge from utilitarian or aesthetic points of view.

You probably can recall a person of whom you were very fond, but after some disappointment he became abhorrent and nothing he did found favour in your eyes. The Nazis even turn this attitude into a principle. They call it the friend-foe theory, maintaining that they may declare anybody friend or foe at will, depending merely on the needs of a political situation.

Right and wrong, good and bad, confront us thus with the same problems as did reality. Just as most people consider the world as something absolute, so also do they regard morals. Even people who realize that the conception of morality is a relative one (that what is "right" in one country may be "wrong" in another) exhibit moralistic standards as soon as their own interests are involved. The motor-car driver, intolerant of pedestrians, will curse motorists when he himself turns pedestrian.

A child's judgment of its mother—as we have seen—depends upon the fulfilment or frustration of its wishes. This ambivalent attitude exists just as much in the parents. If a child fulfils their wish (if it is obedient) and does not even protest against senseless demands, the parents are satisfied, and the child is regarded as "good." If the child frustrates the parents' wishes (even in cases where it is evidently incapable of understanding, far less of fulfilling, what is asked of it, and cannot conceivably be held responsible for its actions or reactions) it is frequently called "naughty" or "bad."

A teacher will classify his pupils as "good" or "bad" according to their ability to fulfil his wishes as regards learning, attentiveness or sitting still; or, if the teacher is interested in sport, he may prefer pupils who share this interest. States with different structures make different demands on their citizens, the "good" citizen being, of course, the one who complies with the laws, whilst the "bad" citizen is called a criminal. The citizen who is satisfied with his government will praise it as "good." If, however, it imposes too many restrictions and demands upon him it becomes a "bad" government.

The State or the average father or the governess—all behave like spoilt children. They take notice of a person only if he comes into the foreground by doing something unusual—a heroic deed, a brilliant achievement in sport, correct behaviour in an extremely difficult situation. On the negative side there is the citizen who becomes a disturbing factor in the smooth functioning of society—the great criminal. He might be given the same front page headline as the hero. An otherwise indifferent father will certainly notice his child when it disturbs his sacred sleep.

In every society there is, in addition to these emotional reactions, a number of demands so inflexible, so deeply rooted, that they have become canons of conduct, dogmas and taboos, and have given our ethical system its fixed and rigid aspect. This rigidity is reinforced by the existence in us of that peculiar moral institution called "conscience." This conscience has static morals. It lacks an elastic appreciation of changing situations It sees principles but not facts, and can be symbolized by the blindfolded figure of Justice.

*   *   *

What have we found so far? Good or bad, right or wrong, these are judgments made by individuals or collective institutions, according to the fulfilment or frustration regarding their demands. They mostly lose their personal character and, whatever their social origin might have been, they have become principles and standards of behaviour.

"An organism answers a situation." Man in general has forgotten that good and bad were originally emotional reactions, and is inclined to accept good and bad as facts. The result of this is that once some person or group is called good or bad, emotional answers are roused (love and hate, ¶ and ‡, cheers and condemnation. Love for the Führer and hatred of the enemy at hand: submission to one's own and disgust with strange gods). Whenever we meet "good" or "bad" we feel the whole scale of emotional reactions, from indignation to vindictiveness, from silent appreciation to the bestowal of high honours.

Calling persons or things "good" or "bad" has more than a descriptive significance—it contains dynamic interference. "You are a bad boy" is mostly charged with anger, even hostility. It demands a change and threatens unpleasant consequences, but the emotional content of "You are a good boy" is praise, pride and promise.

As the intensity of reactions varies, different amounts of ¶ and ‡ come into play. That our reactions towards the good things and persons are ¶, is not difficult to realize. Linked up with the emotional reaction of liking or loving is the tendency to make contact. The mother caresses the good child: the child will show its gratitude towards the governess by hugging and kissing her: the king will shake hands with a hero: the President of France, in bestowing the Legion d'Honneur, will embrace the recipient. With children the contact is often made indirectly, by giving presents to them, e.g. for the stomach (sweets); with adults by presenting them with gifts for their vanity (medals and titles).

At the other end of the scale we find annihilation. The bad thing or person is experienced as a nuisance or disturbing factor to such a degree that the desire is to do away with it. The child wants to throw the "bad" mother out of the window, wishes her dead. (It has to be emphasized that the child really means this during a period of frustration. As soon as the frustration is no longer in the foreground, the death-wish will probably disappear.) The mother, on the other hand, might threaten to leave the naughty child and to deprive it of her own presence, well knowing how much it needs her. The Roman Catholic Church excommunicates its offenders. In oriental tales the despot kills off all who become a nuisance to him. In our time this procedure has reached a climax in the Nazis technique, of destroying opposition (concentration camps, "shot while trying to escape," extermination of whole races).

Reviewing the contradiction which apparently exists in Ethics (the clear-cut unambiguous emotional reactions on the one hand and the relativity of ethical standards on the other) we have found that good and bad are originally feelings of comfort and discomfort. These are projected on to the object that stimulated those feelings and that subsequently is called good or bad. Later on good or bad became terms isolated from the original deeds, but retaining the meanings of signals, the ability to evoke—though in a different context—all the mild or violent reactions of wish-fulfilment and wish-frustration.

VIII

NEUROSIS

I have repeatedly mentioned that our organism is not in the position to concentrate on more than one thing at a time. This deficiency, based upon the figure-background phenomenon, is partially being made good by the holistic tendency of the human mind—by the striving for simplification and unification. Every scientific law, every philosophical system, every generalization, is based upon the seeking for the common denominator, for the fact identical to a number of things. In short, for the "gestalt" common to a number of phenomena.

The objection will be that a number of people can concentrate on several things at the same time. This is not true. They might quickly oscillate between different items, but I have not found anyone who, for instance, in the following figure could see six *and* seven cubes at the same time.

6 CUBES   7 CUBES   6 OR 7 CUBES

The creation of new wholes is not accomplished by fusion but by more or less violent struggles. Although we have to leave much of this theme over for the chapter on Ego-functions, we may hint here at the fact that, e.g., wars often lead to the creation of larger formations or unification of masses. This unification might be extensive or intensive. Although after World War No. 1 Russia as a whole did not expand, the internal incoherent structure became distinctly more integrative and stronger, whilst the present 1942 expansion of Germany is anything but integrative.

The laws of conflict (‡) and integration (¶) become evident in the relationship between individuals as much as in that between groups, and they apply likewise to the interdependency between individual and community.

The most important conflict which can either lead to an integrated personality or to a neurotic one is the conflict between the social and biological needs of man. What is good and bad (mostly called right and wrong) from the social point of view, might by no means be good and bad (healthy or unhealthy) for the organism. Against the biological laws of self-regulation mankind has created the moralistic regulation—the rule of ethics, the system of standardized behaviour.

Originally, leaders (kings, priests, etc.) laid down the law in order to simplify their ruling, and later on the "ruling" classes followed this routine: when, however, the principle of self-regulation was violated up to an unbearable point, revolutions followed. After realizing this fact, the privileged classes more often considered the needs of the ruled classes, at least to such a degree as to prevent revolutions. Such a system is usually called democracy. Under fascism the most vital needs of large groups are frustrated for the sake of a small ruling group, while in socialism (and in the Atlantic Charter) general freedom from want is the foremost aim. This should be remembered by those who put fascism and socialism in the same category! The only sphere in which both are identical is in their appreciation of holism (totalitarianism and planned economy).

In spite of the relative uniformity of human beings (if someone has his heart on the right side, or has six fingers instead of five, he is looked upon as a monstrosity, and a man with two mouths or one eye approaches the limits of our imagination), it is never possible to standardize the behaviour of every member of a group. Some individuals cannot comply with the demands made upon them and are called criminals. If they do not fit into the general pattern they evoke in their rulers rage. Punishment follows, either to "educate" the criminals or to arouse terror and fright in their fellowmen, lest they, too, might become disobedient, "bad."

Often enough, however, the socially required self-control can only be achieved at the cost of devitalizing and of impairing the functions of large parts of the human personality—at the cost of creating collective and individual neurosis.[1] The religious and capitalistic development of society is responsible for the main share in the creation of collective neuroses, of which the suicidal wars now raging throughout the world are sympto-

---

[1] In pre-psycho-analytical times the neuroses were called functional diseases. Neurosis is a disorganization of the proper functioning of the personality within its environment. Although generally no gross physiological changes can be discovered and only minor differences like vaso-motoric instability, disturbances of glandular secretions and muscular mal-co-ordination can be observed—a neurosis has to be considered an illness in the same way as the weakness of the heart is called an illness.

The margin between a proper and insufficient functioning of the heart is rather broad. The strain of competing in a Marathon race would be too much for your heart, if it is not functioning one hundred per cent: on the other hand, a person with damaged heart valves, leading a comfortable, quiet life may live for years. A similarly broad margin exists in the functioning of ourselves within society.

matic. "The world has gone insane," E. Jones once remarked to me, "but, thank Heaven, there are remissions." Unfortunately these remissions are like the return of a pendulum gathering force for new progress—for the Twentieth Century's swing.

The infectious nature of neurosis is based upon a complicated psychological process, in which feelings of guilt and fear of being an outcast (‡) play a part, as well as the wish to establish contact (¶), even if it be a pseudo-contact. The drug addict induces others to indulge in the same habit. Religious sects send missionaries to convert heathens, and the political idealist will try to convince everybody, by any means, that his particular outlook is the only "right" one. *Und willst Du nicht mein Bruder sein, dann schlag ich Dir den Schaedel ein.* (If you refuse to be my pal, I shall be forced to crack your skull.)

A simple example of the spread of neurotic infection was given in a London weekly: the members of a certain heathen tribe practised sexual intercourse before marriage.[1] Missionaries interfered, declaring this to be a sin. The observer describes how these harmless and frank people became shy, avoided the missionaries and became liars and hypocrites. We may assume that later they not only avoided the missionary but also the community, and in the end concealed their sexual needs even from themselves.

If a whole town turns out chanting magic words, making magic gestures and bringing offerings to supernatural beings, in the expectation that this will ingratiate the gods and help to break a drought, and they all have faith in the efficacy of this procedure, none will realize the stupidity of this behaviour, the insanity of such collective neurosis. But if an individual awakens and regains his senses, he will come into conflict with his environment and become isolated from family and friends, a figure outstanding against the background of the community, an object of hostility and perse-

[1] Perhaps the most important of our moral institutions is marriage. Without any question there are many advantages in this institution, but weighing up the beneficial and the detrimental aspects it remains a moot question which side of the scale is the heavier. Were the genuine attraction in the marriage situation so great, it would be unintelligible why the Roman Catholic Church regards it as necessary to make divorce impossible. If somebody likes a place, high walls are not necessary to keep him there.

We find happy marriages exceptional, laudable examples held up to mankind. Then there are a number of tolerably "good" marriages, which are matters of convenience and habit. Few marriages are openly unhappy, but many partners live a marriage full of repressed unhappiness, which finds its outlet in irritability, tendency to domineer each other, etc.; in short, they live in the most intimate hostility. Unfaithfulness, separation, divorce are (mostly unsuccessful) attempts to return to health. The primitive method of having intercourse before marriage until a satisfactory partner has been found by spontaneous contact (in contrast to moral obligations or monetary advantages) gives a much better chance for a continuation of this contact, eventually under the name of marriage. Under these circumstances the people and not the institution are in the foreground.

cution. Possibly, he may develop an individual neurosis, by a process which cannot be fully understood without the knowledge of the paranoic character. The community will be aggressive towards the man who doubts their ideology and will do its utmost to hurt him. And he, in turn, if he is unable to hit back, will either repress his aggression or project it on to his adversaries, thus changing real persecution into persecution mania and fear.[1]

So, an outcast, he withdraws from the world and loses contact; and the fewer chances he has of gratifying his social needs, and the more his instincts are deprived of gratification, the greater becomes the viciousness of the neurotic circle.

For a cure, there are two opposite courses possible: the autoplastic and the alloplastic. Either he gives up his heresy and returns, a prodigal son, into the lap of the collective neurosis (this is difficult after he has gained his insight) or he succeeds in converting the rest of the community to his way of thinking. Such a successful alloplastic cure by winning the others over to his side means not only a justification of his existence, a re-establishment of contact, but also a step in development, regression to nature and health, and progress towards wider knowledge.

This process would correspond to the treatment of the individual neurosis. The progress of the neurosis must be halted, and the regression to the layers of biological health stimulated.

The reader should not take offence if I sometimes refer to him as a neurotic—if the cap does not fit he need not wear it. Since, however, we live in a neurotic civilization, nobody is likely to have escaped some twist or other in his personality. Denial of unpleasant facts, though saving discomfort, creates the illusion of their non-existence—*mais ce ne les empêche pas d'exister!* The majority of mankind has only the choice between individual or collective neurosis (e.g. religion) or individual or collective criminality (gangsterism; hitlerism) or a mixture of both (e.g. most cases of juvenile delinquency). Man is caught between the devil of criminality and the deep sea of neurosis. It is next to impossible to avoid the dangers of social or biological impairment. In such a desperate situation man has developed innumerable devices to protect himself from either danger.

Among the safeguards against "doing wrong" we find police and conscience, against neurosis the "cry for nature" and outlets like the carnivals in Roman Catholic countries. A tolerable existence, however, is possible if we apply safety devices for the avoidance of real dangers. The appreciation of which dangers are real and which imaginary, and the application of this judgment characterizes the healthy individual. Anybody who has ever experienced nightmares or a fear when walking through a dark forest,

[1] Jewish children, for example, readily become neurotic where they are exposed to anti-semitic persecution.

when every crack of a twig, every rustle of the leaves seems to herald an approaching enemy, will realize the unnecessary sufferings imposed upon us by such unreal—imaginary—dangers.

The biological avoidance of dangerous contacts is often of importance to self-preservation, and also to the preservation of things with which we identify ourselves, which lie within our Ego-boundaries (Part II) and are therefore of value to us. Anything threatening to impair the whole or parts of the personality is felt as a danger, as something hostile which has to be annihilated, either by destruction or by avoidance.

A great variety of actions intended to avoid unwanted contacts can be observed, the main ones being protection and flight. In war we find: active defence (personal resistance) and active flight (running away); partial defence (digging in, camouflage) and partial flight (strategic retreat according to plan); mechanical resistance (steel helmets, fortifications) and mechanical flight (vehicles). Artificial fog in flight as well as in attack is produced to deprive the enemy of visual contact. To leave fighting rearguards behind while retreating is a combination of flight and defence. Fundamentally, two trains of development in warfare (and this applies likewise to commercial competition, political intrigue, criminology, character formation, and neurosis) stand out clearly. The combination of attack and defence (e.g. the guns and armour-plate of the tank); and the answer to new weapons of attack with adequate defences.

Animals avoid dangers with the help of their skin and its derivates (shells, horns, senses, etc.); they resort to flight by the muscular system (running and flying away); they have at their disposal camouflage (mimicry) and other means of fooling the enemy's eyes. By pretending to be dead (playing possum) the immobilized animal aims at being overlooked. The octopus applies the fog technique for escape, the rat slips into its dug-out, etc. With the more complicated development of the human organism the means of avoidance, too, become more differentiated. In the legal sphere the task of the defence is often more complicated than that of the aggressor—the crown prosecutor—who himself is the defender of the law, which in turn defends society against criminals who might have defended themselves against starvation. In psycho-analysis expressions like *defensive neurosis* and *phobia* show that Freud attempted to classify the neurosis according to the means of avoidance. But this attempt was not carried through, as is seen from the use of expressions like "obsessional neurosis" or "hysteria."

Anna Freud has demonstrated the defensive dynamics of the conscious personality—*The Ego and its defence mechanism*—as a general law. Defence indeed covers a large proportion of avoidance.

The disadvantage of "avoidance" is the impairment of the holistic function. By avoidance, our spheres of actions and our intelligence disintegrate. Every contact, be it hostile or friendly, will increase our spheres, integrate our personality and, by assimilation, contribute to our faculties, as long as it is not fraught with unsurmountable danger, as long as there is a chance to master it.

One apparent contradiction has to be considered: the avoidance of isolation. This is best represented by a person who cannot say "no" and who apparently is not afraid to make, but rather to lose contact. To this I have to say that contact includes its dialectical opposite: isolation; this fact will become clear only in the course of the discussion on Ego functions. Without the isolation component contact becomes confluence. Even the American isolationists in 1941 wanted to retain commercial contact, while avoiding the clash with the Axis. Exactly the same applies to the person who cannot say "no." His tendency is to avoid hostility.

*   *   *

The means of avoidance are so manifold that it is hardly possible to bring them into any kind of order, yet it might be worth while to approach the problem dialectically. In a scheme (though incomplete) we can put down:

(a) The means which tend towards annihilation, which have a sub-tractive function.
(b) The opposite, the plus function—the hypertrophic growths or additions.
(c) Changes and distortions.

Joining and disjoining functions of course occur always simultaneously. But this is evident only in category (c), whilst in (a) or (b) either addition or subtraction is strikingly in the foreground.

(a) Subtraction:
    (1) Scotoma.
    (2) Selectivity.
    (3) Inhibition.
    (4) Repression.
    (5) Flight.

(b) Addition:
    (6) Over-compensation.
    (7) Armour.
    (8) Obsessions.
    (9) Permanent projection.
    (10) Hallucinations.
    (11) Complaints.
    (12) Intellectualism.
    (13) Mal-co-ordination.

(c) Changes:
   (14) Dis-placement.
   (15) Sublimation.
   (16) Many character features.
   (17) Symptoms.
   (18) Feelings of guilt and anxiety.
   (19) Projection.
   (20) Fixation.
   (21) Indecisiveness.
   (22) Retroflection.

(a) Subtraction.

(1) The simplest means of annihilation is the Scotoma (blind spot, black-out of perceptions). This is one of those conjuring tricks (mentioned before) employed in situations where a real annihilation is impossible. By pretending not to hear or see, the source of unpleasantness seems to disappear. Children often cover their eyes or ears with their hands, displaying the origin of the ostrich policy and hypocrisy which may characterize many later actions. Compensation of a scotoma is found in Korsakow's disease, where a gap in memory is filled with imaginary happenings.

(2) Selectivity is a means of avoiding an objective point of view. Where it is dictated by organismic needs, selectivity belongs to the unalterable biological basis of our existence, but its arbitrary application leads to half truths which are more dangerous than lies. It is applied in propaganda and politeness, war news and rumours, wishful thinking and hypochondria, and reaches its peak in the mentality of the hysterical and paranoic character.

One has the impression that from Bergson's concept of the Unconscious, Freud selected the past, the causality, whilst Adler accentuated the future, the purposefulness.

(3) In Inhibition some expression which should get outside the intra-organismic field is retained—is inhibited but not exhibited. By avoiding e.g. crying, the demand of society for self-control is obeyed. The disadvantage is that this often leads to hysterical symptoms. Inhibited expression might appear as self-consciousness.

(4) Psycho-analysis has proved over and over again that Repressions mean the avoidance of awareness. In the long run nothing is gained by transporting an impulse from the conscious to the unconscious field.

(5) Flight is one of the best known of all avoidances—but nobody can run away from himself. The escapist gains nothing as he carries with him all his unfinished problems. The flight into illness and into the future —at least as far as day-dreams are concerned—has been unmasked by psycho-analysis, but its opposite—flight from the present into the past and into "causes"—has actually been supported by Freudism.

(b) Addition.

(6) The most widely known addition is Over-compensation (Adler). The unpleasant feeling of inferiority must be avoided. A wall of opposites to specific inferiorities is built around the vulnerable spot, the result being a multitude of protective measures, even if entirely superfluous. The masculine protest—the wish for a penis—has to safeguard such attitudes which many women unnecessarily regard as weaknesses (S. Rado).

(7) The Armour (Reich) shows a similar structure. A number of muscular contractions, resulting in mal-co-ordination and awkwardness, are produced to avoid the expression of unwanted "vegetative energies" (by this Reich apparently means all functions except the motoric ones).

(8) In the Obsessional Neurosis the avoidance of contact with forbidden objects (e.g. dirt) and the avoidance of certain wishes (e.g. aggressive tendencies) create a mental neoplasma of ceremonies and "making sure" actions. The development of large parts of the personality is arrested.

(9) That Permanent Projections like the creation of gods are an addition is obvious to anybody who does not turn this fact upside down —who believes that these gods have created man. But even with the believer, religion remains an "as if" fiction, a fact which can be realized by comparing a pious persón with a psychotic suffering from religious delusions, who experiences God as a personal reality. Religion tends to prevent the growing up of mankind, tends to keep believers in an infantile state. "We are all children of one father—God!"

(10) Hallucinations are additional activities, covering up and thereby avoiding, the perception of reality. A woman carrying a piece of wood and addressing it as her child avoids the realization of her baby's death.

(11) The grouser has added a wailing wall to his existence. He prefers indulging in complaints to taking action.

(12) Intellectualism is a mental hypertrophy, and by no means identical with intelligence, a fact which many people dislike admitting. It is an attitude designed to avoid being deeply moved.

(13) According to F. M. Alexander many of our actions are accompanied by a tremendous amount of superfluous activities, this excess being the outcome of avoidance of "sensory appreciation" and appearing as Mal-co-ordination.

(c) In this group plus and minus functions are either mixed, or simple changes take place.

(14) In Displacement we avoid the contact with the original object by directing our attention to a less objectionable one. It is not that the replacement of a father-figure by an uncle happens to Mr. X, but Mr. X purposely diverts his interest from the father to the uncle.

(15) Sublimation resembles displacement in that it substitutes one action for another—for a more objectionable one. It is the original direct action that has to be avoided. It seems problematical whether we are

justified in calling displacement a pathological, and sublimation a healthy function.[1]

(16) Two examples belonging to the Character group and its plus/minus functions:

An overclean person wants to avoid contact with dirt, but at the same time remains intensely interested in all occupations connected with dirt (washing, hypertrophied eagerness to trace the tiniest specks, etc.).

The bully is easily unmasked as a coward. Once he meets someone who refuses to be bullied this character feature will collapse. The sternest conscience, if properly tackled, likewise loses its grip on its victims.

(17) The plus/minus function of Symptoms can be gathered from the following example: A woman shows a functional paralysis of her right arm. This paralysis, though in itself a deficiency, is experienced by her as an additional factor. The analysis reveals that she is short-tempered and still inclined to slap her already grown-up daughter. By paralysing her arm she avoids the expression of her temper—she annihilates the temptation of slapping her daughter's face.

(18) Freedom from Feelings of Guilt and Anxiety are, according to a very primitive psycho-analytical conception, all that is required for the cure of a neurosis. They are indeed very unpleasant phenomena. The feelings of guilt (based upon the projected aggression) drive the "sinner" into avoidance: "I shall not do it again." But often enough, as in the case of chronic alcoholism, these feelings of guilt, though very deeply felt at the time, are not of any lasting consequence. They bribe the conscience or environment for the time being, but recede quickly enough into the background once the situation has changed—once the hangover has passed.

With anxiety we shall deal in the next chapter.

(19) Projection (e.g. of aggression) subtracts a certain amount of aggression from the personality, but adds the same amount to the environment. One avoids the consciousness of being aggressive but adds fear to one's life.

(20) The phenomenon of Fixation exhibits to the casual observer only its hypertrophic character, the tremendous attachment (excessive love, repressed hatred, or feelings of guilt) to one person or situation (e.g. family). Together with this fixation the opposite always appears—the avoidance of contact with anything outside the fixation-boundaries. To decide what comes first, the hen or the egg—the fear of outside contact or the clinging to familiar situations—is not easy.

(21) The perfect example of the tension between plus and minus is

---

[1] Dante and Schubert are said to have owed their artistic achievements to sex-frustration and sublimation. Goethe, however, was very creative, even much more versatile than either of them, in spite (or perhaps because) of his many and often satisfactory love affairs.

provided by Indecision. According to Karl Landauer's observations, very young children show little inclination to avoid dangers: dangers are fascinating and the child runs towards them. Soon, however, it learns to reverse its attitude, to run away. In a state of indecision we are torn between the wish to approach and the urge to flee, between contact and avoidance, but as soon as one side of the scale overbalances the conflict is solved, the indecision disappears.

(22) With Retroflection we shall deal extensively later on.

*   *   *

The object of every treatment, psycho-therapeutic and otherwise, is to facilitate organismic balance, to re-establish optimal functions, to remove the additions and to make up for the deficiencies. Psycho-analysis endeavours to replenish the conscious personality with the addition of those parts which were rejected (repressed or projected). The regaining of awareness is identical with the undoing of a great number of avoidances. For Freud the avoidance or acceptance of awareness is more than a change of a characteristic: it is co-ordination to the systems of Consciousness and Unconsciousness; the unconscious material changes its place under certain conditions, especially in the course of a psycho-analysis. This so-called topical aspect can also be applied to the "instinct cycle" and has a more practical value than the above enumeration of avoidances which serves the main purpose of getting acquainted with the different means of avoidance, demonstrating the simultaneous occurrence of advantage and disadvantage, the hopelessness of achieving any valuable results through the neurotic avoidance.

In Chapter V we have demonstrated that for the achievement of the organismic balance there exists a cycle, which we have called organism/world metabolism, and which consisted of six links.

These were:

(1) The organism at rest.
(2) The disturbing factor, which may be (a) internal or (b) external.
(3) Creation of image or reality (plus/minus function and figure-background phenomenon).
(4) The answer to the situation aiming at
(5) A decrease of tension, resulting in
(6) Return of the organismic balance.

This metabolism is disturbed as soon as its cycle is interrupted at any single point, just as an electric installation can be interrupted anywhere. The contact can be broken in the wire, in the switches or in the globe itself.

Regarding the "instinct cycle," we find the interruption—the avoidance of contact—everywhere except with:

(1) The organism at rest. As this is the zero-point, the question of

avoidance does not arise. Taking boredom or depression for zero-points is a mistake, as both are evidently emotional situations, disturbing factors resulting from certain inhibitions.

Taking the sex instinct as example, we meet quite a number of well-known means of avoiding its demands. We find, as we follow up the instinct cycle:

(2) (a) Training in asceticism, the wish to be castrated, the avoidance of stimulating food and drink, the whole armoury of ideological (mainly religious) oppressions, scotomization, mistaking sex impulses for something else.

(2) (b) What means have husband or wife upon whom a sexual demand has been made of avoiding their "duty"? Rationalization (excuses); symptoms (headaches); muscular armour (vaginism); playing possum (too tired); avoidance of situations (polypragmacy, separate bedrooms); avoidance of stimulation (neglecting make-up); active defence (irritability, ridicule).

(3) Suppression of phantasy; religious taboos; occupations which distract the attention from sexual image formations; avoidance of reality; not seeking the object of love; developing an over-critical attitude; deviating the sex impulse into inadequate channels (masturbation, going to prostitutes, perversions).

(4) Avoidance of sexual feelings or activities in erotic situations: Genital de-sensibilization (frigidity); armour (muscular tenseness); diversion of attention (thinking of something else); displacement (talking or doing something non-sexual); flight, scotomization and projection.

(5) Absence of satisfactory orgasm (W. Reich, *Die Function des Orgasmus*) prevents an adequate lowering of sexual tension. Such insufficient sexual activity might be due to an inability to stand sensations connected with the high tension of the orgasm (short-cut, ejaculatio praecox). Other means of preventing the satisfactory orgasm are: sublimation, avoidance of consequence (coitus interruptus), fear of losing energies (retaining the semen).

Emotions and surplus excitement are often avoided under the inhibiting influence of shame (lack of concentration, fear of being disturbed). "Thinking," among other distractions, is another means of avoiding sexual tension.

In most of these cases gratification is not achieved, the situation remaining incomplete. This in turn leads to permanent sexual irritability, a fact which probably induced Freud to regard libido (among other meanings) as a free floating energy, which can play havoc outside the sexual instinct-gratification cycle.

(6) Any of these avoiding attitudes prevents the return of the organismic balance.

*　　　*　　　*

Once more we find a confusing enumeration of possibilities leaving us dissatisfied, unable to discover a simplifying law. If we start all over again, we find originally social and instinctive demands (not causes, as the answers differ with different groups). These demands, e.g. the ten commandments, canon of conduct, requirements of conscience or surroundings, and likewise the instinctive urges are answered by the organism with emotions: fear, shame and such like, if the demands cannot immediately be accepted. The demanding social institution drives home the acceptance of its demands with punishment and reward, with threat and promise. In order to avoid the punishment and get the reward, the disapproved actions are avoided. The demands of the organism (hunger, need of sleep, etc.) are not less intense and painful than those of society. Hence the frequency of social and neurotic, of external and internal conflicts.

So far the process is simple. It only becomes confusing by the multitude of avoidances entering the scene. The technique of avoidance varies greatly according to the situation and means at one's disposal.

A married woman has a lover. The husband, as it happens, strenuously objects. She might decide to *avoid* her lover altogether, or *avoid* being seen with him or, if discovered, she might faint to *avoid* her husband's outbursts of temper, but eventually on regaining consciousness she might invent lies or reproach him for something or other thereby *avoiding* feelings of guilt or punishment. If, however, she yields to his demands—her fear being greater than her desire—she will become cool and hostile and *avoid* everything that would give him pleasure. In either case he will be the sufferer in the end, having based his relationship on demands and not on understanding.

From all this we can draw two conclusions:

(1) That "avoidance" is a general factor to be found in probably every neurotic mechanism.
(2) That seldom, and only in the case of real danger, is anything gained by avoidance.

7 I

IX

ORGANISMIC REORGANIZATION

In the history of the individual, as well as of whole generations, the ups and downs, the rhythm of action and reaction, are like the movements of a pendulum. It is difficult to remain near the zero-point—not to be lifted to the heights of enthusiasm nor to slide down into the depths of despair. The mechanical thinking of the last century induced in our time its opposite, the development of psychology, and psycho-analysis in particular.

In the sphere of psycho-analysis, the pendulum swung from Freud's historical to Adler's futuristic thinking. After Freud's pessimistic, "We are not masters in our own house!" we meet Adler's protest, lust for power. The purely psychologistic attitude of many an analyst (despising physiology like the ascetics of the Middle Ages) found its repercussions in Reich's attempt to represent character as an armour consisting mainly of muscular contractions.

Outside this progressive development there are those analysts who (over-valuing isolated problems and losing contact with the human personality as a whole) go fundamentally astray, such as O. Rank and partly C. G. Jung. Though making some valuable contributions to psycho-analysis (e.g. Jung's introversion and extraversion) they both enlarge on the dubious parts of Freud's theories. Rank led the historical point of view *ad absurdum*—Jung the conception of libido. The first remained stuck in the throes of the birth trauma, the other inflated the terms *Libido* and *Unconscious* to such an extent that, like Spinoza's concept of God, they covered nearly everything and so explained nothing.

Neither contributes to a holistic understanding of the organism. The contributions of Adler and Reich, however, are of greater value to psycho-analysis in that they provide complementary aspects to certain of Freud's theories. Unfortunately, Freudians and Adlerians either fight each other, or cover their mutual contempt with a pseudo-tolerant yet blind and uninterested attitude, thus living up to the best traditions of sectarianism. Although they are both used to thinking in opposites—Freud generally, Adler occasionally (top/bottom; male/female; superior/inferior)—they refuse to see each other as opposites reciprocally complementary in many respects.

Besides considering the dialectics of the psycho-analytical movement, we can also deal with the dialectics of psycho-analysis itself. Starting

with the word psycho-analysis, we propound the following complementary scheme:

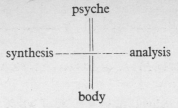

The opposites, psyche and body, have been dealt with as differentiations of the organism. Regarding analysis, Freud maintains that a synthesis
is not necessary—that the libido, once set free, will find its own way of
sublimation. Nevertheless, psycho-analytical circles do speak of re-
education and re-conditioning. Realizing, for instance, that the phobic
attitude (the tendency to avoid the facing of conflicts, instincts, feelings
of guilt, and so on) is an essential part of every neurosis, Freud prescribes
as antidote: contact with the feared things. He persuades a person suffering
from agoraphobia to attempt—after a certain amount of analysis—to
cross a street. Here he is aware that mere talking is insufficient. I doubt,
however, whether Freud was fully aware of the fact that interpretations
are also part of active psycho-analysis, as the patient is brought face to
face with that part of himself which he tries to avoid. This active behaviour
of holding a mental mirror in front of the patient aims at a synthesis,
integration—recontacting the isolated parts of his personality.

Both analysis and synthesis tend to bring order into the patient's
personality, to make his organism function with a minimum of effort.
We may call this process reconditioning or reorganization. Thus polarizing
the word psycho-analysis we arrive at a somewhat clumsy term: Organismic
reorganization of the individual. If we accept these conclusions we have
to broaden the basic rule of psycho-analysis. This rule is in brief. "The
patient shall say everything that enters his mind, even if he feels embarrassment or other refractory emotions, and he shall suppress nothing
whatsoever." Complementing this rule we have to add, firstly, that he is
expected to communicate everything he feels in his *body*. The patient
will, of his own accord, mention any strong physical symptoms, such as
headaches, palpitations, etc., but he will neglect whatever is less obtrusive,
such as a slight itch, restlessness and all the subtler expressions of the
body language, the importance of which has been pointed out by W.
Reich and G. Groddeck. A simple method of covering the whole organismic situation is to ask the patient to convey to the analyst whatever he
experiences mentally, emotionally and *physically*.

The second change which I propose to the basic rule concerns suppression of embarrassment. A patient, eager to comply with the analyst's

demands will swing over to the opposite extreme: instead of holding back, he will *force himself* to say everything. He achieves this by suppressing his embarrassment. The patient very soon acquires a technique of either wording the embarrassing material in a non-committal manner, or of bracing himself and deadening his emotions. So he becomes shameless, but not free from shame; the ability to endure embarrassment, the most valuable result of a proper application of the basic rule, remains undeveloped. The problem of embarrassment will be dealt with in a later chapter dealing with ego-development. Thus we have to make the second change in the wording of the basic rule: we have to impress upon the patient that he must neither suppress nor force anything, and that he must not forget to convey to the analyst every bit of conscious resistance such as embarrassment, shame, etc.

Similarly, the analyst should not put pressure on the patient and persuade him to talk, but should attend to the resistances and avoidances. If one wants to draw water from a tap, one would not dream of squeezing the water out of the pipe; one would simply loosen the resistance, the tap which holds the water back. If Ferenczi maintains that the closing muscle of the anus is the manometer of resistance, and if Reich extends this observation towards every possible contraction, they are both right; but we must not forget for a moment that these muscular contractions are only "means whereby"—that they are functions on behalf of emotions, that they are brought into play in order to avoid the feelings of disgust, embarrassment, fear, shame and guilt.

In addition to the anal resistance there are many other resistances, mainly the resistance of the intake, the oral resistance. A muscular resistance is found in anxiety.

*   *   *

I cannot find a better example than the phenomenon of anxiety to demonstrate the superiority of the organismic conception over a purely psychological or physical approach. The general practitioner with the traditional physiological outlook, coming across anxiety attacks in connection with some disease of the heart, sees in them the effect of the faulty functioning of the cardiac system. If, however, these attacks were an integral part of the disease, they would be permanent, which of course they are not. On the other hand he realizes mostly that an additional factor, excitement, is involved which thrusts an additional load upon the heart, and he warns his patients against this danger. These anxiety attacks come about through the coincidence of heart disease and excitement.

Dealing with the psychological approach to the problem of anxiety, I shall confine myself to a résumé of the psycho-analytical theories. Freud defined the anxiety-neurosis as a disease distinct from other neuroses; and as one could expect from the originator of the libido-theory, he attributed it to suppressed sexual impulses. But *how* these sexual impulses are converted into anxiety he could not reveal. He explained it on the one hand *teleologically*, like Adler (stating that anxiety looks into the future—that it is a danger signal or warning sign produced by the Unconscious), but on the other hand historically, taking over from Rank the idea of the birth trauma as the originator of anxiety. Whenever we get into a dangerous situation, he maintains, our unconscious mind, in order to warn us, quickly recalls the experience of our birth.

Other psycho-analysts put forward different theories about anxiety. Harnick maintains that a suckling, getting his nose blocked by the mother's breast, experiences anxiety, and the later anxiety-attacks are repetitions of these incidents. Suppressed aggression is held responsible for the development of anxiety by Adler, Reich and Horney, whilst Benedikt—following a late theory of Freud's—considers anxiety to be the result of the repressed "death" instinct.

As these theories have been brought forward by prominent scientists, we have to accept their observations as being correct, though valid only for the situations in which they have been made. But we must distrust any kind of speculation which, in science as elsewhere, leads to premature generalizations. Either "anxiety" is a screen word, and the different explanations cover different phenomena, or else the word "anxiety" covers one specific phenomenon, and the different theories are incomplete explanations, probably missing a factor common to all of them—the factor specific for anxiety. Observations tend to indicate that the latter is the case, and that we have to search for the common factor of the hypotheses brought forward.

We have three groups of psycho-analytical theories: the one that anxiety originates with the birth or the breast trauma, the other that anxiety is due to repressed instincts. Then we find the danger theory, which we can omit as not being specific for anxiety. Anxiety is a frequent answer of the organism to a real or a pseudo-danger, but other reactions (presence of mind, suspicion, fear, panic, etc.) are likewise possible.

The first group refers to the supply of oxygen, to the individual's breathing. The change-over from being supplied by the mother's placenta to active pulmonary breathing may indeed deprive the newly-born child of the badly needed oxygen food, and this will create a heavy minus of oxygen and a correspondingly intense *oxygen-hunger*. The same applies to Harnick's theory according to which the mother's breast may hamper the child's breathing and thus create a similar minus of oxygen.

Looking at the second group, we find a clue to the solution of our problem in the general practitioner's warning to cardiac cases against *excitement*, as well as against physical exertion. In the concentrated expression of instincts the same signs are found as in the effort syndrome (increased cardiac and breathing activity occurring already during milder exercises). Both sexual orgasm and outbursts of temper are peaks of excitement.

Eliminating all the incidental factors we realize that excitement and lack of oxygen form the nuclei of the theories mentioned, and when observing an anxiety attack, we invariably find excitement and difficulty in breathing. Yet this does not solve the problem of how anxiety is produced, and what the relation is between excitement and breathing on the one hand, and anxiety and difficulty in breathing on the other.[1]

The picture of excitement, as everyone has experienced, is increased metabolism, increased heart activity, quickened pulse, increased breathing. This is excitement, but not anxiety. If, however, the child during birth or at the mother's breast suffers from insufficient oxygen supply, the situation becomes an anxiety-situation. Yet, when an adult has an anxiety-fit, he is neither being born at that moment, nor is he being choked by a breast. If we could find the same inadequacy of oxygen supply in exciting situations as in the two infantile situations mentioned, we might realize *how* excitement is converted into anxiety, and thus solve a thousand-year-old riddle.

We get a hint from the language, for the word *anxious*—similarly to the Latin word *altus*—has an ambiguous meaning (being in high tension); it is not differentiated into the meanings of being in a state of anxiety and

---

[1] In the case of the effort syndrome and other cardio-vascular weaknesses the heart does not adequately compensate for the increasing metabolism which takes place in excitement and increased muscular activity. This inadequacy becomes particularly conspicuous if the thyroid balance is disturbed—it lies, as I have mentioned before, between the excitability of a ·Basedowic thyreotoxic and the dullness of a myxoedemic type. Any physician will confirm two facts: firstly the ease with which a Basedowic gets anxiety attacks, and the relative immunity of the myxoedemic type against them; secondly, that the former has an increased, the latter a decreased basic metabolic rate.

Metabolism is a chemical process taking place within our organism and producing conditions vital to our existence, e.g. heat. In this respect the organism behaves exactly like a combustion appliance. A stove, in order to burn and to produce heat, requires two kinds of fuel—oxygen and components of carbon. We generally think of the latter only (the coal or wood), and forget about the other fuel (the air), which is available without cost. A stove cannot burn if it has not sufficient solid fuel or if it lacks the necessary quantity of air. The burning up of substances in the human body takes place in the tissues. The carbon fuel is our food, which has been liquified by a complicated process of assimilation—to be considered later in detail. The oxygen is brought to the tissues by the red blood corpuscles.

Excitement is identical with increased metabolism, increased combustion, increased need for liquid fuel and oxygen. To comply with this increased demand, the blood must rush up more oxygen to the tissues. The pump—the heart—must accelerate and the blood vessels must enlarge to cope with the fuller blood-stream as it is physiologically impossible for the single blood-corpuscles to carry more oxygen. The greater demand for oxygen must be met by the lungs through intensifying the breathing (either by more rapid breathing or by increasing the volume of each breath or both).

being in a state of excitement. It is related to the Latin word *angustus* (narrow), thus pointing to a feeling of narrowness in the chest. In a state of anxiety we "contract," we "narrow" our chest.

There are many situations in which people do not allow themselves to *exhibit* excitement and its symptoms, especially the noisy and intensified breathing. Take the case of the masturbating boy who is afraid that his panting may be heard and give him away. In the development of a "controlled" character (cool, calm and collected) the repression of excitement is often overdone. This avoided excitement can produce a frigid character but not anxiety; but if in spite of all training such a person gets excited, he suppresses its expression, e.g. his breathing. He reduces his oxygen supply by making his muscular system (as far as it is connected with breathing) rigid, compressing the chest instead of expanding it, drawing the diaphragm upwards, thus stopping the expansion of the lungs. He puts on an armour, as Reich calls it. (This term is not quite correct, as an "armour" is something mechanical.)

In a state of anxiety an acute conflict takes place between the urge to breathe (to overcome the feeling of choking), and the opposing self-control.

If we realize that the restricted supply of oxygen results in the speeding up of the heart pump (in an attempt to rush sufficient oxygen to the tissues), we understand the palpitations of the anxiety-attack. A number of complications may occur, e.g. constrictions of the blood vessels which the medical man will often relieve by specific medicines. But in every case our problem can be solved by the formula: *Anxiety equals excitement plus inadequate supply of oxygen.*

There is one more symptom to be found in the anxiety attack, namely restlessness. This restlessness is commonly present in that state of excitement which does not find its natural outlet. Excitement is produced by our organism in situations which require an extraordinary amount of (mostly motoric) activity. A state of rage is identical with the desire to attack, and with the mobilization of all available muscular power. Cases are known in which, in despair or in the state of insanity, people "go all out" and show a superhuman strength. If the excitement is diverted from its real aim, the motoric activity disintegrates and is partly used for bringing into play the counter-muscles, i.e. those muscles needed for restricting the motoric action, for exercising "self-control." But enough excitement is left to cause all kinds of in-coordinated movements, like waving of the arms, walking to and fro, tossing from one side of the bed to the other. On account of this surplus of excitement the organismic balance cannot be restored. By preventing the discharge of this excitement, the motoric system of the organism does not come to rest, but remains *restless.*

For this state, Freud has coined the term "free floating anxiety," a conception typical of the isolationist outlook. A piece of anxiety cannot float about independently in the organism.

The pre-different stage of anxiety is apparent in stage-fright and examination fever. Stage-fright (excitement before a performance) is experienced by most actors; their complaints about it, however, are not justified, for without this excitement their performance would be frigid and lifeless. The danger is that they may try to suppress their excitement, not understanding its meaning and being unable to stand the suspense of both waiting *and* being excited. This suspense will often, by means of self-control, turn the excitement into anxiety, unless they choose the outlet of intense restlessness or hysterical outbursts. We need not go into details of the examination fever. The more a person looks upon an examination as upon something decisive, the more energies will his organism mobilize. The less he is able to stand the tension, the more readily will his excitement change into anxiety.

Though we may be able to trace this change in the history of the person, the actual anxiety attack is not a mechanical copy of a previous one, but is newly produced at any particular present moment. Anxiety can often be dissolved and re-changed into excitement without necessarily delving into the past. The past may have no other significance than to illuminate the circumstances under which the habit of inhibiting the breathing was formed.

One can learn to overcome anxiety by relaxing the muscles of the chest *and* giving vent to the excitement. Often no deep analysis is required, but if unconscious spasms of the chest and diaphragm muscles have become fixed habits, concentration therapy may be indicated.

In order not to muddle the picture of anxiety, I have refrained from dealing with certain complications, e.g. the fact that the carbon-dioxide content of the blood will be upset, and that a forced hyper-ventilation cannot be a cure for anxiety. The organism will not function normally, before the muscular spasms are dissolved or as long as the patient emphasizes the inhalation in his breathing technique. The details of the cure and of proper breathing will be given in the last part of the book.

The following statement by a patient gives conclusive evidence of the interchange between anxiety and excitement.

"My first recollection of my suppression of the emotion of excitement or anticipation was some seventeen years ago, just prior to my writing the matriculation examination. I felt the excitement in my chest, but felt at the same time that I was bottling this feeling up and not allowing any expression until about nine years ago, when it reappeared during certain tennis matches. I found, when merely looking on, that the excitement or anticipation (whatever one may call it) was so great that it developed into anxiety, and then became absolutely unbearable. I suppressed the emotion and allowed no expression for it. Whenever the match depended on one, set, I found the excitement too much to bear, and I walked about like a caged lion, unable to sit or stand still. I would often walk away from the tennis courts and return when I thought the set was over and the results decided. I was completely tense, contracting every possible muscle (more especially those in the chest) with the result that I became short-winded even before five or six points had been played. This feeling eventually became so acute, owing to the continued suppression, that I did all in my power to force my small tennis club to desist from playing in these matches, and even resorted to all kinds of subterfuges to attain this object. This trait has unfortunately now followed me on the golf course and I cannot, of course, obtain any relief by walking away, with the result that I contract the chest muscles so severely that I eventually find difficulty in hitting the ball correctly. On some occasions I contracted the chest so much that a pulse started beating in my throat and increased to such an extent that it almost choked me. On one occasion I had to pass a small examination, consisting of a written paper in the morning, and oral in the afternoon. The day before the examination I experienced the usual sinking feeling in the pit of my stomach accompanied by a feeling of excitement, but to try and describe the way I felt between the morning and afternoon is almost impossible. My chest felt constricted so that I could scarcely breathe, I would not stand or sit and was pacing the building like a lunatic, and when I was eventually called in by the examiner I was practically speechless and shaking life a leaf. I experienced the same emotions and sensations at a race course: having won the first leg of a double ticket I found I could not even bear to watch the second leg of the double and walked away to return after the race. I could relate many more experiences of a similar nature; whenever I have a feeling of anticipation, excitement or anxiety I feel that terrific pressure in my chest, I cannot give expression to the emotion and eventually I succeed in depressing myself, and find that I have lost all courage to face any situation in which any of these three emotions are present."

On the phenomenon of anxiety I intended to demonstrate the great changes in theory and practice which were the consequences of apparently small alterations of the basic rule of Freud's theory. But they also involve a switching over from the technique of "free associations" to a "concentration therapy" which has been inaugurated by W. Reich, and which I am trying to develop systematically. The ultimate aim of the new technique is to cut down the time of the neurosis-treatment and to build a basis for the approach to certain psychoses.

X

CLASSICAL PSYCHO-ANALYSIS

Our attitude towards the good and bad things of life goes—as we have seen—hand-in-hand with reactions in opposites. Strictly speaking, these reactions are not reactions but concurrences, "good" corresponding to love, liking, pride and pleasure, and "bad" to hatred, disgust, shame and pain; they are variations of the ¶ and ‡ respectively, and play their part in the fulfilment or frustration of every wish, of every instinct.

There is no doubt that the expressions of the sex instinct are very powerful, and that ¶ and, to a lesser degree, ‡ participate in its function. But love, liking, pride and pleasure, are they all expressions of the sex instinct, as Freud's libido-theory maintains?

In the course of my observations I found that the hunger instinct and Ego-functions played a much greater part in nearly every psycho-analysis than I was led to expect. Whenever I tried to learn something about the hunger instinct from psycho-analytical literature I found the analysis of hunger was always mixed up with one or another libidinal aspect. Serious attempts were made to approach the problem of Ego-functions, but Freud had assigned to the Ego the part of a second fiddle, with the Unconscious in the lead. I could not get away from the impression that in psycho-analysis the Ego was an inconvenience and, unfortunately, one which persisted in making itself felt, scientifically and practically, in every existence.[1]

Finally I reached a point where the libido-theory—in spite of being a valuable aid in acquiring knowledge of pathological characters of the oral, anal, narcissistic and melancholic type—became more of a handicap than an assistance. I then decided to view the organism without libidinal spectacles and I experienced one of the most exciting periods in my life, receiving, as it were, a shock and a surprise. The new outlook exceeded all my expectations. I found I had overcome a mental stagnation and achieved new insight. I began to see contradictions and limitations in Freud's outlook which for twenty years had been hidden from me by the magnificence and daring of his concepts.

[1] The other day, an eminent analyst compared the Unconscious with an elephant and the Ego with a little baby trying to lead the elephant. What an isolationist conception! What a disappointment to the ambition to be omnipotent! What a split in the personality!

Then I took stock. I had studied with a number of psycho-analysts for years. With one exception—K. Landauer—all those from whom I have derived any benefit have departed from the orthodox lines. In the few decades during which psycho-analysis has existed, a great number of schools have developed. This proves, on the one hand, the tremendous stimulation which emanated from Freud but, on the other, it proved the incompleteness or insufficiency of his system. In other new branches of science, e.g. bacteriology and cytology, the development of different schools was either negligible, or reconciliation resulted in a unified line of research.

While I was living entirely in the psycho-analytical atmosphere, I could not appreciate that the great opposition to Freud's theories might have some justification. We used to brush aside any doubt as "resistance." But in his later years Freud himself became sceptical as to whether a psycho-analysis could ever be finished. This confession struck me as an obvious contradiction to the theory of repression. If the neurotic conflict was a fight between the repressing censor and the repressed sex instincts, then either the adequate release of the sex instinct should provide a cure, or else the silencing of the censor should be sufficient. If the censor was merely taken over (introjected) from the environment, it could not be difficult to mitigate his demands and to release the repressed instincts. In practice, one finds very rarely a neurosis which corresponds entirely to this theory. Usually neither the analysis of the censor (conscience) nor of the transference nor of the sex instinct comprehends the neurotic field. My experiences as a psychiatrist in the South African Army reveal that only about 15 per cent of the neuroses show disturbances of sexual gratification, while only in 2 to 3 per cent could hysteria symptoms be traced to actual sex-frustration.

From this another problem arises. When there is no sex-repression, what happens? Does concentration on the sex instinct contribute in every case to adjustment and stabilization? Certainly it was not so in my personal case. On the contrary; only after having dropped the libido theory and the overvalued importance of sex could I find a sound bearing —a harmony of myself, my work and my environment. Within the last few years I have come to the following conclusions:

The principal approach of Freud in the case of psycho-genic diseases is correct. A neurosis makes sense; it is a disturbance of development and adjustment; the instincts and the Unconscious play an immeasurably greater part in man than was ever dreamt of. Neuroses are the outcome of a conflict between organism and environment. Our mentality is determined more by instincts and emotions than by reason.

On the other side of the balance sheet we find that Freud over-estimated the causality, past, and sex instincts, and neglected the importance of purposiveness, present, and hunger instinct. Furthermore his technique aimed originally at concentration on the pathological symptom. By going into the details of the symptom (so-called associations) such material as the patient had difficulties in revealing was brought to the surface. This concentration on the pathological sphere became distorted into thinking in "free" associations resulting in a race between the wits of the analyst and the patient. The psycho-analytical technique developed thus from the original concentration on the symptom to a *dis*-centration, leaving it to chance and to the pressure of the Unconscious as to how much of it would come to the surface and would be dealt with.

Parallel with this avoidance of facing the symptom goes the avoidance of facing the analyst: the patient has to lie in a position in which the analyst cannot be seen. The psycho-analytical interview has changed from a consultation to a (nearly obsessional) ritual in which a number of unnatural—nearly religious—conditions have to be observed.

Great as the service is which Freud has rendered to mankind by unchaining the sex instinct, the time is ripe—to quote Bertrand Russell— "for the analysis of other instincts, and foremost of the hunger instinct." But this will only be possible by confining the sex instinct to its own sphere, namely to sex and nothing but sex.

The physical aspect of this instinct is based upon the function of the procreative glands. If there is any sense in organismic thinking we have to limit the term libido to the psycho-chemical aspect of the sex instinct, and we should conclude that castrated animals (oxen, etc.) or castrated human beings (eunuchs, etc.) would not be able to experience love, liking or any other form of "sublimated" libido.

Let us compare two situations! A young man, greatly disturbed by his sexual tension, feels the urgent impulse to have sexual intercourse and visits a prostitute. Having achieved gratification, he experiences relief, perhaps also a certain gratitude for this, but often he feels disgusted and experiences a strong desire to push the girl away—to get rid of her as quickly as possible. The situation is different if a man has sexual intercourse with the girl he loves. He is not disgusted but happy to remain with her.

What is the decisive difference? In the first case the man does not like or accept the "personality" of the prostitute. If we deduct the sex impulse, there is nothing left which would make him seek her presence. The beloved, however, is accepted in situations free from sexual urge, her presence *in itself* being gratifying.

In the first case the disgust is not repressed. It has only become a "background" against the domineering "figure" of the sexual desire. If the disgust does not remain in the background, it intermingles with the sex impulse, disturbs the sexual activity, and may even become a foreground figure, making the man sexually impotent, or so confused through "double-conditioning," that he may abandon his object altogether.

Freud says that many a young man in our society cannot desire, where he loves, and cannot love, where he desires. This looks like a split of the libido into animalistic and spiritual love. If love were the outcome of the flooding of our organism with sex hormones, this sublimated spiritual love would disappear as the physical urge vanishes. Yet it does not. Affection remains or even increases, particularly after a perfect orgasm.

The proximity of the emotion called love to the sex instinct made Freud commit his fundamental mistake. The child which loves its mother for all the satisfaction it gets from her, will turn to her—to the one who provides food, shelter and warmth—for the gratification of his first conscious sexual desires (usually between the fourth and sixth year).

We now see how important it is to take the term "sex instinct" as a mere abstraction. If an instinct is not a definite reality, Freud was at liberty to include as many organismic functions in his concept of the sex instinct as he required for his theory. We have to examine how many of such organismic functions (called partial instincts) should be included in the bundle of "sex instincts," and how many should come under a different heading. Freud erroneously interprets love during the period preceding this sexual development (the so-called pre-Oedipus stage) as being also of a sexual nature. He finds a way out of the ensuing complications by calling the *pre-sexual* love *pre-genital*, maintaining that the body openings, the oral and the anal zones, harbour the pre-stages of genital energy.

These openings, the oral and anal zones, are indeed of great importance, not in the development of sexual energy, but in the development of the Ego. They lend themselves readily to sexualization, though *originally* they have no "libidinal kathexis."

In his observations of a case of hysteria, Freud realized that a connection between this illness and sex starvation existed, and on the basis of this case he developed his method for treating hysteria and later other neuroses. Every analyst knows that results in these cases are often excellent and lasting, *if* the patient takes up a healthy sex life.

The general opinion among analysts is that hysteria has largely disappeared from their clientele, because the Unconscious has been warned and has regressed to a more complicated neurosis. This, as a rule, is not the case. We rather have to look for an explanation in the social development: Sexual taboos in our time have been relaxed, and women have achieved a greater economical and, through this, a greater sexual freedom. The knowledge of Freud's findings has spread, and "marriage" is more readily advised by the general practitioner in obvious cases of sex starvation. On the other hand I have had the experience, and so have other psycho-therapists, of cases of hysteria which are very refractory. These cases, particularly of juveniles with so-called "moral insanity," show, in spite of good sexual development and orgasmic potency, definite disturbances of their Ego-development.

Four factors determined Freud's further research: the rôle of the libido in hysteria, the existence of repressed, unconscious parts of our personality, the fact that all mental processes make sense and are determined, and the knowledge that organic beings develop from lower to higher levels. He was confronted with the question: where does the libido come from? It could not, in his opinion, spring suddenly into existence, as his observations clearly showed that children show sex curiosity and impulses long before the time of puberty.

Formerly, puberty (with its development of the procreative function and violent disturbances in the development of the personality) was acknowledged as the beginning of sex life in the rites of all peoples, and was celebrated accordingly. An excitability of the genitals can, however, be observed even in babies. In Cuba, nurses calm the baby by playing with its genitals, just as we give a baby a dummy.

From the infant's "*Wonneludeln*" (lustful sucking of the thumb) Freud concluded the existence of a zero-point differentiating into the hunger instinct as *one* branch, and the libido as the *other*.

There are several objections to this theory:

(1) The differentiation already starts in the foetus, with the development of the alimentary and uro-genital system respectively.

(2) The analysis of the hunger instinct isolated from any libidinal kathexis is hardly considered by psycho-analysis. All conceptions connected with the functions of the alimentary channel like introjections, cannibalism, and defaecation are always tinged with a sexual by-taste.

(3) *The normal assimilation is overlooked*, and perverted conceptions, like pleasure of retention, or inhibition of oral development (e.g. cannibalism) are called normal. In reality retention is painful, and relief pleasant. Retention can provide a pleasure of secondary nature, such as proof of one's will-power or obstinacy.

(4) The libido theory is a biological conception, but certain social aspects are mixed up with it. The anal zone has definitely received its neurotic importance as a result of civilization.

(5) Freud inflates the term "libido" to such an extent, that it sometimes stands for something like Bergson's *élan vital* or for the psychological exponent of the sex-urge—to which connotation its use is restricted in this book. Sometimes it means gratification or pleasure, and it also can jump on to the object of love (cathexis), but without the corresponding hormones.

The more one tries to get to the bottom of the meaning of "libido," the more one gets confused. Sometimes libido is a prime mover, a creative power, and at other times it is a substance being moved about. By what? It seems to me that Freud's "libido" conception tried to cover both the universal ¶ function discussed earlier, and the organismic sex-function, and that only by using the word "libido" without a definite referent could he build up his libido-theory.

(6) In the German language "lust" denotes an instinctive urge, as well as pleasure (cf. the derivatives *luestern* "lustful" and *lustig* "gay"). Correspondingly, the term "libido" among other meanings, stands for sexual energy and also for gratification. Hunger-gratification and defaecation are, however, in themselves pleasurable, like every other restoration of the organismic balance, and there is no need to invest them with an additional sexual energy. The complication of simple biological facts leads to unnecessarily complicated explanations.

To show that I am not exaggerating, I quote a leading psycho-analyst, Marie Bonaparte: "The indication for the gratification of the need for food is the pleasure, in the service of which is the oral libido, which causes living beings to find pleasure in the oral intake. The process of secretion, too, can produce intense pleasure, and the anal and urethral libido express, in their way, the satisfaction of the organism whose digestive functions are in order."

This is an instructive example showing how the libido-concept is bound to lead to confusions:

(1) Libido causes pleasure.
(2) Libido expresses satisfaction.

Replacing this by two other words:

(1) I cause pain,
(2) I express pain,

reveals that (1) and (2) are two entirely different experiences. By attributing the pleasure to the gratification of every instinct, we can undo the unnecessary complications arising from the monopoly of the libido.

K. Abraham, who made very valuable contributions to our knowledge of character formation, encounters similar difficulties when trying to fit his observations into Freud's hypothesis. Here is one very simple example to demonstrate what mental somersaults are performed to bolster up the libido-theory:

"Weaning is the original castration."

(1) Castration is a pathological, weaning a biological phenomenon.
(2) Castration means taking away the genitals or parts of them.

(3) Weaning means depriving the suckling of the mother's breast. To call this deprivation a castration is like calling all dogs fox-terriers.
(4) Birth—and not weaning—is the original separation which the child has to suffer.

*   *   *

In spite of all these theoretical complications and contradictions, Freud's libido-theory and psycho-analytical technique were of tremendous value. He was the Livingstone of the Unconscious and created the basis for its exploration. The result of his theory was a re-orientation in the approach to neurosis and psychosis. The research yielded a number of most valuable observations and facts. Not only a new science, but a new outlook on life was created.

Freud has shifted the orientation of our personal existence from the periphery of consciousness to the Unconscious, just as Galileo dethroned the Earth from the centre of the Universe. And just as astronomy—having to acknowledge ever more "fixed points" and systems as merely relatively "absolute"—had previously taken its stand on the conception of the ether, so Freud created his libido-theory. But πάντα ῥεῖ: every new theory is superseded by a still newer one, and under the impact of new scientific facts the trenches of ether-theory and libido-conception have to be evacuated.

An observation of Leverrier gave Einstein the basis for exploding the phantasy of the ether. To dispose of the libido-theory is much simpler. Confining ourselves to one of the many contradictions, to the equation: libido = gratification = sexual energy, we find that libido is, on the one hand, regarded as a general organismic experience, on the other as an energy. Freud applies this energy in the sense of Bergson's *élan vital*. Admittedly, the original foundation of Freud's libido-conception is an organismic one, but the use of this term has become more and more that of a mystical energy, isolated from its material basis.

Ultimately the libido receives a meaning approaching that of ¶. Whilst the libido is the representative of an instinct, ¶ is a universal cosmic function belonging also to the inorganic world. The opposite of ¶ is ‡ for which Freud correctly has the name destruction, but destruction, too, is an instinct to him.

In order to show the difference between Freud's conception and mine I quote what Freud wrote in the *Encyclopaedia Britannica* on this subject:

"An empirical analysis leads to the formation of two groups of instincts: the so-called 'Ego instincts,' which are directed towards self-preservation and the 'object instincts,' which are concerned with relations to an external object. The social instincts are not regarded as elementary or irreducible. Theoretical speculation leads to the suspicion that there are two fundamental instincts which lie concealed behind the manifest ego instincts and object instincts: Namely (a) Eros, the instinct which strives for ever closer union, and (b) the instinct for destruction which leads towards the dissolution of what is living. In psycho-analysis the manifestation of the force of Eros is given the name '*libido*' . . ."

Let us try to see some of the contradictions which are involved in the above theory and in other aspects of psycho-analysis.

(1) According to Freud the Ego is the most superficial portion of the "Id," but the *instincts* belong to the deepest layers of the organism. Thus how can an Ego have instincts?

(2) "Ego instincts which are directed towards self-preservation." Self–preservation is granted by the hunger instinct and by defence. In both items destruction plays a great part but not as an instinct— only in the service of hunger and defence. In Freud's theory destruction is opposed to the object instincts, but destruction without an "object to destroy" cannot exist.

(3) The arrangement in the above quotation hints that Ego instincts correspond to Eros, and object instincts to destruction. Freud probably meant it the other way round.

(4) ¶ and ‡ are, as mentioned before, universal occurrences. Eros in Freud's terminology is applied as a general term, but the instinct for destruction is intentionally restricted to living beings. This instinct in other places is called death instinct. (A refutation of this *Thanatos* theory will be found in another part of this book.)

(5) I have to emphasize over and over again that the important hunger instinct is not even mentioned. Without considering the hunger instinct the question of destruction and aggression can as little be solved as our social and economical problems.

(6) I confess that I am old-fashioned enough to look upon the problems of instincts from the point of view of survival. To me the sex instinct is the representative of species-preservation, whilst the hunger instinct and the instinct for defence stand for self-preservation.

Ego and Self are by no means identical. The Ego-functions occur in both sex and the hunger instincts. Conscious wishes about self or race preservation seldom exist; we are only aware of desires and needs which want to be gratified.

* * *

How is it possible that the above-mentioned weaknesses in Freud's system have not been clearly set out? My opinion is that most people who came into contact with psycho-analysis have been so fascinated by the new approach, which was far superior to the prescribing of bromides, to hypnosis and to the persuasion therapy, that it became a religion to them. The majority swallowed Freud's theories hook, line and sinker, without realizing that this blind acceptance formed the root of a narrow-mindedness paralysing many of the potentialities of his ingenious discoveries. A sectarianism resulted, characterized by an almost religious credulity, by a passionate search for further proofs and by a patronizing refusal of any facts apt to disturb these sacrosanct ways of thinking. Additional theories complicated the original system, and, as always with sects, each one became intolerant of any other which deviated from the accepted principles. If anybody did not believe in the "absolute truth," a theory was handy which put the responsibility on the complexes and resistances of the sceptic.

There is another point in classical psycho-analysis which cannot stand the scrutiny of dialectical thinking—Freud's "archaeological" complex, his one-sided interest in the past. No objectivity, no real insight into the working of the dynamics of life is possible, without taking into account the counter-pole, that is the future, and, above all, the present as zero-point of past and future. We find the condensation of Freud's historic outlook in the concept of transference.[1]

The other day, whilst waiting for a tram, I pondered over the word transference, and I realized that there would have been no tram, if it had not been transferred from the factory or other tramway lines to the rails in front of me. But the running of a tramway line is not explained by this transference alone. It is a coincidence of several factors, e.g. functioning of electric current and the presence of a staff. These factors, however, are only "means whereby," while the decisive factor is the need for conveyance. Without the passengers' requirements the tram service would be quickly abolished. It would not even have been created.

It is unfortunate that one has to mention such platitudes to demonstrate how selected and comparatively unimportant a part the transference plays in the whole complex. And yet, whatever happens in psycho-analysis is not interpreted as a spontaneous reaction of the patient in answer to the analytical situation, but is supposed to be dictated by the repressed past. Freud even goes so far as to maintain that a neurosis is cured once the childhood amnesia is undone, once the patient has gained a continuous knowledge of his past. If a young man, who has never found anybody to understand his difficulties, develops a feeling of gratitude towards the analyst I doubt whether there exists a person in his past from whom he transfers his thankfulness to the analyst.

On the other hand it is silently acknowledged that the futuristic, the teleological thinking plays its part in psycho-analysis. We analyse a patient *in order* to cure him. The patient says many things *for the purpose of*

[1] According to Freud, a neurosis rests on three pillars: sex instinct, repression and transference.

covering up essential things. The analyst *aims at* stimulating and completing developments which have been arrested.

Besides transference, spontaneous reactions and futuristic thinking, there are the projections which play a very great part in the analytical situation. The patient visualizes disagreeable parts of his own unconscious personality in the analyst, who can often search till he is blue in the face for the original from whom the patient has transferred his image.

A mistake similar to the over-estimation of causes and transference occurs in the concept of "regression." Regression in the psycho-analytical sense is a historical regression, a sliding back to infancy. Is there not a possibility of interpreting it differently? Regression might mean nothing more than a falling back to the true Self, a breakdown of pretences and of all those character features which have not become part and parcel of the personality and which have not been assimilated into the neurotic's "whole."

In order to understand the decisive difference between *actual* and *historical* regression and *actual* and *historical* analysis we have to direct our attention first of all to the time factor.

XI

TIME

Everything has extension and duration. We measure extension in length, height and width; duration in time. All these four dimensions are measures applied by man. This chair opposite me *is* not forty inches high, but *I* can so measure it and, if I throw the chair over, its height is only twenty inches, the previous height becoming the width. Time is measured in one dimension—length. We say a long and a short time ago, but we never speak of broad or narrow time. The expression "it is high time" has its origin probably from high tide or from the water-clock. Whilst for objective measuring, we take fixed points (B.C. and A.D., a.m and p.m.), the psychological zero-point is the ever present, reaching, according to our organization, forward and backward like the maggot that eats its way through cheese, leaving traces of its existence behind.

Omitting the dimensions of time leads to fallacies in logic, to cheating in arguments: Logic maintains that a = a, that, e.g., an apple can replace itself in another context. This is correct so long as the extension only of the fruit is considered, as is mostly done. But it is incorrect as soon as its duration is taken into account. The unripe apple, the tasty fruit and the rotting one are three different phenomena of the time-space event "apple." But being utilitarians we take of course the edible fruit as referent when we use the word "apple."

As soon as we forget that we are time-space events, ideas and reality clash. Demands for lasting emotions (eternal love, loyalty) might lead to disappointment, vanishing beauty to depression. People who have lost the rhythm of time, will soon be out of date.

And what is this rhythm of time?

Apparently our organization has an optimum in the experience of the sense of time—of duration. In language this is expressed as passing—pastime—the past; (in French, *le pas—passer—passe*; in German, *ver-*"*gehen*"—*Ver-*"*gang*" *enheit*). The zero-point is thus, for us, the walking speed. Time marches on! Time which is flying, or crawling, or even standing still denotes the plus and minus deviation. Such a judgment contains its psychological opposite; we would like the flying time to slow down, and to hurry it up when it is crawling.

Concentration on things as time-space events is experienced as patience, a tension between a wish and its fulfilment, as impatience. Apparently, in this case, the image exists merely in extension, the time component being split off as impatience. In this way time awareness, or the sense of time, enters the human life and psychology.

Einstein is of the opinion that the time sense is a matter of experience. The small child has not yet developed it. The awakening of a suckling occurs when the hunger tension has become so high as to interrupt sleep. This is not due to any sense of time: on the contrary, the hunger helps to create such a sense. Although we do not know of any organic equivalents of the time sense, its existence has to be assumed, if not by anything else than by the accuracy with which some people can tell the correct time.

The longer the delay of wish gratification, the greater the impatience, when the concentration remains on the object of gratification. The impatient person wants the immediate, *timeless* joining of his vision with reality. If you wait for a tram, the idea "tram" might slide into the background and you might entertain yourself by thinking, observing, reading or whatever pastime is at hand until the tram arrives. If, however, the tram remains a figure in your mind, then ¶ appears as impatience, you feel like running to meet the tram. "If the mountain does not come to Mohammed, Mohammed must go to the mountain." If you suppress the tendency to run towards the tram (and this self-control has become, with most of us, automatic and unconscious) you become restless, annoyed; if you are too inhibited to let off steam by swearing and becoming "nervous," and if you repress this impatience, you will probably transform it into anxiety, headache or some other symptom.

Someone was asked to explain Einstein's theory of relativity. He answered: "When you spend an hour with your girl, the time flies; an hour seems like a minute; but when you happen to sit on a hot stove, time crawls, seconds seem like hours." This does not conform to the psychological reality. In an hour of love, if the contact is perfect, the time factor does not enter the picture at all. Should the girl, however, become a nuisance, should contact with her be lost and boredom set in, then you might start counting the minutes until you can get rid of her. The time factor will also be experienced, if time is limited, when you want to cram as much as possible into the minutes at your disposal.

There are, however, exceptions to the rule. The repressed memories in our Unconscious are, according to Freud, timeless. This means that they are not subject to change as long as they remain in a system isolated from the rest of the personality. They are like sardines in a tin which apparently remain for ever six weeks old or whatever their age was, when they were caught. As long as they are isolated from the rest of the world very little change takes place until (by being eaten up or oxydized) they return to the world metabolism.

The time centre of ourselves as conscious human time-space events is the present. *There is no other reality than the present.* Our desire to retain more of the past or to anticipate the future might completely overgrow this sense of reality. Although we can isolate the present from the past (causes) and from the future (purpose), any giving up of the present as the centre of balance—as the lever of our life—must lead to an unbalanced personality. It does not matter if you sway over to the right (over-conscientiousness) or to the left (impulsiveness), if you over-balance forward (future) or backwards (past), you can lose your balance in any direction.

This applies to everything, and, of course, to the psycho-analytical treatment as well. Here the only existing reality is the analytical interview. Whatever we experience there, we experience in the present. This must be the basis for every attempt at "organismic reorganization." When we remember, we remember at that very second and to certain purposes; when we think of the future we anticipate things to come, but we do so at the present moment and from various causes. Predilection for either historical or futuristic thinking always destroys contact with reality.

Lack of contact with the present, lack of the actual "feel" of ourselves, leads to flight either into the past (historical thinking) or into the future (anticipatory thinking). Both "Epimetheus" Freud and "Prometheus" Adler, co-operating with the neurotic's desire to dig into the past or to safeguard the future, have missed the Archimedic point of readjustment. By giving up the present as a permanent referent the advantage of going back to the past in order to profit from our experiences and mistakes, changes into its opposite: it becomes detrimental to development. We become sentimental or acquire the habit of blaming parents or circumstances (resentment); often the past becomes a "consummation devoutly to be wished for." In short, we develop a retrospective character. The prospective character, in contrast, loses himself in the future. His impatience leads him to phantastic anticipations which—in contrast to planning—are eating up his interest in the present, his contact with reality.

Freud has the correct intuition in his belief that contact with the present is essential. He demands free-floating attention, which means awareness of all experiences; but what happens is that slowly but surely patient and analyst become conditioned to two things; firstly, to the technique of free associations, of the flight of ideas and, secondly, to a state in which analyst and patient form, as it were, a company fishing for memories, the free-floating attention floating away. Open-mindedness is in practice narrowed down to the almost exclusive interest in the past and the libido.

Freud is not exact about time. When he says the dream stands with one leg in the present, with the other in the past, he includes the past few days into the present. But what happened even only a minute ago is past, not present. The difference between Freud's conception and mine may seem irrelevant, yet actually it is not merely a matter of pedantry, but a principle involving practical applications. A fraction of a second might mean the difference between life and death, as we have seen in Chapter I, in the coincidence of the falling stone killing a man.

The disregard of the present necessitated the introduction of "transference." If we do not leave room for the spontaneous and creative attitude of the patient, then we have either to search for explanations in the past (to assume that he transfers every bit of his behaviour from remote times to the analytical situation) or, following up Adler's teleological thinking, we have to restrict ourselves to finding out what purposes, what arrangements the patient has in mind, what plans he has up his sleeve.

By no means do I deny that everything has its origin in the past and tends to further development, but what I want to bring home is, that past and future take their bearings continuously from the present and have to be related to it. Without the reference to the present they become meaningless. Consider such a concrete thing as a house built years ago, originating in the past and having a purpose, namely to be lived in. What happens to the house if one is satisfied with the historical fact alone of its having been built? Without being cared for, the house would fall into ruin, subjected, as it would be, to the influence of wind and weather, to dry and wet rot, and other decaying influences which, though small and sometimes invisible, have an accumulative effect.

*   *   *

Freud has shaken up our concepts of causality, morality and responsibility; but he stopped half-way: he has not driven the analysis to its ultimate conclusions. He said we are not as good or bad as we believe we are, but we are unconsciously mostly worse, sometimes better. Accordingly, he transferred responsibility from the Ego to the Id. Furthermore, he unmasked intellectual causes as rationalizations and decided that the Unconscious provides the causes for our actions.

How can we replace causal thinking? How do we overcome the difficulties of taking our bearings from the present and achieving a scientific understanding without asking for reasons? I have mentioned before the advantages that accrue from functional thinking. If we have the pluck to attempt to follow modern science in its decision that there are no ultimate answers to the "Why?" we come across a very comforting discovery: all relevant questions can be answered by asking: "How?" "Where?" and "When?" Detailed description is identical with concentration and increased knowledge. Research requires detailed descriptions, without neglecting the context. The rest is a matter of opinion or theory, faith or interpretation.

By applying our ideas of the present we can improve our memory and powers of observation. We speak of memories coming into our mind: our Ego is more or less passive towards them. But if we go back into a situation, imagining that we are really on the spot, and then describe in detail what we see or do, using the present tense, we shall greatly improve our capacity for remembering. Exercises on these lines will comprise the last part of this book.

The futuristic thinking, which in Adler's psychology stands in the foreground, is in Freud's conception relegated to secondary importance (e.g. secondary gain from illness). He stuck to causes, although in the *Psycho-Pathology of Everyday Life* he has brought many examples to show that forgetting and memories have tendencies and not only causes. On the one hand the memories determine the neurotic's life, and on the other he remembers or forgets for certain purposes. An old soldier might remember deeds he can boast about—he might even invent memories *for the purpose of boasting*.

Our manner of thinking is determined by our biological organization. The mouth is in front of us and the anus at the back. These facts have something to do with what we are going to eat or to meet, and also of what we are leaving behind or what we pass. Hunger certainly has some connection with the future, and the passing of the stool with the past.

XII

PAST AND FUTURE

Although we do not know much more about time than that it is one of the four dimensions of our existence, we are able to define the present. The present is the ever-moving zero-point of the opposites past and future. A properly balanced personality takes into account past and future without abandoning the zero-point of the present, without seeing past or future as realities. All of us look both backward and forward, but a person who is unable to face an unpleasant present and lives mainly in the past or future, wrapped up in historic or futuristic thinking, is not adapted to reality. Thus reality—in addition to the figure-background-formation, as shown previously—gets a new aspect provided by the sense of actuality.

Day-dreaming is one of the few occupations which are generally recognized as flight from the zero-point of the present into the future, and in such a case it is customary to refer to this as escape from reality. On the other hand, there are people who come to the analyst, only too willing to comply with the popular idea of psycho-analysis—namely to unearth all possible infantile memories or traumata. With a retrospective character the analyst can waste years in following up this wild-goose chase. Being convinced that digging up the past is a panacea for neurosis he merely collaborates with the patient's resistance of facing the present.

The constant delving into the past has a further disadvantage, in that it neglects to take into account the opposite, the future, thereby missing the point in a whole group of neuroses. Let us consider a typical case of anticipatory neurosis: A man, on going to bed, worries about how he will sleep; in the morning he is full of resolutions as to the work he is going do in his office. On his arrival there he will not carry out his resolutions, but will prepare all the material he intends conveying to the analyst, although he will not bring forward this material in the analysis. When the time comes for him to use the facts he has prepared, his mind occupies itself instead with his expectation of having supper with his girl friend, but during the meal he will tell the girl all about the work he has to attend to before going to bed, and so on and on. This example is not an exaggeration, for there are quite a number of people always a few steps or miles ahead of the present. They never collect the fruits of their efforts, as their plans never make contact with the present—with reality.

What is the use of making a man, haunted by unconscious fear of starvation, realize that his fear originated in the poverty experienced in his childhood? It is much more important to demonstrate that by staring into the future and striving for security he spoils his *present* life; that his ideal of accumulating superfluous wealth is isolated and separated from the sense of life. It is essential that such a man should learn the "feel of himself," should restore all the urges and needs, all the pleasures and pains, all the emotions and sensations that make life worth living, and which have become background or have been repressed for the sake of his golden ideal. He must learn to make other contacts in life besides his business connections. He must learn to work *and* play.

Such people develop an open neurosis once they have lost their only contact with the world—the business contact. This is known as the neurosis of the retired business-man. Of what use is an historical analysis to him, except for providing a pastime to fill a few hours of his empty life? Sometimes a game of cards might serve the same purpose. At the seaside one often finds this type of man (having no contact with nature), who would refuse to leave the stuffy cardroom, to have a look at the beauty of a sunset. He would rather stick to his senseless occupation of exchanging cards, of holding on to his "dummy" than to face contact with nature.

Other types that look into the future are the worriers, the astrologists, the safety-first-never-take-a-chance fellows.

Historians, archaeologists, explanation seekers and complainers look in the other direction, and most attached to the past is the person who is unhappy in life, "because" his parents have not given him a proper education, or who is sexually impotent, "because" he acquired a castration complex, when his mother had threatened to cut off his penis as a punishment for masturbation.

Seldom is the discovery of such a "cause" in the past a decisive factor in the cure. The majority of people in our society have not had an "ideal" education, and most people have experienced castration threats in their childhood without becoming impotent. I know of a case in which all the possible details of such a castration complex came to the surface without essentially influencing the impotency. The analyst had interpreted the patient's disgust towards the female sex. The patient had accepted the interpretation, but never managed to feel, to experience nausea. So he could not change disgust into its opposite, appetite.

The retrospective person avoids taking the responsibility for his life and actions; he prefers placing the blame on something that happened in the past instead of taking steps to remedy the present situation. For manageable tasks one does not need scapegoats or explanations.

In the analysis of the retrospective character one always finds a distinct symptom: the suppression of *crying*. Mourning is a part of the resignation-process, necessary if one is to overcome the clinging to the past. This process called "mourning labour" is one of the most ingenious discoveries of Freud. The fact that resignation requires the work of the whole organism demonstrates how important the "feel of oneself" is, how the experience and expression of the deepest emotions is needed to adjust oneself after the loss of a valuable contact. In order to regain the possibility of making contact anew, the task of mourning must be finished. Though the sad event is past, the dead is not dead—it is still present. The mourning labour is done in the present: it is not what the dead person meant to the mourner that is decisive, but what he still *means* to him. The loss of a crutch is of no importance if one was injured about five years ago and has since been cured; it matters only if one is still lame and needs the crutch.

Although I have tried to deprecate futuristic and historical thinking, I do not wish to give a wrong impression. We must not entirely neglect the future (e.g. planning) or the past (unfinished situations), but we must realize that the past has gone, leaving us with a number of unfinished situations and that *planning must be a guide to, not a sublimation of, or a substitute for, action.*

People often make "historical mistakes." By this expression I do not mean the confounding of historical data but the mistaking of past for actual situations. In the legal sphere laws are still valid which have long since lost their *raison d'être.* Religious people, too, dogmatically hold on to rites which once made sense but which are out of place in a different civilization. When the ancient Jew was not allowed to drive a vehicle on the Sabbath, it made sense, for the beast of burden should have a day's rest, but the pious Jew of our time submits to unnecessary inconvenience by refusing to use a tram which runs in any case. He changes sense into nonsense—at least so it appears to us. He looks at it from a different angle. Dogma could not retain its dynamic, could not even exist, if it were not supported by futuristic thinking. The believer holds up the religious law *in order to* be in "God's good books," to gain prestige as a religious man or to avoid unpleasant pricks of conscience. He must not feel the historical mistake he makes, otherwise his life-gestalt, the sense of his existence, would fall to pieces, and he would be thrown into utter confusion by the loss of his bearings.

Similar to the historical are the futuristic mistakes. We expect something, we hope for something, and we are disappointed, maybe very unhappy, if our hopes are not fulfilled. We are then very much inclined to blame either fate, other people, or our own inabilities, but we are not prepared to see the fundamental mistake of expecting that reality should coincide with our wishes. We avoid seeing that we are responsible for the disappointment which arises from our expectation, from our futuristic thinking, especially if we neglect the actuality of our limitations. Psycho-analysis has overlooked this essential factor, although it has dealt abundantly with disappointment "reactions."

The most important "historical mistake" of classical psycho-analysis is the indiscriminate application of the term "regression." The patient evinces a helplessness, a reliance on his mother, unbefitting an adult, becoming to a child of three. There is nothing to be said against an analysis of his childhood (if the patient's historical mistake is sufficiently emphasized), but in order to realize a mistake we must contrast it with its opposite, the correct behaviour. If you have spelt a word wrongly you cannot eliminate the mistake unless you know the correct spelling. The same applies to historical or futuristic mistakes.

The patient in question has perhaps never reached the maturity of an adult and does not know what it feels like to be independent of his mother, how to make contact with other people; and unless he is made to feel this independence, he cannot realize his historical mistake. We take it for granted that he has this "feel," and we are only too ready to assume that he has reached the adult position and has regressed to childhood only temporarily. We are inclined to overlook the question of situations. As his behaviour is normal in situations representing no difficulties or in matters requiring reactions similar to those expected of a child, we take it for granted that he is essentially grown-up. When more difficult situations arise, however, he proves that he has not developed a mature attitude. How can we expect him to know how to change if he does not realize the difference between infantile and mature behaviour? He would not have "regressed" if his "self" was already mature, if he had assimilated and not only copied (introjected) adult behaviour.

We may conclude then that the immediate future is contained in the present, especially in its unfinished situations (completion of the instinct cycle). Large parts of our organism are built for "purposes." Purposeless, e.g. senseless, movements can range from slight peculiarities to the inexplicable behaviour of the insane.

Conceiving the present as the result of the past we find as many schools of thought as we find causes. Most people believe in a "primary cause" like a creator, others fatalistically stick to the inherited constitution as the only recognizable and deciding factor, whilst for others, again, the environmental influence is the only cause of our behaviour. Some people have found economics to be the cause of all evil, others the repressed childhood. The present, in my opinion, is the coincidence of many "causes" leading to the ever changing, kaleidoscopic picture of situations which are never identical.

XIII

PAST AND PRESENT

Whilst it is not possible as yet to give a full account of the relations between past and present, enough material is available to attempt an incomplete classification as follows:

(1) The influence of the constitution (inheritance).
(2) The training of the individual (conditioning through environmental influence).
(3) Futuristic memories.
(4) The compulsion of repetition (the incompleteness of situations).
(5) Accumulation of undigested experiences (traumata and other neurotic memories).

(1) In regard to *constitution* the relationship between past and present is rather obvious. Let us take the functioning of the thyroid gland as an example. Cretinism (myxoedema) is due to something that happened in the past. Will delving into the past have any value except to gratify our scientific curiosity or to teach us about the illness' origin, so that this knowledge may help us to cure it to-day? We continually add thyroid hormones to comply with the *present* thyroxin deficiency.

(2) The *training of the individual* can be compared with the building of roads; the aim is to direct the traffic in the most economical way. If, however, the conditioning is not a very deep one, it is liable to deteriorate just as badly built roads are likely to break up. Deterioration tends towards annihilation. Old roads will disappear; our minds will forget. Some roads, however, are built like the old Roman highways. Once we have learned to read, many years of not reading may still leave the reading capacity intact.

If, however, a reconditioning takes place, if the traffic is directed on to new roads, the situation will be different: if we are compelled to speak a foreign language and make little use of our native tongue, we experience a deterioration of the latter, and after some years we may often find it difficult to remember words which were formerly automatically at hand. The reconditioning, on the other hand, the switching back to the native tongue, would take less time than it originally took to learn it in childhood.

When we attempt to stop the progress of a neurosis we try to recondition the patient to the biological, usually called normal or natural, functions. At the same time we must not forget the training, the conditioning of undeveloped attitudes. We can appreciate F. M. Alexander's methods from the point of view of reconditioning, if we don't forget the need to dissolve at the same time the dynamic influence of the wrong *gestalt*. If we merely superimpose one *gestalt* on to another, we encage, repress, but nevertheless keep alive, the wrong gestalt; by dissolving the latter we set free energies for the functioning of the whole personality.

(3) The expression *teleological, futuristic memories* sound paradoxical, but we often remember past experiences for future purposes. From the psycho-analytical point of view the most interesting category of this kind is the danger signal. If several motor-car accidents have occurred at the same place on a highway the authorities may put up a danger signal. These danger signals are erected not in memory of those killed; they are created for the "purpose" of safeguarding against future accidents.

The danger signal for the neurotic is not, as Freud says, the anxiety attack. The nervous person puts his *memories* as stop signals all over the place, wherever he scents the possibility of danger. To him this procedure seems reasonable; he appears to act according to the proverb: "Once bitten, twice shy." He may, for instance, have fallen in love and been disappointed. He therefore takes great care that such a "disaster" should not happen again. As soon as he feels the slightest sign of affection he produces (consciously or unconsciously) the memory of his unpleasant experience as a red stop light. He completely disregards the fact that he makes an historical mistake, that the present situation might differ considerably from the previous one.

Unearthing traumatic situations from the past might provide even more material for danger signals, might restrict even more the neurotic's activities and spheres of life, as long as he has not learned to differentiate between previous and present situations.

(4) A very delicate matter to deal with is the *compulsion of repetition*, in itself an amazing discovery of Freud's which he unfortunately carried to absurd conclusions. He saw in the monotony of the repetitions a tendency towards mental ossification. These repetitions, Freud contends, become rigid and lifeless, like inorganic matter. His speculations about this life-denying tendency led him to the conjecture that there is a definite urge working behind the scene: a death or nirvana instinct. He concluded further that just as the organismic libido is turned outwards as love, so the death instinct turns outwards as a tendency to destroy. He even went so far as to explain life as a permanent struggle between the death instinct and the disturbing libido. This anti-religious man re-enthrones Eros and Thanatos, the scientist and atheist regresses to the gods which he had fought a lifetime to destroy.

In my opinion Freud's construction contains several mistakes. I do not agree with him that the gestalt of "compulsion of repetition" has the character of rigidity, although a distinct tendency towards ossification exists in *habits*. We know that the older a person grows or the less elastic his outlook on life is, the more impossible any change of habits becomes. When we condemn certain habits and call them vices we imply that a change is desirable. In most cases, however, they have become part of the personality to such a degree that all conscious efforts fail to change them and that all efforts are confined to ridiculous resolutions which bribe the conscience for the moment without influencing the issue.

Principles are no less obstinate. They are substitutes for an independent outlook. The owner would be lost in the ocean of events if he were not able to orientate himself by these fixed bearings. Usually he is even proud of them and does not regard them as weaknesses, but as a source of strength. He hangs on to them because of the insufficiency of his own independent judgment.

The dynamic of habits is not homogeneous. Some are dictated by economy of energy and are "conditioned" reflexes. Habits are often fixations or have originally been fixations. They are kept alive by fear but might be changed into "conditioned" reflexes. This insight involves that a mere analysis of habits is as insufficient for "breaking" them as are resolutions.

The structure of the "compulsion of repetition" proper is quite different from that of habits and principles. We have previously chosen the example of a man who becomes disappointed again and again in his friends. We would hardly call this a habit or a principle. But what then is this compulsory repetition? To answer this question we have to make a detour.

K. Lewin carried out the following memory experiments: A number of people were given some problems to solve. They were not told that it was a memory test but were under the impression that an intelligence test was being carried out. The next day they were asked to write down the problems they remembered, and, strangely enough, the *unsolved* problems were far better remembered than those which had been solved. The libido-theory would lead us to expect the opposite, namely that narcissistic gratification would make people remember their successes. Or did they all have Adler's inferiority complexes and did they only remember the unsolved tasks as a warning to do better next time? Both explanations are unsatisfactory.

The word "solution" indicates that a puzzling situation disappears, is dissolved. With regard to the actions of the obsessional neurotic it has been realized that the obsessions have to be repeated until their task is finished. When a death wish is dissolved, psycho-analytically or otherwise, interest in the performing of the obsessional rites (the "undoing" of the death wish) will recede into the background and later disappear from the mind.

If a kitten tries to climb a tree and fails, it repeats its attempts over and over again until it succeeds. If a teacher finds mistakes in the pupil's work he makes him re-do it, not for the sake of repeating mistakes, but to train him in the proper solution. Then the situation is completed. Teacher and pupil lose all interest in it, just as we do after having solved a cross-word puzzle.

Repeating an action to the point of mastery is the essence of development. A mechanical repetition without perfection as its aim is contrary to organic life, contrary to "creative holism" (Smuts). The interest is held only as long as the task in hand is unfinished. Once it is completed the interest disappears till a new task creates interest again. There is no savings bank from which the organism (as the libido theory suggests) can draw the required amount of interest.

Compulsory repetitions, too, are by no means automatic. On the contrary, they are vigorous attempts at solving relevant problems of life. The need for a friend is, in itself, a very healthy expression of the desire for human contact. The permanently disappointed man is wrong only in so far as he looks for this *ideal* friend over and over again. He might deny the unpleasant reality in day-dreams or even in hallucinations; he might try to become this ideal himself or to mould his friends to it, but he cannot come to a fulfilment of his desires. He does not see that he makes a fundamental mistake: he looks for the cause of his failure in the wrong direction—outside instead of inside himself. He looks upon his friends as the causes of his disappointment, not realizing that his own expectations are responsible. The more idealistic his expectations are, the less they conform to reality, the more difficult the contact problem will become. This problem will not be solved and the compulsion of repetition will not cease before he has adjusted his expectations of the impossible to the possibilities of reality.

The compulsion of repetition is thus nothing mechanical, nothing dead, but is very much alive. I fail to see how one can deduce from this a mystical death instinct. This is the one instance where Freud left the solid ground of science and wandered off into regions of mysticism, as did Jung with his special development of the libido theory and his conception of the Collective Unconscious.

It is not for me to find out what made Freud invent this death instinct. Perhaps illness or approaching old age made him wish for the existence of such a death instinct which could be discharged in the form of aggression. If this theory were correct, anyone sufficiently aggressive would have the secret of prolonging life. Dictators would live *ad infinitum*.

Freud alternatively uses the terms "nirvana" and "death instinct." While nothing could justify the conception of the death instinct, the nirvana instinct might find some justification. One must protest against the word instinct and apply rather the word tendency. Every need disturbs the equilibrium of the organism. The instinct indicates the direction in which the balance is upset—as Freud has realized with regard to the sex instinct.

Goethe had a theory similar to Freud's, but to him not libido, but destruction, symbolized by Mephistopheles, appeared as the disturber of man's "love for unconditional peace." But this peace is neither unconditional nor lasting. Gratification will restore the organismic peace and balance until—soon enough—another instinct will make its demands.

To mistake the "instinct" for the tendency towards equilibrium is like mistaking the goods which are being weighed on a pair of scales for the scales themselves. We might call this inherent urge to come to rest through gratification of an instinct, "striving for nirvana."

The postulation of the nirvana "instinct" may also have been the outcome of wishful thinking. Those short periods in which the scales of our organism have regained their balance are the moments of peace and happiness, only too soon to be disturbed by new demands and urges. Often we would like to isolate this restful feeling from its place in the instinct-gratification cycle and make it last longer. I understand that Hindus in their disapproval of the body and its sufferings, in their attempts to kill all desires, declared the state of nirvana to be the ultimate aim of our existence. If the striving for nirvana is an instinct, I am at a loss to see why they have put such an amount of energy and training into achieving their aim, since an instinct takes care of itself and does not require any conscious effort.

A great deal more could be said about the so-called death instinct.[1] The insight into its true nature could have been gained long ago, had not Freud's pupils, fascinated by his greatness, swallowed everything he said as a religion—much as I myself did in former years.

(5) This swallowing of mental material brings us to another form of the past-present relations: the large class of *traumatic and introjected memories*.

A simple example is the stupid pupil with the excellent memory, who learns whole passages by heart and can repeat them easily on the examination papers, but is at a loss to explain the meaning of what he has written. He has taken in the material without assimilating it. Common to this class of memories which more than anything else has attracted the interest of Freud is the fact that they all lie in a kind of mental stomach. Three things can happen: either one vomits this material up (like a reporter), or defaecates it undigested (projection), or suffers from mental indigestion,

[1] In my opinion ¶ as well as ‡ forces are responsible for death, but death is not responsible for aggression. In the case of the hardening of the arteries a certain amount of calcium joins in the tissues of the arteries and makes them rigid, thus disturbing the proper nourishment of the tissues. A simple example of the ‡ energy is the ulcer of the stomach, where the stomach juices destroy the walls of the organ.

a state which is covered by Freud's remark, "the neurotic suffers from memories."

To understand this mental indigestion fully and to provide a cure for it, we have to consider the details of hunger instinct and organismic assimilation. Disturbances in assimilation will—on the psychological side —promote the development of paranoia and paranoic character. The examination of this problem will be the pivot of the second part of this book.

PART TWO

MENTAL METABOLISM

"Any element of a foreign, alien or hostile character introduced into the Personality creates internal friction, clogs its working and may even end in completely disorganizing and disintegrating it. The Personality, like the organism, is dependent for its continuance on a supply of sustenance, intellectual, social and suchlike, from the environment. But this foreign material, unless properly metabolized and assimilated by the Personality, may injure and even prove fatal to it. Just as organic assimilation is essential to animal growth, so intellectual, moral and social assimilation on the part of the Personality becomes the central fact in its development and self-realization. The capacity for this assimilation varies greatly in individual cases. A Goethe could absorb and assimilate all science and art and literature.

He could assimilate this vast mass of experience, could make it all his own, and make it all contribute to that splendour and magnificence of self-realization which has made him one of the greatest among men."—

(J. C. Smuts.)

I

HUNGER INSTINCT

If we cut through the three dimensions of a cube of one inch (Figs. I and II), we are left with eight cubes instead of one; the volume remains the

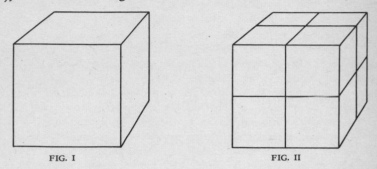

FIG. I   FIG. II

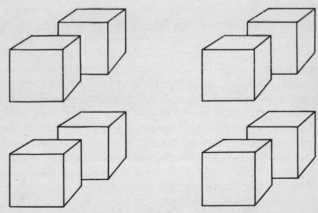

FIG. III

same, but the surface area is doubled (Fig. III). Fig. I shows a surface of six square inches; Fig. III shows eight cubes, each having six sides measuring half an inch: $8 \times 6 \times \frac{1}{2} \times \frac{1}{2} = 12$ square inches. Having thus doubled the surface of the original cube, we can continue the subdivision, thereby increasing the surface.

The advantage of a large surface is its quick and thorough reaction to physical and chemical influences. A tablet of aspirin dissolves more quickly when crushed. A piece of meat, put into a mild acid, requires a long time to dissolve, for the acid attacks the surface only, leaving the inside untouched. If it is minced and spread, however, all the substance will dissolve in the same time as was necessary to penetrate the surface in the first instance.

This ‡ plays the major part in the process of food consumption. The ¶, however, is not to be ignored, as it is present in the approach to food (appetite), in tasting and in certain synthetic chemical reactions within our organism. These functions are relatively insignificant in the foetus, but in the post-natal individual they play an ever increasing rôle.

In the first stage we find the embryo, which is like any other tissue of the mother; it gets all the food it requires *via* the placenta and umbilical cord—the liquified and chemically prepared meal as well as the necessary amount of oxygen. In the early stages both these foods are delivered to the tissues without any effort whatsoever on the part of the foetus, while later the embryo's heart takes part in the distribution. With birth, the umbilical cord ceases to function, the life-line between mother and child is cut, and, in order to keep alive, the newly-born child is faced with tasks which—simple to us—may be difficult for the little organism. It has to provide its own oxygen, that is, to start breathing, and it has to incorporate food. Breaking up solid structures, as shown in the beginning of this chapter, is not yet required, but the molecules of the proteins, etc., of the milk have to be chemically reduced and broken up into simpler substances. There is, however, one conscious active part which the suckling has to perform: the *hanging-on bite*.

In the next phase, the baby's front teeth erupt, and the first means of attacking solid food appear. These front teeth act as scissors, involving also the use of the jaw muscles, though in our civilization their use is often replaced by that of the knife, with a resulting impairment of the teeth and their function. The task of the teeth is to destroy the food's gross structure, as shown in Figs. I to III.

The mother's nipples become a "thing" to bite on. "Cannibalism," as this stage is wrongly called in psycho-analysis, comes into play. The biting of the nipple may be painful to the mother. Not realizing the biological nature of the child's biting impulse, or perhaps having a painful nipple, the mother may become upset and even smack the "naughty" child. Repeated smacking will condition the child to an inhibition of biting. Biting becomes identified with hurting and being hurt. The retribution trauma, however, is not as frequently encountered as the traumatic frustration through the withdrawal of the breast (premature or sudden weaning). The more the activity of biting is inhibited, the less will such a child develop the ability to tackle an object, if and when the situation calls for it.

In this case a vicious circle is started. The small child cannot repress[1] its impulses, nor can it easily resist such a powerful impulse as that of biting. In the very small child the ego-functions (and with them the ego-boundaries) are not yet developed. As far as I can see, it has at its disposal only the means of projection. The child cannot, at this stage, distinguish between the internal and external world. The expression "projection" is, therefore, not quite correct, as it means that something that should be felt in the *internal* world is experienced as belonging to the *external* field; but for practical purposes we may use the word "projection," instead of "pre-differential state of projection." (See Chapter X of this Part.)

The more the ability to hurt is inhibited and projected, the more will the child develop a fear of being hurt; and this fear of retaliation, in turn, will produce a still greater reluctance to inflict pain. In all such cases an insufficient use of the front teeth is to be found, together with a general inability to get a grip on life, to get one's teeth into a task.

Another outlet for the inhibited aggression is "retroflection," for which I have reserved a special chapter.

If dental development stopped after the appearance and use of the front teeth we would be able to bite a biggish lump into small pieces, but the digestion of such pieces would strain our chemical apparatus and require considerable time. The finer a substance is ground, the larger is the surface it presents to chemical action. The task of the molars is to destroy the lumps of food; mastication is the last stage in the *mechanical* preparation for the forthcoming attack by *chemicals*, by body juices. The best preparation for proper digestion is to grind the food into an almost fluid pulp, mixing it thoroughly with saliva.

Few people realize that the stomach is just a kind of skin, unable to deal with lumps. Sometimes the organism, in order to compensate for the lack of chewing, produces an excessive quantity of stomach acid and pepsin. This adjustment, however, entails the danger of the development of a gastric or duodenal ulcer.

The different stages in the development of the hunger instinct may be classified as *pre-natal* (before birth), *pre-dental* (suckling), *incisor* (biting) and *molar* (biting and chewing) stages. Before going into the details of the psychological aspect of these different stages, I should like to dwell on a theme touched on before—the theme of impatience. Many adults treat solid food "as if" it were liquid, to be swallowed in gulps. Such people are always characterized by impatience. They demand the im-

[1] Repression is originally based upon the control of the closing muscles of mouth, anus and urethra.

mediate gratification of their hunger—they have not developed an interest in destroying solid food. Their impatience is combined with greediness and inability to achieve satisfaction, a fact we shall illustrate later.

In order to realize the close relation between greed and impatience, one has only to watch the suckling's excitement, greed and impatience when he drinks. The *contact* function of the suckling is confined to the hanging-on bite, the rest of the feeding is *confluence* (fluere = to flow). When adults are very thirsty they behave in a similar way without seeing anything wrong in it. But people who gulp solid food mistake solids for fluids, with the result that they neither develop the ability to chew, to work anything through, nor the ability to stand suspense.

Compare the impatient eater (who will of course always find an excuse for his haste, such as "having no time") with the person waiting for the tram. To the mind of the greedy eater the filling of the mouth is as much a "figure" as the tram is to someone impatiently waiting for it. In both cases the confluence, here the flowing together of image and reality, is expected, and remains the primary urge. The filling of the mouth does not recede into the background, as it should do, and the pleasure of tasting and destroying food does not become the centre of interest—the "figure."

Above all, *the destructive tendency, which should have its natural biological outlet in the use of the teeth, remains ungratified*. We find here the same plus and minus functions as in avoidances. The destructive function, although in itself not an instinct but a very powerful instrument of the hunger instinct is "sublimated"—turned away from the object "solid food." It evinces itself in harmful ways, such as killing, waging of wars, cruelty, etc., or, by means of retroflection, as self-torture and even self-destruction.

Purely mental experiences (wishes, phantasies, day-dreams) are often treated "as if" they were objective realities. In obsessional and other neuroses one can, for instance, notice that a wish to do something forbidden is treated and punished by the conscience in a similar way as the real misdeed is punished by the legal authorities. As a matter of fact, many neurotics cannot differentiate between an imaginary and a real misdeed.

In the psychoses the confluence of imagination and reality often leads the patient not only to expect, but to inflict real punishment for imaginary deeds.

Hunger for mental and emotional food behaves like physical hunger: K. Horney observes correctly that the neurotic is *permanently* greedy for affection, but that his greed is never satisfied. One decisive factor in this behaviour of the neurotic is that he does not assimilate the affection offered to him. He either refuses to accept it, or he deprecates it, so that it becomes distasteful or valueless to him as soon as he has obtained it.

Furthermore, this impatient, greedy attitude is responsible more than anything else for the excessive stupidity we find in the world. Just as such people have no patience to chew up real food, so they do not take sufficient time to "chew up" mental food.

As modern times promote hasty eating to a large extent, it is not surprising to learn that a great astronomer said: "Two things are infinite, as far as we know—the universe and human stupidity." To-day we know that this statement is not quite correct. Einstein has proved that the universe is limited.

II

RESISTANCES

The libido-theory maintains that the evolution of the sexual instinct passes through an oral and an anal stage, and that disturbances or fixations during these phases prevent the development of a healthy sex life. Both observation and theoretical considerations compel me to contradict this hypothesis. If a person's main interest lies in his oral or anal functions, this amount of interest might diminish his sexual interests; and if sexual taboos are accepted, the interest in eating and—at least in our civilization —in defaecation might increase. The oral and anal characters are often the results of push and pull—away from the genitals, and towards the alimentary openings.

To take the genital character as the highest form of development is quite arbitrary. Reich, for instance, by glorifying sexual potency, gives the impression of building up an ideal not existing in reality. I agree with him that any disturbance in the function of the orgasm will, at the same time, disturb other functions of the personality, but so will any disturbance of the ego-functions, of the hunger instinct, and, as F. M. Alexander and Reich himself have shown, of the motoric system. I have treated cases of hysteria in which the sexual difficulties were overcome very quickly—yet their analysis proved to be difficult because of their badly developed ego-functions.

Within our civilization we certainly find typical oral and anal characters, but we do not find many references to the anal complex in the Bible or among many primitive races. Defaecation has become a nuisance, and since the discovery that the faeces act as germ-carriers in typhoid, cholera, etc., they have become subject to a hygienic taboo and are deeply despised. We find the opposite anal behaviour among the Chinese, where it is not shameful to defaecate on the host's field; on the contrary, it is regarded as a favour, for dung is scarce and therefore highly esteemed.

Though classifying human beings into oral, anal and genital characters, psycho-analysis has never concerned itself with the different forms of resistance correlated to those three types. *Oral* and *genital* resistances are neglected, and every resistance is seen as an *anal* resistance, as an unwillingness to give away, or as a tendency to keep back one's mental, emotional and physical contents. Freud treated his patients like children sitting on the chamber-pot, persuading, urging them to bring out whatever was in their minds without yielding to their embarrassment.

If we acknowledge difficulties in the oral and genital behaviour of a person, would we not look for resistances specific to these types? A genital resistance need not necessarily be meanness, which is a typical anal resistance. A person who masturbates does not always avoid intercourse for fear of losing his precious semen—his resistance might be due to shyness, or fear of contagion or other genital resistances of which frigidity and sexual impotence are typical results.

In the oral type we find cases of obvious oral resistances dovetailed with insufficient development of the biting functions. A primitive oral resistance is hunger-strike, either conscious, as in prisons (in order to enforce certain demands), or unconscious, in the form of lack of appetite. If a husband is annoyed with his wife, his aggression may not go into his teeth, his temper may not find its way into tackling but into refusing her food—"he just can't swallow one bite." I have just come across a reference showing that W. Faulkner found local contractions (spasms) of the oesophagus in people receiving unpleasant news, and it is obvious that they resisted the swallowing of unpalatable information.

An oral resistance of outstanding importance is disgust. It is (mainly as fed-up-ness) a leading symptom in neurasthenia. *Repressed* disgust plays an essential part in the paranoic character. I observed a border-line case between paranoia and a paranoic character who suffered from recurrent vomiting but without the emotional experience of disgust. No "organic" foundations could be found. Disgust is essentially a human phenomenon. Although some observations on animals (mainly domesticated) exist in this direction, one can, as a general rule, say that for the animal there is no need to return food which it dislikes. It does not eat any food for which it has not a craving. According to the instinct theory represented in this book, a piece of meat lying in a meadow does not exist for the cow, it never becomes "figure," it is not eaten and therefore cannot produce disgust. In the training of the human being, however, disgust plays an important part.

Disgust means the non-acceptance, the emotional refusal of food by the organism proper, whether the food be *really* in the stomach or throat, or only *imagined* to be there. It has, so to say, escaped the censorship of taste and got as far as the stomach. If a person seeing some putrefied matter (or whatever arouses his aversion) is disgusted, he behaves "as though" the disgusting material were already in his stomach. He has sensations varying from slight discomfort to biliousness—he might even vomit, although the disgusting matter is actually outside him. This kind of resistance belongs to the class of annihilation. Disgust signifies the undoing of the oral contact, parting from something which has become a part of ourselves—"and the Lord spat him out of His mouth."

Disgust at the faeces is the emotional motive behind the training of the child in cleanliness, and though originally an oral resistance, it forms the nucleus of the anal complex. The child becomes estranged from its own physical products and the process of producing them.[1]

An additional resistance, a *resistance against resistance*, is of special importance: the repression of disgust. For example, a child who thoroughly dislikes certain food, might feel disgusted, and vomit it up. The child is punished, for it is supposed to eat everything, and is forced, again and again, to eat food it dislikes. So, looking for a way out of the conflict it gulps the food down quickly (in order to avoid the disgusting taste), and tries, mostly successfully after a time, not to taste anything at all. Thus it develops a lack of taste, an oral frigidity. I intentionally use the term frigidity, as this process is very similar to that by which a woman, afraid for various reasons of her genital sensations, develops frigidity, thus enabling her, on the one hand, to "suffer" the sexual approach of the man, and, on the other, sparing her the conflicts which would arise between them, were she to yield to her disgust and fear.

I have only touched on the question of oral, anal and genital resistances, and I shall have more to say, especially about the dental resistance, for I maintain that the use of the teeth is the foremost biological representation of aggression. The projection, but also the repression of (or the resistance to) their aggressive functions is largely responsible for the deplorable state of our civilization.

Before entering the discussion of this phenomenon, however, I have to emphasize once more that it is difficult for most people to accept the structural similarity of mental and physical processes. One who takes for granted the theory, or rather the superstition that mind and body are two different things, joined together, will not easily be convinced of the correctness of holistic thinking. Accepting the indivisibility of the organism for situations only in which it suits you, does not mean that you "have" it. As long as you accept holism with your brain only, and believe in it in an abstract non-committal way, you will be surprised and fall back upon your scepticism each time you come into contact with physico-mental facts.

The statement that a person without the proper taste for food will also show lack of taste—or, as people say, show "bad" taste—in things concerning art, clothing, etc., might provoke a great deal of argument. Without a considerable amount of observations it will be difficult to

---

[1] Its disinterested and insensitive attitude towards its own product provides a perfect preparation for the life of the modern industrial worker, whose output is treated similarly to the faeces of the child. As soon as it has been produced, it is removed without arousing any interest. In striking contrast stands the case of the medieval artisan, who had personal contact with his work and who saw his products valued by others.

appreciate the fact that our attitude towards food has a tremendous influence upon intelligence, upon the ability to understand things, to get a grip on life and to put one's teeth into the tasks on hand.

Anyone not using his teeth will cripple his ability to use his destructive functions for his own benefit. He will weaken his teeth, and contribute to their decay. The fact that he does not thoroughly prepare his physical food for assimilation will have repercussions on his characterological structure and mental activities. In the worst cases of dental under-development people remain, as it were, sucklings throughout life. Although we seldom encounter anyone who has remained a complete suckling, who never makes some use of his teeth, we find many people who restrict their dental activities to soft food which liquifies easily, or to crisp food, which conveys the feeling that the teeth are being used but which does not require the investment of any substantial amount of effort.

The suckling at the mother's breast is a parasite, and persons who retain this attitude during a life-time remain *unrestricted parasites* (e.g. blood-suckers, vamps or gold-diggers). They always expect something for nothing; they have not attained the balance necessary for the life of an adult, the principle of give and take.

As people are not likely to get very far with such a character, they either cloak it, or pay for it indirectly. These people are recognized by their exaggerated modesty and lack of back-bone. At table, such an *inhibited parasite* is embarrassed with every dish offered to him, but closer observation will soon reveal the greed behind the modesty. He snatches sweets when no one is watching, and he will emerge slyly and very apologetically with ever increasing demands. Give him an inch and he will take an ell. The smallest favour he does is inflated to a sacrifice, for which he expects to be rewarded by gratitude and praise. His gifts are mostly empty promises, clumsy flatteries and servile behaviour.

His opposite is the *over-compensated parasite* who does not take food for granted, but lives in a permanent unconscious fear of starvation. He is often found among public servants, who sacrifice their individuality and independence in exchange for security. He lies at the breast of the state, relying on an old age pension, and thereby having his food secured for the rest of his days. A similar anxiety compels many to accumulate money, and still more money, in order that the interest (milk) of the capital (mother) may flow unceasingly.

So much for the *characterological* side of the picture. The finding of origins in the past is not identical with a cure for the present. Historical thinking merely helps to *understand* the parasitic character. The mere realization of his under-development (the feel of it, as I call it; or the transposition from the Unconscious into the Conscious, as Freud calls it), may make the patient either feel ashamed of, or accept his oral character.

Only by learning how to apply his biting tools, the teeth, will he be enabled to overcome his under-development. His aggression is thereby put to work in its proper biological place; it is neither sublimated, nor exaggerated, nor is it suppressed; therefore it harmonizes with his personality.

There can be no doubt that mankind suffers from suppressed individual aggression and has become the executor and the victim of tremendous amounts of released collective aggression. Anticipating a thesis to be proved later, I might say: *Biological aggression has turned into paranoic aggression.*

Intensified paranoic aggression is an attempt to re-digest projections. It is felt as irritation, rage or a wish to destroy or to conquer. It is not experienced as dental aggression, as belonging to the alimentary sphere, but is directed as personal aggression against another person, or against a collection of individuals, acting as screens for the projections.

People who condemn aggression and yet know that repressions are harmful, advise sublimation of aggression, as prescribed by the psychoanalysis for the libido. But can one advocate sublimation of aggression, at *any* price?

With sublimated libido one cannot propagate a child—with sublimated aggression one does not assimilate food.

The *re-establishment of the biological functions of aggression is*, and remains, *the solution of the aggression problem.* Very often, however, we have to resort to sublimation of aggression, usually in cases of emergency. If a person suppresses aggression (which is thus not at his disposal) as in cases of obsessional neurosis, if he bottles up his rage, we have to find an outlet. We have to give him an opportunity of letting off steam. Punching a ball, chopping wood, or any kind of aggressive sport, such as football, will sometimes work wonders.[1]

Aggression has one aim in common with most emotions: not senseless discharge, but rather application. Emotions may be surpluses of the organism (i.e. the organism may have the urge to get rid of them), but there is a distinct difference between emotions and mere waste matter. The organism has to get rid of certain waste matter, such as urine, and it does not care where and how it achieves this end—but there is no biological contact between urine and the outside world.[2] Most emotions, on

[1] A woman once complained to me that, although she liked her husband, she was always irritable with him when he came home, and every night they had unpleasant scenes. I advised her to scrub the floors in the afternoon, and the next day she told me with pride that her floors had never before looked so nice and clean. I asked her about her husband, and she said: "Oh! yes I quite forgot to tell you—it was the first nice evening we have spent together for years."

Another less pleasant way of sublimating aggression is shown by the fate of galley slaves. When whipped by the overseer, they were, of course, enraged against him, but their only outlet was to vent their wrath on the oars, and this application was exactly the purpose the whipping was meant to achieve.

[2] The connection between urinating and extinguishing fire, as remarked upon by Freud, is not a biological, but a cultural phenomenon.

the other hand, require the world as object. One may choose a substitute such as stroking a dog instead of a friend, as affection needs some kind of contact; but, like other emotions, it will not give satisfaction if it is senselessly discharged.

In the case of sublimated aggression, an object is easily procured: a problem may be a hard nut to crack, the drill of a bore bites into metal, the teeth of the saw cut wood. All these are excellent outlets for aggression, but they will never equal dental aggression, the application of which will serve several purposes: one rids oneself of irritability and does not punish oneself by sulking and starving—one develops intelligence, and has a good conscience, because one has done something "good for one's health."

I have stated that aggression is *mainly* a function of the hunger instinct. In principle, aggression can be part of any instinct—take, for example, the part that aggression plays in the pursuit of the sexual object. The terms destruction, aggression, hatred, rage and sadism are used in psychoanalytical literature almost as synonyms, and one never knows definitely whether reference is made to an emotion, to a function, or to a perversion. Though our knowledge is not sufficiently advanced for clear-cut distinctions, we should nevertheless try to bring some kind of order into this terminology.

If the hunger tension becomes high, the organism marshals the forces at its disposal. The emotional aspect of this state is first experienced as undifferentiated irritability, then as anger, and finally as rage. Rage is not identical with aggression but it finds its outlet in aggression, in the innervation of the motoric system, as the means of conquering the needed object. After the "kill," the food itself has to be attacked; the tools, the teeth, are ever ready, but they require the motoric forces to do the job. Sadism belongs to the sphere of "sublimated" aggression, and is mostly found mixed with sexual impulses.

The sublimation of the hunger instinct is, in some ways, easier, and in some ways more difficult, than that of the sex instinct: easier in that we always find objects for aggression (all work, especially all manual labour, sublimates aggression—a non-aggressive blacksmith or wood-cutter is a paradox). Sublimation is more difficult in so far as dental aggression always *requires* an object. Self-sufficiency, as it is sometimes found in connection with the sex instinct, cannot exist. There are people who live a sex life without any object in reality, contented with phantasies, masturbation and nocturnal emissions, but nobody can gratify the hunger instinct without *real* objects, without food. Freud gives a convincing illustration of this fact in the story of the dog and the sausage,[1] but again he takes it

---

[1] For a considerable time one can make a dog pull a cart, just by dangling a sausage before his nose; but sometimes one actually has to give the dog something to eat!

as proof for the urgency, not of the *hunger*, but of the *sex* instinct and the impossibility of its frustration.

There is not the slightest justification for calling only the sex instinct an object instinct. Aggression is at least as much object-bound as sex, and it can in the same way as love (in narcissism or in masturbation) have the "Self" as object. They both may become "retroflected."

Our plight began   ns such an overwhelming
number of rules   food as the Mosaic one.
Some of them,   , appear to be rationally
justified by late   nevertheless quite possible
that Moses im   himself was very fussy about
it, and either   anted to make sure that the
tithe (the 10   s received) suited his taste.

In additio   which complicates the picture.
The Jew   o classes of food "milky" and
"meaty."   ction between the food of the
suckling   se desire to eat its mother must
be stopp   hough not entirely prohibited, is
strictly   emains partly unexpressed. This
unexpr   stimulated the opposition of the
Jews

Ev   he aggression of the oppressed class,
and   aggression (which he unconsciously
enh   s a danger to himself. If the aggressive
ter   mes too strong, the rulers usually divert
it   They stir up a war or look for a scape-
g   or creed. Moses, however, used another

          fetishes for help in their distress, and the
          be ineffectual, is discarded. The ancient
          t their gods were too well *established* to be
          were so many of them. Thus, if one felt
          ne god, one switched over to another and
          rder not to become the object of such disloyal
          Moses—projecting himself into Jehovah declared
Him to be   Once he was infuriated when, during his absence,
the Jews built a   od, the Golden Calf, a god they could see and
touch—and one which has remained till to-day, though not openly
worshipped as such. To secure his leadership, Moses applied the trick
of *retroflecting* the aggression.

Retroflection means that some function which originally is directed

THIS BOOK

IS THE

PROPERTY OF

_____

I BOUGHT IT

FROM

BUSCK & O'GARA
BOOKSELLERS

✦

Who sell

NEW, OLD and RARE
BOOKS

✦

MUSIC

✦

PRINTS

at

326 S. Wabash Ave.
CHICAGO, ILL.
WEBster 3990

from the individual towards the world, changes its direction and is bent back towards the originator. An example is the narcissist a person who instead of directing his love outwards to an object falls in love with himself.[1]

Whenever a verb is used in connection with a reflexive pronoun, we may look for a retroflection; if a person talks to "himself," he does so instead of talking to someone else. If a girl, disappointed by her lover, kills "herself," she does so because her wish to kill him is retroflected by the wall of her conscience. Suicide is a substitute for homicide or murder.[2]

We understand now what Moses achieved by retroflecting the aggression of his followers. The religious Jew does not blame Jehovah for any failure or misfortune. He does not tear out *His* hair, does not belabour *His* chest—he retroflects his own annoyance, blames himself for every mishap, tears his own hair, beats his own chest.[3]

This retroflected aggression was the first step in the development of our paranoic civilization. The "means whereby" for the "end gain" of repression came into existence. This repression starts a vicious cycle. With the help of retroflected aggression, another wave of aggression is stifled and again retroflected, and so it goes on.

Moses' intention was apparently to do away with aggression only as far as it threatened his authority. In the Christian religion, however, the process develops further: all instincts must be repressed, and a split between body and soul is inaugurated; the body as the carrier of the instincts is despised and condemned as sinful. Sometimes even exercises are prescribed to deaden the body and its functions.

At the same time another mistake is made. The emotional equivalent of aggression is hatred. Instead of allowing outlets for aggression the dogma is introduced that hatred can be compensated, or even replaced, by love; but in spite of, or perhaps because of, vigorous training in charity, increased intolerance and aggression result. These effects are not neutralized by love, but directed against the "body" and against those who do not believe in the truth of that special branch of religion. This mistake, this belief that one can neutralize aggression by love and religion

[1] Psycho-analysis acknowledges two kinds of narcissism, primary and secondary. The term narcissism should be reserved for what psycho-analysis calls "secondary" narcissism. The "primary narcissism" has nothing to do with the behaviour of the Greek youth, who retroflected the love for his twin sister on to himself. In "primary narcissism" there is no retroflection. It is identical with what I call senso-motoric awareness.

[2] Retroflection shows a dialectical complication, which can be neglected in this context, but will be dealt with in the last part of this book.

[3] If the Jews would call a halt to such retroflection and turn their aggression into its original direction, they would attack Moses-Jehovah; with this their religion would fall to pieces, but so would their melancholia.

gains increased significance in our present time. Two writers of high distinction, A. Huxley and H. Rauschning, are completely at a loss as to what to do with aggression. They, too, see no other way of dealing with it than by prescribing idealism, love and religion.

After aggression had been suppressed, the body disavowed and the "soul" glorified, the age of industrialism brought about a new difficulty: to-day the soul of the workman is of no interest to the manufacturer. He needs the functions of the "body" only, and especially of those parts of the organism that are required for the work (factory *hands*; Charlie Chaplin in *Modern Times*). Thus devitalization progresses further: individuality is being killed. This process affects highly specialized workers as well, upsetting the harmony of their personality.

More and more activities are projected on to, and invested in, the machine which thus assumes a power and life of its own.[1] It joins hands with religion and industrialism, joins in the destruction of mankind: every time we use a lift or a motor car the leg muscles become slightly more atrophied, or at least, lose the opportunity of becoming stronger. That the wholesale destruction of mankind is not yet done by machines is really a miracle, but it has already been demonstrated *ad nauseam* that tanks and aeroplanes are more important than mere man-power.

This is what we call progress!

[1] The usefulness of machines (like that of religion and other projections) is more than compensated for by its disadvantages.

IV

MENTAL FOOD

In addition to the characterological and social results of dental inhibition, there is a further consequence: Stupefaction. Without understanding this fact, we cannot comprehend why the majority of mankind fail to notice the decay of civilization.

"Though the mills of God grind slowly, they grind exceedingly small." Man is crushed between the jaws of war and exploitation, in spite of all the advantages of civilization and in spite of all the delusions with which our pride in "progress" tries to drown the "discontent within our civilization." Our despair of finding salvation remains unabated, the dream of regaining lost contact with Nature is still a dream, while every attempt to have recourse to religion, to a creed, whether it be communism, fascism, theosophy, psycho-analysis or philosophy, will break down sooner or later. It will either lead to contradictions within the very systems, or clash with reality, with collective destruction.

The Christian religions attach the utmost importance to faith. They maintain: faith is power, belief is virtue. Criticism is forbidden; independent thinking is heresy.

What has this to do with dental inhibition? The rite of the Lord's Supper provides the answer to this question. With the aid of projection the believer experiences the hallucination that a wafer is the body of Christ—he projects his phantasy of Christ into the wafer and incorporates (introjects) this image afterwards. In some churches he has to swallow the wafer without touching it with his teeth. If he bit and tasted, the wafer would become an ordinary wafer, a banal piece of food, and the symbolic illusion of the procedure would be destroyed. The sense of this ceremony is essentially a training in gulping down whatever Religion preaches.

This attitude is adopted not only in religion, but also in the education of children, by asking them to swallow any nonsense such as the story of the stork and babies. Genuine interest is often squashed: "Curiosity killed the cat." In Germany, where the only mental food for the people is provided by the government (mainly through newspapers and radio), the average German "goebbels" down whatever is dished out to him; he consumes and absorbs the Nazi slogans and ideologies to the same degree as his chewing powers, his critical attitude is impaired. Even if mental assimilation is imperfect, *aliquid semper haeret*, something must enter the system, particularly when it is presented to people who suffered traumatic food experiences during and after the last war.

Nazi propaganda sees to it that the mental food should be such as will go down easily. Its promises, flatteries and "sweets" for vanity, like the "Herrenrasse theory," are eagerly swallowed. Aggression and cruelty are first "sublimated" on Jews and Bolsheviks, then on small, and finally on big nations.

My experiences in psycho-analysis were influenced by my own oral under-development. Believing, as I previously did, in the libido-theory (especially in Reich's ideal of the genital character), and not realizing its implications, I made a kind of phallic religion of it, rationalized and justified by what seemed a sound scientific foundation. By chewing psycho-analytical theories, however, and by pondering over every undigested morsel, I found myself becoming more and more capable of assimilating its valuable parts, and of discarding its errors and artificial constructions. As this process is still going on, this book, at least in parts, must needs be of a sketchy character. It may contain contradictions which have escaped my observation; but since this new approach (though it merely covers a fraction of the organismic functions) has already met with good practical results in refractory cases and with enthusiasm from people who certainly showed no signs of a "positive transference," I decided that it was time to draw attention to the necessity of a "psycho-analysis" of the hunger instinct and the disturbances of mental assimilation.

The mental metabolism must be low in those extreme cases of dental inhibition provided by that type which is over-fond of sweets, swallows only the easiest mental food (like magazine stories), and is incapable of digesting anything that requires thinking or that has a remote resemblance to science or "highbrow" literature. Such people, however, have at least the sound instinct not to swallow things which do not agree with them, in contrast to those who gulp down mental food and retain undestroyed morsels in their mental intestines. As they cannot stomach them they usually vomit them up and constantly repeat them. The ambiguous meaning of the word "repeat" indicates the indigestibility of such "brought-up" material.

An example of this type is the average reporter. He rushes through the town, greedy for news, but does not use the acquired knowledge for himself. He does not enrich his own personality, but spits out what he has learned in the pages of next morning's paper. People who compile compendia are often of the same type. They bring up other people's knowledge, but its assimilation, the real "having" of it, remains very small. Gossiping is a further example. Here, however, the woman who reports the latest scandal to her girl friend often adds quite a dose of gall to her acid remarks.

The last examples do not belong to the complete-dental-inhibition group. They refer to people who use their front teeth, but not the grinding molars. They have morsels in their stomach, but not big lumps.

For the psycho-analytical situation, too, the correlation of mental and dental behaviour is of great importance. Frequently a person who is being analysed, tells after the interview all his interesting experiences to his wife or friends. He may think (and herein fool even the analyst) that his behaviour is a sign of interest in the treatment, but the analyst soon discovers that the patient has accepted very little of his statements; by reporting the details of the interview to someone else the patient gets rid of all he has taken in, and nothing remains to be assimilated. So it is small wonder that the cure makes very little progress.

Observations of this nature may have induced Freud to remark that the interpretations alone are insufficient, as the patient does not really accept them; but except for the "transference" slogan, Freud omits to show "how" interpretations are accepted, and which resistances prevent the patient from digesting the mental food. I have not found any remark showing concern about the details on which the patient's willingness and ability to accept the analyst's words depend. Although under the influence of "positive transference" (enthusiasm), the patient is more prepared to accept interpretations, it is equally true that he will react with hostility if the analyst says something distasteful to him. This reaction is a spontaneous defensive impulse, and not the sudden appearance of "negative transference."

No one can easily accept interpretations of his repressed Unconscious, i.e. of those parts of one's personality one avoids facing by every means. If one could, there would be no need for repressions and projections. Thus the demand that the patient should accept exactly what he wants to avoid is paradoxical. Reich's method of trying to bring home the truth through concentration on the armour is certainly progress, which, however, is largely undone by pushing the mental food down the patient's throat, by mocking and even bullying. By brushing aside the oral resistances and making the patient swallow ideas which he cannot digest, artificial attitudes and actions are induced instead of an organic development of the personality. I had occasion to observe this fact on two of Reich's former patients.

In contrast to Reich, the *orthodox* psycho-analyst pretends to demand nothing from the patient, but actually demands the impossible—namely, the compliance with the basic rule and the acceptance of his interpretations. My advice is to deal not with the Unconscious but, as far as possible, with the Ego. Once a better functioning of the Ego is achieved, and the ability to concentrate is restored, the patient will be more willing to co-operate in the conquest of the Unconscious. The readiness with which a person considers the statements of someone else depends largely upon his oral development and freedom from oral resistances.

The simplest form of oral resistance is direct avoidance. Children close their mouths tightly when they are asked to eat something distasteful to them, just as they close their ears with their hands whenever they do not want to listen. As adults are usually better versed in the technique of politeness and hypocrisy, it is often difficult to distinguish whether they are genuinely uninterested (no mental appetite—lack of figure-background formation), or merely repressing a potential interest. Such inhibitions of contact are: ignoring the presence of others; mind wandering; polite, but indifferent listening; pretence of interest; obsessional contradicting. In everyday life one often hears the remark: "What did you say? I have been miles away! Please say it again." This does not happen if a person is interested—if the topic suits his taste.

No one sends out messages without being reasonably sure that they will reach their destination. How can the analyst be sure that a patient who says "yes, yes" all the time, has received the message—for instance an interpretation? In order to establish a sound mental appetite and assimilation, we have to recondition our patient; we have to correct his "wrong" attitude towards physical and mental food. But we cannot correct a "wrong" attitude without:

(1) Providing the contrast of the "right" one.
(2) Realizing that to the feeling of familiarity we give the term "right" and to the feeling of strangeness the name "wrong" (F. M. Alexander). Our conscious feeling is usually not right, but righteous. The phase of the so-called "negative transference" coincides with the patient's or pupil's unwillingness to part with his familiar thoughts and feelings. What the analyst or teacher says at that stage sounds "wrong" to him.
(3) Draining the "energies" and fixations from the "wrong" and opening the road for the "right" behaviour.

One seldom accepts an opinion contrary to one's own conviction; this is readily observed in every discussion. Therefore I do not take it for granted that the patient will accept what I say, but make it my task to pay not less attention to his *oral* resistances than is usually given to the *anal* ones. For many cases I consider it as bad analytic technique to say a few sentences only at the end of the session, leaving it to chance whether the analyst's résumé or interpretations are accepted or not. True enough, if one keeps the patients mentally starved for a whole hour, some will be hungry to hear what the analyst has to say: but those who can be treated in this summary way are the exceptions. In the majority of cases one has to watch carefully the oral resistances, and one has to differentiate between the hopeless situation of complete lack of interest and the promising one, in which the patient's interest is merely inhibited. If I notice mind-wandering I ask the patient to repeat what I have said. He will soon realize his lack of contact and his inattentiveness; and with patience one can induce him to remember bits and pieces—to recall half-heard sentences and to rehash them. By this method he regains much material which he would otherwise have lost. Once patients realize their inattentiveness, the cure of their "bad memory" begins.

On the other hand, if there is a resistance against the resistance—if, for instance, the patient *forces* himself to listen like a student to a tedious lecture—he might suffer torture, and as he takes it in without appetite he will derive little benefit. The analyst must have a clear idea of the patient's digestive tolerance, and dose his mental medicine and food accordingly. "Sweets," e.g. praise in the proper place, will be useful in showing appreciation of a genuine effort in a difficult situation (Adler's encouragement). Sometimes a patient is fed with such an amount of psycho-analytical wisdom, that he gets "fed up," disgusted with the analyst, and leaves the analysis. Subsequently a miraculous improvement *might* take place which is not seldom attributed to non-analytical circumstances. What actually happened is that the "hoarded" material has afterwards been assimilated, and the knowledge acquired through—but away from—the analytical treatment has enabled the former patient to solve his conflicts on his own.

An oral resistance well known to the analyst is the intellectual resistance. Everything the analyst says is accepted and the patient talks very intelligently with pleasing readiness about analytical theories—about his incest wishes, his anal complex, etc. He advances as many childhood memories as the analyst may like, but everything is "thought" and not "felt." This type has an intellectual stomach like the rumen of a cow. The wisdom, although ruminated, does not pass through the intestinal walls and never reaches the tissues of the organism proper. Nothing is ever assimilated, nothing reaches the personality, but all remains in the mental rumen—the brain. Such greed for knowledge is deceptive. These intellectuals can swallow anything, but they do not develop a proper taste, an opinion of their own; they are ever ready to hang on to this or that "ism" as their specific dummy (cf. Chapter VI). When they switch over from one intellectual dummy to another, it is not that they have assimilated the content of one "ism" and are ready for new mental food. The old dummy has become distasteful to them mostly as a result of disappointment, and they get hold of another "ism," with the deceptive hope that the new dummy will be more satisfactory.

When they bring forward their empty theories, the analyst should make them explain in detail what they really mean. He should even embarrass them by making them realize the contrast between their complicated phrases and little meanings. Only if they learn to chew and taste every word they speak, and if, at the same time, they feel the un-destroyed morsels of food—of the real food—going down their throat, is there a hope of their understanding or assimilating what the "ism" means.

Only those who grind their mental food so thoroughly, that they get the full value of it, will be able to assimilate and reap the benefit of a difficult idea or situation. Everyone will gain much more for his knowledge and intelligence by reading one good book six times than by reading six good books once. The chewing applies likewise to criticism: if someone is touchy, and his dental aggression projected, every critical opinion is experienced as an attack and this often results in inability to stand even benevolent criticism. When, however, dental aggression is functioning biologically, one does not shun, one even welcomes, criticism. One cannot learn much from careless praise, but criticism may contain something constructive, thus converting even the most mischievous attack into a benefit. Criticism should be neither refused, nor swallowed, but should be chewed up carefully and should in every case be taken into consideration.

V

INTROJECTION

Those to whom I have shown the importance of the analysis of the hunger instinct—the structural similarity of the phases of our food consumption with our mental absorption of the world—have been surprised that Freud should have missed this point. Compared with the fact that Freud discovered the implications and complications of sexual repression, this is of minor importance. After the complete analysis of one group of instincts, the analysis of other groups was bound to follow sooner or later. The material which Freud had at his disposal for building up his theories was poor and faulty (e.g. the association psychology). Though I consider the libido theory to be out of date, I am not blind to the fact that it was the most important step in the development of psycho-pathology, and had Freud not concentrated on it, psycho-analysis might never have been born.

Many people, expecting an integration of their Weltanschauung from the study of man's objective and subjective worlds, have tried to make the body of their philosophy walk on two legs—Marxism and Freudism. They have tried to build bridges between the two systems, but failed to see that the economical complications with which Marx was concerned resulted from the instinct of self-preservation. Although fully realizing man's basic need for food, clothes and shelter, Marx did not follow up the implications of the hunger instinct in the same way as Freud did with the sex impulses—his sphere of research was mainly that of social relations and only rarely the individual.

Little has been said in communist and socialist literature about sexual needs and problems—about the instinct of race-preservation—compared with what is written about the feeding problem—starvation, self-preservation or reproduction of working power. Freud has sexualized the hunger instinct, whereas communism passed through a period when sex problems were looked upon "as if" they belonged to the sphere of hunger (glass-of-water-theory), just as many people in our civilization speak of sexual appetite and thus confound sex instinct and hunger instinct.

The psycho-analysis of Marxism has as little influence on economic issues, as the Marxist denotation of psycho-analysis as a product of bourgeois idealism diminishes the value of Frued's findings. Declaring the castration complex to be the mechanism by which the oppressed classes are kept down—as Reich does—is as arbitrary as assuming that neuroses will automatically disappear in a classless society.

Marx was in a way a forerunner of Freud: "Marx discovered the simple fact (heretofore hidden beneath ideological overgrowths) that human beings must have food, drink, clothing and shelter first of all, before they can interest themselves in politics, science, art, religion and the like. This implies that the production of the immediately requisite material means subsistence, and therewith the existing phase of development of a nation or an epoch, constitutes the foundation upon which the state institutions, the legal outlook, the artistic and even the religious ideas are built up. It implies that these latter must be explained out of the former whereas the former have usually been explained as issuing from the latter." (F. Engels.)

This is the common basis of Freud and Marx: the needs of man (for Freud the instincts of race preservation and for Marx the instincts of self-preservation) are primary; the intellectual super-structure is determined by the biological structure and by the need of gratification of these two groups of instincts.

Although some wars are known to have started from libidinal causes, like the Trojan war, most are waged as fights for hunting grounds and other means to feed the people, or, in modern times, to feed industries or the insatiable greed of morbid conquerors.

Freud's attitude to communism was hostile—at least during one period of his life. In the Russian revolution he saw mainly destruction. He had an emotional aversion to destruction, as shown by his peculiar theory about death as well as by his archaeological interests. The past for Freud must not be past, it must be salvaged and brought back to life. Above all, this aversion to destruction manifested itself in his attitude towards *introjection*.

*　　　*　　　*

Freud certainly made most valuable discoveries regarding introjection, as in the case of melancholia, which he realized as an unsuccessful attempt to destroy an introjected love-object. He as well as Abraham maintained, however, that introjection in itself can be a normal process. They overlooked the fact that *introjection means preserving the structure of things taken in, whilst the organism requires their destruction*. Partial introjection is conceived by psycho-analysis as part of the normal psychological metabolism, whilst I consider this theory to be fundamentally wrong, mistaking a pathological process for a healthy one. Introjection—in addition to its occurrence in melancholia, formation of conscience, etc.— is a part of a *paranoic pseudo-metabolism*, and is in every case contrary to the requirements of the personality.

Take the instance of the Ego. According to Freud the normal Ego is built up by a number of identifications. Helene Deutsch, in striking contrast, considers the *pathological* nature of ego-identifications, and even holds that identifications can accumulate to such a pathological degree, that such "as-if" personalities (who quickly, but superficially, accept any rôle required by a situation) cannot be psycho-analysed successfully. I have proof, however, that the "as-if" personality can be analysed, provided one approaches the problem not from the libido theory, but from the point of view of mental assimilation.

The intake of the world shows three different phases: *total introjection*, *partial introjection* and *assimilation*, corresponding to the suckling, "biteling" and "chewling" phases (the pre-dental, incisor and molar stages). The relations of the attacking subject and the attacked object are simple in the instances of Figs. I to III.

In Fig. I we have the straightforward aggression, which in Fig. II is retroflected (e.g. self-destruction). In Fig. III, aggression is projected: aggressor and victim have apparently changed parts; the aggressor experiences fear in place of the desire to attack.

Complications arise once we take into account

TOTAL INTROJECTION

To anyone of the pre-dental group—behaving "as though he had no teeth"—the introjected person or material remains intact, isolated as a foreign body in the system. The object has been gulped down. It has evaded contact with the aggressive teeth, as demonstrated by the instance of the Lord's Supper. The image is incorporated more or less *in toto*.

(a) *In melancholia* (Fig. IV), *the impulse to attack is directed against the introjected object.* It is retroflected from the real food (laziness in using the muscles of the jaw; often hypo-tonus of the face muscles).

(*b*) *In* the case of a severe *conscience* (Fig. V), *aggression is projected on to an introjected subject*, which as conscience then attacks those parts of the personality that meet with its disapproval; these attacks range from slight pricks to the most cruel punishment. The "Ego" answers with remorse and feelings of guilt. The German *Gewissensbiss* (being bitten by the conscience) expresses the oral origin of the conscience, as does the English remorse (murder-bite).

(*c*) *In the "as-if" personality* (Fig. VI), *aggression or love is projected on to a person who is afterwards introjected*. By this means the "as-if" person avoids the fear of attack, and retains the benevolence of his environment. The dynamics involved in this process are too complicated to be dealt with in this context.

In the last three instances mentioned the "introject" is not dissolved. The result is a temporary or permanent fixation; as destruction is avoided and assimilation does not take place, the situation remains necessarily incomplete.

PARTIAL INTROJECTION

corresponds to the "biteling" stage, and is regarded by Freud as normal. Here only parts of a personality are introjected. For example, if a person speaks with an Oxford accent, and his friend envies him, the latter might mimic the accent but not the whole person in question. To regard this as a healthy ego-development is paradoxical. The Oxford accent may by no means be an expression of the friend's self. An "Ego" built up of substances, of introjections, is a conglomerate—a foreign body in the personality—just as is the conscience or the lost object in melancholia. In every case we find foreign, unassimilated material within the patient's system.

ASSIMILATION

Psycho-analysis does not pay attention to the differentiation of the dental stage, and therefore the development of the total and partial introjective phases is not pursued to the state of assimilation. Instead of paying attention to this very important feature of living beings (scotoma), a switchover is made in psycho-analytical theory from the mouth to the anus. Van Ophuijsen was the first to see that the anal-sadistic phase originates in the oral aggression, just as Freud realized that the anus learns many of its functions from the mouth. The mouth, however, neither ceases functioning nor developing with the beginning of what Freud calls the anal stage. The source of aggression is neither the anal zone nor any death instinct. The assumption that oral aggression is a mere transient phase in the development of the individual would amount to maintaining that dental aggression does not exist in adults.

Any introjection, total or partial, must go through the mill of the grinding molars, if it is not to become, or to remain, a foreign body—a disturbing isolated factor in our system. The "Ego," for instance, as I intend showing later, should not be a conglomerate of introjections, but a *function*, and to achieve a proper functioning of the personality one has to dissolve, to analyse such a substantial Ego and reorganize and assimilate its energies, much as Reich puts the energies invested in the muscular armour to better use.

Emergency actions, like vomiting or diarrhoeic defaecation of unused morsels, will not further the development of the personality. The psycho-analytical equivalent to this, the catharsis, has been abandoned, since it was realized that the cathartic success was as short-lived as the intro-jective treatment of hypnosis.[1] One of my most difficult cases was an elderly man suffering from a stomach-neurosis and a jealousy-paranoia. He was quite satisfied to make a clean breast of everything that had happened to him. He always collected and produced all kinds of patho-logical material and felt tremendously relieved when he could just confess and spit out all his trouble. But when I stopped him, and made him chew the "cud," he became obstinate. The progress of his cure was very slow, and depended on the amount of aggression we could set free and invest in his chewing abilities. Simultaneously, as was to be expected, his stupidity, which previously had been immeasurable, decreased.

If Freud's statement—that the neurotic suffers from memories—is not taken as an explanation of the neurosis, but as an indication of a symptom, we realize the great (though limited) therapeutic value of classical analysis. But if tackled piecemeal it is a Herculean task to dispose of the Augean mess—the undigested rubbish we carry with us from the past, all the unfinished situations and unsolved problems, all the grudges and unpaid debts and claims—the unmaterialized retaliations (revenge and gratitude). This task, however, is much simplified if, instead of tackling each item singly, we restore the full organismic assimilation once and for all. This can only be done if we take into account the mental metabolism and look upon psychological material in the same way as upon physical food. We must not be satisfied with making unconscious material conscious, with "bringing up" unconscious material. We must insist that it should be re-hashed, and thus be prepared for its assimilation.

If this holds good already for partial introjection it applies much more to the total introjection, or to total inhibition of dental aggression. The destructive use of the teeth in melancholia (and other instances of total introjection) is so inhibited, that the unemployed aggression turns into self-destruction of the individual. Contact with any introjected material is usually impotently aggressive, manifesting itself as spitefulness, grum-

[1] The promising features of narco-analysis must not deceive us. It is a purely symptomatic treatment and cannot bring about permanent changes in the per-sonality.

bling, nagging, worrying, complaining, irritation, "negative transference" or hostility. This corresponds exactly to the unused potential of the physical destruction of the food. It is the distorted application of ‡ in the psychological metabolism.

Melancholia is mostly a phase of cyclothymia of the maniac-depressive cycle. In the maniac period the unsublimated, but dentally inhibited aggression is not retroflected as in melancholia but is directed in all its greediness and with most violent outbursts against the world. A frequent symptom of cyclothymia is dipsomania which is on the one hand a sticking to the "bottle" and on the other a means of self-destruction.

Through the treatment the introjected material—by being split up— is differentiated into assimilable material, contributing to the development of the personality, and into an emotional surplus to be discharged or applied. In psycho-analytical terminology: remembering is of therapeutic value only when it is accompanied by emotions.

Increased mental metabolism is accompanied by hyper-acidity, increased movement of the bowels and excitement which may change into anxiety if the oxygen supply is impaired. Reduced metabolism is characterized by depression, deficient flow of digestive juices, dryness in the mouth, hypo-acidity and dry aspastic constipation.

The phenomenon of introjection is a comparatively recent discovery, but folklore shows that it has been well known through the ages. The figures in fairy tales often have a more or less fixed symbolic meaning. The fairies stand for the good mother, the witch or step-mother for the bad one. The lion stands for power and the fox for shrewdness. The wolf symbolizes greediness and introjection. In the story of Little Red Riding Hood the wolf introjects the grandmother, copies her, behaves "as-if" he was she, but his real self is soon unmasked by the little heroine.

In a lesser known of *Grimm's Fairy Tales* the Wolf swallows seven kids. The kids are rescued and replaced by pebbles—a good symbol indeed for the indigestibility of the introject.

In both stories the introjected objects, though having been swallowed, are not assimilated, but remain alive and intact. Or is the libido-theory correct; was the wolf not hungry at all, but in love with grandma?

VI

THE DUMMY COMPLEX

Perhaps the most interesting of all oral resistances is the "dummy" attitude. While our knowledge of it is still scanty, sufficient observations are at hand to warrant their publication. The discovery of the dummy complex has shed light on a number of obscure analyses, and I hope—once it has been checked up by other analysts—that it will bring further contributions mainly to the question of fixations.

In order to understand the dummy attitude we have to return once more to the suckling and its difficulties in attaining the biteling stage. The main activity of the suckling is confined to the hanging-on bite, which is not a "bite through," not a biting off of a part of the breast but which establishes *confluence* between mother and child. Thus only the beginning of the feeding process presents any conscious difficulty; once the baby has made a vacuum pump of his mouth and the milk begins to flow, no further effort on its side is required. The sucking movements are subcortical, automatic, and while the feeding takes place, the child gradually falls asleep. Only a few weeks after the birth other conscious activities—like consciously expelling the nipple from the mouth, or consciously making sucking movements—can be observed in connection with the feeding process.

A conflict may arise when the child's teeth start growing. If the flow of milk is insufficient, the child will be provoked into mobilizing all the means at its disposal for achieving satisfaction, which implies the use of the hardened gums and the attempt to bite. Any frustration at that stage, any withdrawal of the breast without immediate substitution of more solid food will lead to dental inhibition. The child will get the impression that through the attempts to bite, its equilibrium will not be restored, but will rather be further upset and that, therefore, the milk-yielding object must not be approached in any manner different from before. *The differentiation into breast, which must be left intact, and food, which must be bitten and chewed and destroyed, does not take place.*

This early dental inhibition leads to the development of two distinct character features: a hanging-on attitude (fixation) on the one hand, and the "dummy" attitude on the other.

People with these characteristics hang on to a person or a thing and expect this attitude to be sufficient to "make the milk flow" by itself.

They might take great pains to get hold of something or someone, but they will relax their efforts as soon as they have achieved this. They try to stabilize any relationship at the very first phase of contact; thus they may have hundreds of acquaintances, but none develops into a real friendship. In their sexual relations only the conquest of the partner matters, but consequent relationship quickly becomes uninteresting and they become indifferent. There is a striking discrepancy in the attitude of such persons before and after marriage. A proverb says, "Women can make nets but not cages."

The attitude of such cases towards study and work suffers from similar difficulties. They know something about everything, but they cannot appropriate anything which can be achieved only with a specific effort. Their work is rather uncreative, mechanical (automatic), limited mainly to routine. In short, their aim is still—like a baby's—the successful hanging-on bite, which restores equilibrium and dispenses with the necessity for further effort (biting).

But in the life of grown-up people the hanging-on attitude can only very occasionally be completely successful. In most situations one has to make proper contact—one has to tackle the matter on hand, to "put one's teeth into it," e.g. one has to sustain one's interest and activity over a period of time—in order to derive any benefit for one's own personality.

How do people cope with the failure of the hanging-on attitude? How can they get round the necessity to bite? How can they dispose of the surplus aggressiveness, which must arise from the dissatisfaction with the hanging-on relationship (resentment), without incurring the danger (as they feel it) of causing change and destruction?

If there is a fixation to the infantile hanging-on attitude, we may expect that the means whereby this attitude is maintained are equally infantile. The frustrated and dissatisfied infant looks for—and sometimes is even given a dummy, something indestructable, to which biting can be applied without repercussions. The dummy allows for the discharge of a certain amount of aggressiveness, but, apart from that, it does not produce any change in the child, that is, it does not feed it. The dummy represents a serious impediment in the development of the personality, because it does not actually satisfy the aggressiveness, but deviates it from its biological aim, namely the gratification of hunger and the achievement of the restoration of the individual's wholeness.

Anything that the baby gets hold of may be used as a dummy—a pillow, a teddy bear, the cat's tail (as in *Mrs. Minniver*), or the baby's own thumb. Later on in life, any object might become "dummified" if only the hanging-on bite is applied to it. In such instances the individual lives in mortal fear of the dummy developing into the "real thing" (originally the breast) and that the hanging-on bite might turn into a "first bite." He is afraid that the fixation object might be destroyed. This object can be a person, a principle, a scientific theory or a fetish. At the time of my writing, the British people have suffered great distress in relinquishing the idea that the battleship was invaluable. The battleship had become a fetish to them, but in practice it is a very expensive nuisance, only "good to be sunk," as a prominent politician has characterized it.

Parliamentary discussions often become dummified (and even mummified). Instead of being developed into action, matters are talked to death, or brought to a standstill by being pushed from a commission to a sub-commission and from there to another sub-sub-commission. Instead of progress and integration a deadlock is the result, a state of affairs which is mostly justified by a conservative tendency, by the wish to keep everything intact and unchanged. The present system must under no circumstances be destroyed; the dummy or fetish must be saved.

The dummy as an object which remains whole and undestroyed provides a perfect screen for the projection of the individual's holistic tendency. The more the holistic functions are projected, the more are they lost for the building-up of the personality, the greater will be the disintegration, and the more marked the danger of developing a schizophrenia. As long, however, as reality provides the dummy, it serves a very useful purpose; it prevents the individual from sliding off into a true paranoia (an extensive projection of aggression) by keeping him busy with some real though unproductive occupation.

But all the attempts of such types—like the obsessional character—to preserve things in their original state are doomed to failure. The lack of change, that is the non-application of aggressiveness in the service of individual holism, disintegrates the personality, thus defeating its own ends. Only by re-establishing the destructive tendency towards food as well as towards anything that presents an obstacle to the individual's wholeness, by re-instating a successful aggression, the re-integration of an obsessional, and even of a paranoid, personality takes place.

There is hardly anything that cannot serve as a dummy, as long as it helps to avoid changes in reality. Take for instance the obsessional thoughts, which can go on for hours and hours, keeping the patient busy without leading to a decision or conclusion (chronic doubting). Take the sexual fetishism, the fixation of a man, for instance, on girls' panties or shoes as a safeguard against real sexual contact. Take the day-dreamer who prefers his phantasies to the "real thing." Further, take those patients who for years and years continue to see a psycho-analyst and imagine that their mere attendance at the sessions is sufficient proof of their intention to change their attitude to life. Actually they have only exchanged one dummy for another, and as soon as the analyst touches some essential complex, the patient generally manages to avoid being impressed by dummifying himself.

An extreme case of this sort was provided by a patient, who, whenever he had to face any difficulty in life, became completely wooden. He felt as if he were a doll, and all his complaints, all his interests were centred in his dummy, in his own mummified personality. Another patient, in any difficult situation, produced the obsessional idea of imagining knives going through him without causing pain or drawing blood. In this phantasy he became the perfect dummy whom no amount of aggressiveness could destroy. Other cases just feel sleepy or drowsy, whenever they perceive the "danger" of provocation in any situation.

The classical psycho-analytical situation, in which the patient is hardly aware of the analyst's presence, lends itself particularly to dummification. Here the patient is actually encouraged to regard the analytical situation not as a "real" situation and the analyst not as a "real" person; thus the whole relationship between patient and analyst becomes "un-real," that is something that in itself is of no importance and of no consequence. Every emotion or reaction is interpreted as a phenomenon of "trans-ference," i.e. as something that does not directly apply to the actual situation. Thus the analytical situation presents itself as the perfect dummy, for which all obsessional and paranoid characters are looking. This accounts for the fixation of those patients to the analysis which might go on for years on end, in spite—or rather because—of the lack of success.

VII

THE EGO AS A FUNCTION OF THE ORGANISM

(a) IDENTIFICATION/ALIENATION

When we attempt to put into practice the conclusions from the previous parts an apparent contradiction is met: the statement that the healthy Ego is unsubstantial seems to be at variance with my demand that the analyst should deal with the Ego rather than with the Unconscious. This contradiction is removed if we word the demand: the analyst should make use of the Ego-functions rather than appeal to the Unconscious.

The function of the lungs is mainly the exchange of gases and vapour between organism and environment. Lungs, gases and vapour are concrete, but the function is abstract—yet real. The Ego, so I maintain, is similarly a function of the organism. It is not a concrete part of it, but is, rather, a function which ceases, for instance, during sleep and coma, and for which no physical equivalent can be found either in the brain or in any other part of the organism.

In psycho-analytical theory, the conception of the Ego as a substance is fairly generally accepted. To quote one instance: Sterba interprets the psycho-analytical cure as a building up of isolated islands of Ego, which, in the course of time, will consolidate into one solid, reliable unit.

Another analyst, Federn, likewise assumes the substantiality of the Ego. For him the Ego consists of that mysterious material called libido. The libido in addition to being capable of occupying images and erogenetic zones, of energizing many activities and being the representative of the object instincts, is now credited with the ability to expand and contract. At the same time the dualistic concept of libidinal object instincts as opposed to the Ego instincts is conveniently forgotten. In spite of the theoretical confusion there is, however, a valuable nucleus in Federn's observation: the fact that his libidinal Ego has changing boundaries. Once we discard the libido-theory we shall see that the concept of the Ego-boundaries will assist us considerably in the understanding of the Ego.

Two of Freud's statements add to the confusion: (a) the Ego is differentiated from the Unconscious; (b) the Unconscious contains repressed wishes. If a wish has been repressed, it must have been strong enough to have Ego quality ("I" want . . .). The contradiction, however, disappears as soon as we realize that we have two kinds of Unconscious: the biological

Unconscious (in the sense of the philosopher Hartmann), and the psycho-analytical Unconscious, which consists of previously conscious elements. We may conclude then: the Ego is differentiated from the biological Unconscious, but consequently certain Ego aspects have become repressed, and now constitute the psycho-analytical "Unconscious." To the observer the Ego quality of the latter remains obvious, but not to the patient. If, for example, an obsessional neurotic says: "There is a vague feeling at the back of my mind that I may experience an impulse through which some harm might befall my father, whom I dislike thoroughly because of his unpleasant habits!" he originally means: "I would like to kill that swine."

Freud says further about the Ego that it has command over the motoric system. This statement indicates that the Ego is not identical with the whole personality. If "I" command the motoric system, "I" must be different or apart from it: a general commanding an army is a part of, but apart from the rest of the army.

Yet, if I say: "I am travelling to the city of X," the Ego stands for the whole personality. A confusing number of statements without any central conception! To demonstrate my own conception of the Ego I have first to add to this confusion, not by piling up more theoretical statements, but by giving further practical aspects of the Ego.

Below a number of Ego aspects are enumerated in such a way as to show each aspect against its opposite as background, as we have previously done with the term "actor."

The Ego is	In Opposition to
a function	a substance
a contact function	confluence
a figure/background formation	de-personalization and dreamless sleep
elusive	stable
interfering	organismic self-regulation
the awareness of the self	awareness of another object
instance of responsibility	the Id
the boundary phenomenon itself	an object having a boundary
spontaneous	dutifully attentive
servant and executive of the organism	master in its own home
appearing in the ectoderm	mesoderm and endoderm
identification/alienation	the feel of indifference

We may obtain some provisional orientation from the psycho-analytical classification of the *Id*, the *Ego* and the *Super-Ego* or *Ego-Ideal* constituting the human personality.

Freud uses the two terms Super-Ego and Ego-Ideal almost synonymously; but, nevertheless, we may differentiate them as *conscience* and *ideals*, and characterize them as follows:

The conscience is aggressive, and expresses itself mainly in words; the aggression is directed from the conscience to the "Ego," the tension between conscience and Ego being experienced as feeling of guilt.

Ideals mainly exist in pictures; the emotion involved is love, its direction being from the Ego towards the ideal; a tension between Ego and ideal is felt as inferiority.

The Id represents the instincts, expressing themselves in sensations; the tension between Ego and Id is called urge, drive, wish, etc.

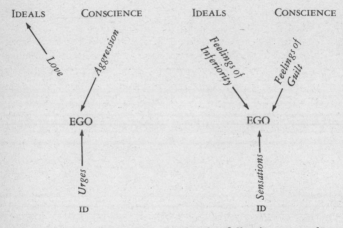

We can now apply this conception in the following example: a little boy feels the desire to "pinch" some sweets. Also, like many children, he is obsessed with the ideal of being grown up, but big people, in his imagination, don't crave for sweets; so he thinks he should fight his appetite. In addition his conscience tells him that stealing is a sin. Feeling these three experiences simultaneously his poor Ego would be caught between three fires. He, however, does not experience his Ego as a *substance*. The healthy child does not think "an ideal is obsessing me; the hunger is torturing me and my conscience forbids me to steal sweets." He experiences: "*I* want to be grown-up; *I* am hungry but *I* must not steal sweets."

From an objective point of view, his conscious experience is determined by conscience, ideals and Id, but subjectively he is hardly aware of that. He achieves this subjective integration by the process of identification— the feeling that something is part of him or that he is part of something else.

Thus I agree with Freud that the Ego is closely related to identification.

Freud, however, overlooks the one fundamental difference between the healthy and the pathological Ego. In the healthy personality identification is an Ego-function, whereas the pathological "Ego" is built up of introjections (substantial identifications) which determine the personality's actions and feelings, and limit their range. Super-Ego and Ego-Ideals invariably contain a number of permanent, partly unconscious, identifications; but the Ego becomes pathological if its identifications are permanent ones instead of functioning according to the requirements of different situations, and disappearing with the restoration of the organismic balance.[1]

A difficulty arises from the term "identification" itself, which has different aspects, e.g. copying somebody, siding with someone, concluding that two things are the same, sympathy (Einfuehlung) or understanding. The different aspects of the same word are responsible for two opposing theories in psycho-analysis: Freud's and Federn's.

Freud's opinion that every Ego is built up of identifications or introjections (in the sense of imitating someone, behaving "as if" one is somebody else) applies only to types which have developed a kind of Ego conglomeration—a fixed outlook on life, or a rigid, or an artificial character. In a rigid character we see that the Ego-functions cease almost completely, as the personality has become conditioned to habits and behaves automatically. Freud has realized this fact by saying that analysis can only be successful as long as the character has not become petrified. The complete identification (e.g. with conventions) will, in such a person, occasion intense conflicts as soon as the Ego has to function as the executive of (and identify itself with) an instinct of which he disapproves according to his principles. He might find himself starving, but to appropriate a loaf of bread would be such a horrible crime to him, that he would alienate this urge. He would rather die of starvation than risk going to jail for a few days.

In education, such stern morals may lead to severe misunderstandings. If carbohydrate hunger makes a child take sweets, wherever it can find them, the parents (projecting their legalistic outlook on the child) may be very worried over the "criminal". they have produced.

(b) BOUNDARY

As the term "identification" has become synonymous with introjection, Federn (possibly realizing that introjection is not the only existing form of identification) created the conception of the Ego and its boundaries.

---

[1] A simile might at least hint at this difference. One of the functions of the kidneys is the excretion of salts. The salts are merely passing through the urogenital system. Under certain pathological conditions the salts precipitate and form a solid, foreign body in the organism and interfere with the well-being, and eventually with the functions, of the kidney.

His theory assists us greatly in understanding some Ego-functions, provided we eliminate certain mistakes of his.

A physical phenomenon may serve to demonstrate the dialectic of the Ego-boundaries:

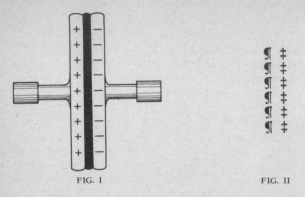

FIG. I   FIG. II

Two metal plates, A and B, are separated by an insulating layer. If one condenser plate is charged with positive electricity, negative electrons will gather on the opposite plate; but if there is a direct contact, positive and negative electrons will neutralize each other (Fig. 1). Ego-boundaries behave in exactly the same way. We have only to replace + and — by ¶ and ‡, which appear in the psycho-analytical terminology as libido and hostility (Fig. 2).[1]

Federn assumes that the Ego is a libidinal substance with permanently changing boundaries. By this he means that we identify ourselves with everything we accept as familiar or as belonging to us. Our Ego, according to Federn, can withdraw its boundaries within our personality, or stretch them beyond it.

Especially in obsessional neurosis the Ego has limited functions: a death wish, as mentioned previously, is disowned; it is not acknowledged as belonging to the Self. The obsessional character refuses to identify himself with, or take responsibility for such thoughts, responsibility and blame being the same to him. *Every inhibition and repression narrows down the Ego-boundaries.*

We enlarge our Ego-boundaries when we identify ourselves with *our* family, *our* school (old school tie traditions), *our* football club, *our* country. A mother may defend her child "as though" she were fighting for herself; if a football club has been slighted, any one of its members may take revenge, "as if" he himself had been insulted.

In all these instances the object of identification remains outside the

[1] Photographs of electrons show that (+) electrons have ¶ and (—) electrons ‡ character.

personality. It is not introjected and the identification is a fictitious one ("as if," "as though"). The mother was not attacked, and nobody had insulted the club member himself.

Mr. X sees a house and says, "I see a house." He does not say, "The optical system in Mr. X's organism sees a house." He identifies himself with this system of his. The next moment the house might recede into the background of his consciousness and he might find himself concentrating on some voices. He then quickly identifies himself with his acoustic apparatus and with his curiosity about these voices. He might say, "I hear *voices!*" or else, "*I* hear voices," thereby emphasizing that he stands in contrast to others who may not have heard a sound.

Now let us assume he heard voices but there were none. If he identifies himself with the fact that he is imagining, and says "I imagined that I heard voices," his Ego is functioning correctly; but if he identifies himself with the content of his hallucination when he lacks the insight into the fact that he has a fictitious, an "as if" identification, he behaves "as if" he heard voices.

The "as if" identification itself is not pathological; only the mistaking of a fictitious for a real identification falls under this category. Sometimes the fictitious identifications can accumulate to such a degree that we speak of an "as if" character (H. Deutsch). "As if" identifications are found in introjections (the child who plays mother) as well as in the enlargement of the Ego-boundary.

The corresponding "as-if" *alienation* is present in repressions, projections, and in a similar narrowing down of the Ego-boundaries. Although the patient expresses that such and such thoughts and wishes are not his, they belong, in fact, to his personality: alienation by repressing and projecting is, in the end, always unsuccessful. Psychoanalysis recognizes this fact as "return of the repressed."

In the identification/alienation function we see once more the working of holism. We see the formation of wholes—the oneness of mother and child, the integration of a number of people to a club; the greater the identification of the members with the club the more solid will be its structure, sometimes even to the point of petrification. The narrowing down of boundaries is also done in order to preserve a whole. Those parts of the personality which apparently endanger the accepted whole are sacrificed. ("And if thine eye offend thee pluck it out.") A similar idea is found in political purges.

Federn's theory shows a definite mistake and a one-sidedness. The mistake is that he considers the Ego as a substance with boundaries, while, in my opinion, only the boundaries, the places of contact, constitute the Ego. Only where and when the Self meets the "foreign" does the Ego start functioning, come into existence, determine the boundary between the personal and the impersonal "field." Federn is one-sided in that he considers only the integrative energy of the libido and neglects the simultaneous appearance of ‡.

The members of a football club tend to melt together into one unit (¶). Members of a clan are more attached to each other (¶) than those of another clan. Ideologies unite those who believe in them (¶). In times of danger when the security of a country is threatened, the unity of its citizens is of the utmost importance in its defence.

A sound holism requires mutual identification. The club which does not identify itself with its members—protecting their interests and compensating them for their devotion—will disintegrate. The ‡ which, in collective group, is added up and found on the outside of its boundaries returns to the individuals.

Federn does not look at the Ego-boundary from without, where the ‡ gathers. Just as the accumulation of positive electricity on one condenser plate is accompanied by that of its opposite on the other plate, so the integrative energies within the Ego-boundaries are complemented by hostility without.

Wherever two holistic structures meet, they themselves are kept together and separated from each other by more or less pronounced hostility. Two football clubs show this in a mild form of rivalry towards each other in general, and in their matches in particular. Between schools we see competition; between nations, wars. Family Smith feels superior to Family Brown, who in turn despises the members of the Smith family. The Montagues and Capulets are examples of hostile clans; but Romeo and Juliet break through the boundaries, their desire to join each other being so much stronger than their family ties.

The more hostility threatens from without the greater will be the integrative function of individuals and groups. In the moment of danger the organism will marshal all faculties at its disposal; whenever a country is attacked this aggression from outside may result in uniting its citizens. The mother who has just been angry with her child will the next moment protect it against an extraneous insult.

Love is identification with an object ("mine"); hate alienation from it ("away from me!"). The wish to be loved is the desire that the object should identify itself with the subject's wishes and demands. Intense mutual love is expressed in terms like, "one heart and one soul," "hand in glove," etc. In sexual intercourse mutual identification is imperative; "to be one flesh," reads a passage in the Bible.

The boundary between two farms is formed by a fence. This fence indicates the contact between the two farms, but isolates them from each other at the same time. In nomadic times there were no boundaries, there was a confluence. With personal ownership there came the division of land and the creation of friendly or hostile neighbours. If to-day the farmers joined in a collective group, the confluence would be re-

THE EGO AS A FUNCTION OF THE ORGANISM

established, but the boundaries between the collective farms (cf. the socialist competition in Russia) would remain. There would also be a confluence if a farmer coveted his neighbour's farm and incorporated it into his own property.

Isolation emphasizes separation, whilst contact emphasizes the approach, aiming at undoing the isolation either by withdrawing hostility, and replacing the *I* and *You* by *We*, or by making the whole complex *mine* or, by surrender *yours*.

Does ¶ create ‡ or vice versa? Both assumptions are incorrect. There is no causal connection between these two functions. Wherever and whenever a boundary comes into existence, it is felt both as contact and as isolation. Usually neither contact nor isolation exists, as there is a confluence but no boundary. This confluence is interfered with by (¶) and (‡), libido and aggression, friendship and hostility, sense of familiarity and of strangeness or whatever one chooses to call the energies forming the boundary.

A good example of the simultaneity of ¶ and ‡ is embarrassment. Here one finds simultaneously the tendencies to make contact (exhibition) and to hide. Its pre-differential stage is shyness. Both possibilities, attachment as well as separation, are open to the shy child. Shyness is therefore a normal phase in the child's development; but making friends with every Tom, Dick and Harry or shrinking from every contact are unhealthy extremes if they are permanent attitudes instead of adequate responses.

By exclusively identifying itself with the demands of the environment, by introjecting ideologies and character features, the Ego loses its elastic power of identification. As a matter of fact, it practically ceases to function other than as the executor of a conglomeration of principles and fixed behaviour. Super-Ego and *character* have taken its place, in a similar way as in our time machine-made articles have replaced individual handicraft.

VIII

THE SPLIT OF THE PERSONALITY

There is a well-known proverb which declares that a bundle of sticks is stronger than the same number of single sticks. Does this proverb imply a mere scientific fact? Certainly not. Proverbs have a moral. This one implies: join a number of sticks and they will have more power to resist and to attack! Or vice versa: if you need a strong stick a number of thinner ones joined together will serve the same purpose!

Such an integrative function is another aspect of the Ego. The Ego in a kind of administrative function will connect the actions of the *whole* organism with its foremost needs; it calls, so to speak, upon those functions of the whole organism which are necessary for the gratification of the *most urgent* need. Once the organism has identified itself with a demand, it stands as wholeheartedly behind it as it is hostile towards anything alienated.

A man makes two statements: "I am hungry," and later on, "I am not hungry." From the logical point of view this is a contradiction, but only as long as we regard this man as an object, and not as a time-space event. Between the two statements he has had something to eat. So both times he is telling the truth. A more complicated situation is met with, if we put a hungry person in an airtight box. He who has just said, "I am hungry," feels now, "I am choking," and not even, "I am hungry *and* I am choking." From the survival point of view breathing is more important than eating.

How is it that we do not experience such contradictory statements as incompatible facts? Identification (and what is said about identification applies in every case to alienation as well, since both are mutually necessary counter functions) follows the figure/background formation. A healthy Ego-function answers the subjective reality, and the needs of the organism. If, for instance, an organism develops hunger, food becomes "gestalt"; the Ego identifies itself with the hunger ("I am hungry") and answers the gestalt ("I want this food").

In the case of the person who would rather die than steal the bread, the Ego alienates the taking of food. Without the figure/background formation, however, he would neither see nor imagine the bread, and there would be no possibility of the Ego alienating the impulse to take the bread, and identifying itself with the law.

Were the Ego-functions *identical* with the figure/background formation, they would be superfluous, but they are indispensable for the administrative task to direct all available energies to the service of that organismic need which is in the foreground. With this fact we encounter a further bi-functional aspect—that of master and servant. Freud's remark, "We are not master in our home," is correct in so far as the Ego accepts orders from the instincts within the biological field, and from conscience and environment within the social field. The Ego, however, is not merely a servant of instincts and ideologies; it is also a middleman with many responsibilities. (Pushing the responsibilities on to causes does not further the Ego-development.)

The desire to master ourselves results from insufficient co-operation between organism and Ego-function. If someone, for instance, decides that defaecation is a nuisance, and that his intestines have without fail to do what he wants, this mastering attitude is a mis-application of the Ego-functions. His Ego-functions ought to secure the adequate gratification of the defaecation urge, with a minimum of energy and an optimum of organismic functioning. A dictatorial, bullying self-controlling Ego (which, correctly expressed, means the identification function with a bullying conscience), far from taking the responsibility for the organism, pushes it (mostly as blame) on to the Id or the "body," as if it was something not belonging to the Self.

The concept of the "Id" is possible only as a counterpoint to the concept of the Super-Ego. Thus it is an artificial, un-biological construction created by the alienation function of the Ego. A boundary appears between the accepted and refused part of the personality, and a split personality develops.

In other words, by taking the Ego as a substance we have to admit its incompetence. We have to accept the Ego's dependency upon the demands of instincts, conscience and environment, and we have to agree fully with Freud's poor view on the Ego's power. Once, however, we realize the Ego's power of identification we acknowledge that our conscious mind is left with an instance of very considerable importance—with the decision to identify itself with whatever it considers as being "right."

We find in this identification/alienation function the beginning of a "free will." This function is often misapplied, but this does not alter the fact that in it we have encountered the principle of the conscious control of the human Self. Society has to determine which identifications of the individual are desirable for its smooth holistic function, without damaging the individual's development, its physical and mental health. Although this programme sounds simple, it is outside the scope of mankind at the present stage of our civilization. In the meantime the individual can do no more than to avoid multiple identifications which without fail must lead to the impairment of the personal holism—which must result in internal conflicts, splits of the personality and increasing unhappiness. These splits, conflicts and unhappiness in the individual are the microcosmic equivalent of the present world situation.

> "Dissenting clamours in the town arise;
> Each will be heard and all at once advise.
> One part for peace and one for war contends;
> Some would exclude their foes, and some admit their friends."
>
> *Virgil.*

*   *   *

The intuitive knowledge of these ¶ and ‡ functions, forming the boundaries, is Hitler's great advantage. His aggression not being invested in its dental outlet (bad teeth—porridge eater) finds its way basically into crying and shouting. When he does not get what he wants he becomes irritable, first whining, then shouting and screaming at the top of his voice, until the whole of his environment becomes panicky and does everything to pacify the cry-baby (you can't hurt an innocent baby and Hitler always pleads innocence). Later he finds, the more followers he gets the more aggression he can apply; the more aggression he can apply the stronger become the internal ties of his group. He finds the uniting symbol of the gallows-cross, the slogan, "One people, one country, one leader," an ideological term which attracted many classes of the German people. Finally, he supplies the emotional food for the German vanity: the idea of the "master race."

Parallel with the application of ¶ goes his knowledge of the working of ‡. Recognizing the importance of wholes, he knows that unity makes strength; so he sets out to destroy every powerful adverse organization, be it an industrial council, a trade union or the Church. He cracks the nutshell and throws away the indigestible material, he swallows the members and assimilates the money of the broken up organizations. "One by one," he tackles first the internal, then the external organizations and states. He applies the oral technique in strategy as well. He cuts the hostile armies up with the incisors of his blitz and grinds them down with the molars of his tanks. If his incisors—the spearheads—are blunted, if the molars of his bombardment are not successful enough to grind the enemy to pulp, then he is lost. The best he can do is to hang on with his teeth, trying not to let go.

One essential aim of his technique is to split wholes—for instance nations—with the help of the fifth column. The idea is, on the one hand, to join all the members of the fifth column in a solid unit by stirring up their common grudges and hatreds, by stressing their own relationship with each other, and by presenting himself as the only saviour. On the other hand, he encourages the training in destruction which, in turn, increases the cohesion of the fifth column. The greater the oral under-development (e.g. the lack of reasoning power or the dependency on Church and State) which he encounters, the easier it is for him to find sufficient people who "believe" in him.

*   *   *

Only the conscious exploitation of the Ego-boundary phenomenon is Hitler's privilege. The boundaries occur, of course, everywhere and range from the split which, especially in times of election, goes through the U.S.A. to the split personality.

If a football club is not keeping up its aggression in competition and there are no other attractions to keep the members together, the club will either disintegrate or, at least, break down into fractions. People with certain affinities will draw together and form cliques. They will start teasing each other, quarrelling about small items and, finally, if there is no occasion to re-establish the common outside boundary, they will fight each other. The result will be a split, or even a separation.

If separation takes place the hostility will cease, but only under one condition—that no contact remains. The boundaries with their ¶/‡ functions come into existence only where some contact is left.

Where both a split *and* contact exists there will always be the boundary-function either as open or latent hostility or, as the inhibited tendency to re-integration by identification, as latent friendship or love. The place of contact in such cases is identical with the place of conflict. "It takes two to make a quarrel."

A split between the individual and the world exists in the case of an imprisoned criminal, whose isolation is materialized by the prison bars. A friendly attitude by either side (mercy and repentance respectively) may remove the separation and re-establish contact. But the *contact-phenomenon* is not permanent; it is constituted by the experience of re-union, and will be replaced by *confluence*, once the former "criminal" is again accepted by society.

In the case of the criminal the split is inaugurated by society, but the individual can likewise create such splits. The desire for solitude brings about a boundary as a passing phase, whilst misanthropy or a generalized persecution idea leads to a more permanent isolation. A political conviction which is different from the majority may create a new party, a new creed will create a new sect.

In order to avoid conflicts—to remain within the bounds of society or other units—the individual alienates those parts of his personality which would lead to conflicts with the environment. *The avoidance of external conflicts*, however, *results in the creation of internal ones*. Psycho-analysis has correctly stressed this fact over and over again.

A child badly wants a certain toy. He does not get it, but knows it is possible to buy it with money which is in Daddy's pocket. To take this money, he knows, would lead to a serious conflict with his father, who says that stealing is a sin and that one gets punished for it. Identifying himself with the father's dictum he must alienate—suppress—his desire. He must either destroy it by resignation and crying, or throw it out of his Ego-boundary—by repressing or projecting it. Repression is done by retroflecting his aggression which originally was directed against the frustrating father and is now directed against his desire. Projection—by a different and more complicated process—restores the harmony between himself and the father but at the cost of destroying his own.

Holism requires internal peace. An internal conflict is opposed to the very essence of holism. Freud once said that a conflict in the personality is like two servants quarrelling all day long; how much work can one expect to get done? If a split exists within the personality (for instance, between conscience and instincts), the Ego may be either hostile toward the instinct and friendly towards the conscience (inhibition), or vice versa (defiance).

How the same act evokes different reactions, evaluations and even conflicts, and how the varying reactions depend on the mode of identification, may be shown in the following examples of killing:

(1) Someone has shot his neighbour. Society or its representative, the crown prosecutor who identifies himself with the victim calls it murder and demands punishment. (2) Someone has shot his opponent in a war. Society identifies itself with the soldier, the victim this time being outside the identification boundaries. The soldier might receive a reward. (3) The same as (1) but here the judge, on learning that our "killer" had been deeply offended by the neighbour, might sympathize with the accused. By identification with both the killer and the killed the judge will be in a conflict about the accused's guilt. (4) The same as (2) but the soldier's Super-Ego has retained the dogma that killing is a cardinal sin. He will likewise be in conflict by identification with both his country's and his conscience's demands.

In (3) the judge says, "I condemn you," and "I do not condemn you." In (4) the soldier feels, "I must kill," and "I must not kill." Such double identifications are intolerable for the organism. A decision is required. One of the identifications must cease. In fact, only by understanding the possibility to refuse identifications as undesirable and as dangerous, and to alienate them, can we grasp the true sense of the Ego and its development as selector or censor.

Identification with organismic needs is originally effort-free, but alienation is not. The closer a wish is to organismic needs, the more difficult becomes alienation when the social situation demands it. Most of us have experienced how difficult it is to dissociate oneself even from a morbid curiosity of staring at a deformed person. In spite of all efforts to turn one's eyes away, one discovers oneself looking again and again in the disapproved direction. If it is already nearly impossible to alienate such morbid curiosity or an unpleasant habit such as a tic or stammering, how much more difficult must it be to alienate a really powerful impulse. "Would you stop for a candy?"

I have mentioned before that in the identification function we have the nucleus of a "free will," which will come into being as soon as in the process of reconditioning we replace "right" and "wrong" by "identification" and "alienation" respectively. Having identified ourselves with certain methods, we call them "right" and alienate others, calling them "wrong." This "feel" of right and wrong is often deceptive, as familiarity or habits are perceived as right, and strange or unaccustomed attitudes as wrong. F. M. Alexander has made an excellent study of these difficulties encountered in the process of reconditioning.

Such mistaking of the familiar attitude for the "right" one is daily encountered in analysis. Many analysts speak of this as lack of the patient's insight into his illness. This reproach entirely misses the point. The biologically correct attitude might have been alienated to such an extent that the patient cannot any more conceive it as being natural. His resistance is an identification with certain ideological demands which he does not experience as a changeable identification—but as a fixed "right" outlook.

The analysis of a symptom may elucidate the meaning of the foregoing, and show how the mobilization of the Ego-functions is necessary for the re-establishment of the healthy functioning of the whole personality.

Mrs. A suffers from a headache, after a girl friend has insulted her. She is unaware of the fact that she herself is producing the headache, and is not willing to take responsibility for it—she rather blames her constitution, her proneness to headaches, or her inconsiderate friend. Psycho-analysis, too, relieves her of responsibility by finding the cause in converted libidinal energy. If she took more responsibility for her headache (and less aspirin), and if she knew exactly how she produced it, she might decide not to produce it at all.

She says that after the friend's insult she felt like crying, but did not shed a single tear. This looks as if crying were converted into headache. But just as I cannot conceive how repressed libido can change into a headache, so I cannot accept such a conversion of crying. Every conjuring trick has its rational explanation. Identified with dignity and pride, she was incapable of identifying herself with the biological need of finding relief in crying, so she contracted her eye and throat muscles to stop the flow of tears. Intense muscular contraction leads to pain; the squeezing of head muscles results in headache. Anyone may convince himself of this "production of pain" by tightening a fist as hard as possible.

To return to the patient: without dissolving the Ego-conglomeration (in this case, the permanent contractions) she cannot yield to the impulse of crying and acquire adequate Ego-functions, i.e. identifications with her actual needs. Her headache is the signal of an unfinished situation; she is unable to finish, get rid of her resentment, because she has a tremendous reluctance to let herself go.

In this reluctance she is assisted by her senso-motoric system.

IX

SENSO-MOTORIC RESISTANCES

When the analyst points out to the patient that he has a resistance or is in a state of resistance, the patient often feels guilty "as if" he should not have such unacceptable characteristics. Psycho-analysis concentrates correctly to a great extent on resistances, but often with the idea that they are something unwanted—something that can be done away with, and that should be destroyed wherever they are met with, in order to develop a healthy character. Reality looks somewhat different. One cannot destroy resistances; and in any case, they are not an evil, but are rather valuable energies of our personality—harmful only when wrongly applied. We cannot do justice to our patients as long as we do not realize the dialectics of resistance. The dialectical opposite to resistance is assistance. The same fort which resists the aggressor assists the defender. In this book we can retain the term "resistance," as we are essentially the enemies of the neurosis. In a book on Ethics we would prefer the term "assistance" for those mechanisms which help us in repressing the condemned character features. It should, however, be kept in mind that without appreciating the patient's outlook on his resistances as assistances we cannot successfully deal with them.

The rigidity of the resisting energies presents the cardinal difficulty. If a motor-car brake or a water tap is jammed, adequate functioning of car or water supply is impossible. The analytical situation has the task of recovering the elasticity of such rigid resistances. It is not that the internal resistance disappears and that a negative transference is created. It is rather that, in addition to the Ego-boundary which lies between the disturbing internal wish and the conscious personality, another boundary (between patient and analyst) comes into existence. The analyst is looked upon as an ally of the forbidden impulse, and is consequently alienated. The censor, full of mistrust and hostility, is on guard against the disturber, lest identification with the "strange" ideas of the psycho-analyst should take place. The organism identifies itself with this hostility and resists or even attacks the analyst.

The figure-background formation has one serious drawback. The organism concentrates on one thing at a time. It achieves thus a maximum of action on one place but a minimum of attention for the rest. Any unforeseen attack thus constitutes a danger. The unexpected—the surprise attack—is as detrimental for the individual as it is for any army or nation. Just as fortifications and permanent defences compensate for a weakness in man-power, so we find in the individual organism skin and shells on the physical, character formation on the behaviour plane. But, as mentioned before, the boundaries cannot be hermetically sealed. Some contact with the world must remain. A castle must have communications like doors to receive food or to send messages. A big breach on the wall, instead of a door, would constitute an open communication, a *confluence*. If, for instance, the fence of a farm were broken, the cattle could escape through this confluence with the outer world, and the farmer would have to fall back from the mechanical guard of the fence upon a living defender, a watchboy or a dog. These, however, might fall asleep and the opening remain unguarded, the confluence thus being re-established.

Such guarded communications are the body openings. They require quite an amount of conscious attendance (Ego-functions) otherwise they might become places of confluence. Using the simile of the castle, pathological resistances may be compared with locked doors (the key of which has been mislaid), and total absence of resistances corresponds to the gaps in the wall resulting from the complete removal of the doors. The impulsive irresponsible character, as found in cases of "juvenile delinquency," clearly shows the absence of necessary resistances, the lack of brakes which he should apply to safeguard himself against the retaliation of society. By analysing resistances on the assumption that they should not exist, we run great risks. It will often happen that resistances are not fully dealt with, but are repressed and over-compensated—embarrassment by pseudo-courage, shame by impudence, disgust by indiscriminate greediness. In "juvenile delinquency" the repression of resistances appears often as defiance and heroism making itself shown as "tough guy" ideal.

The mere dissolution of the resisting energies entails another danger. Many people have developed hardly any other Ego-functions than those of resistance, be it against their own impulses, or against demands made on them. They aim at developing a strong Ego, a character full of "will-power." To them an efficient personality is identical with a "strong" character—one able to suppress smoking, sex-impulses, hunger and so forth.

If one deprives them of these resisting and domineering functions, there is nothing left in which they are interested. They have never learned how to enjoy themselves, how to be aggressive, or how to love, and while their resistances are being analysed, they become completely confused, while their identification with those vital functions has not yet been established.

Moreover, the resisting energies of such people are very valuable, and if they have good domineering and resisting qualities, they will find ample opportunity of using them beneficially. What must be achieved is the undoing of retroflections. The patient must learn to direct the resisting energies towards the outside world, to apply them in accordance with the demands of the situation, to say "No" when a "No" is required. If one has to deal with a drunken, incapable person, it is more important to control, even to get rid of, his molestations, than to control oneself. A child which always complies with the often idiotic and irresponsible demands of its parents and resists its own impulses, will cripple its personality and become a meek and dishonest character. If, at times, it manages to resist their demands, if it puts up a fight, it will in later life be in a better position to stand up for its rights. The actual situation is the criterion as to whether resistance is useful or not. Obstinacy, a concentrated conscious resistance, has likewise to be judged from the point of view of its usefulness. Obstinacy about taking good advice is different from the obstinacy of a determined nation against unprovoked attacks.

If we fully understand two facts, the centrifugal sensoric and motoric functions, and the phenomenon of retroflection, we get a clear conception of the somato-neurotic resistances. Of these the motoric resistances, consisting mainly of increased muscular tension, have been dealt with extensively by Reich's armour theory. What I have to add is that these cramps are in fact retroflected squeezing. They are symptoms of a hanging-on attitude (hanging-on bite; hanging on to a person or to one's possessions, faeces, breath, and so on; cf. Imre Hermann's analysis of the clinch reflex).

*　　*　　*

Of the sensoric resistances, the most frequent is scotomization, a minus or a deficient function by which the perception of certain things is avoided. Less well known is the fact that increased sensoric activity is likewise a resistance. We all know people who are touchy, over-sensitive and easily hurt. Their touchiness, highly developed and cultivated, serves as a means of avoiding situations which they do not want to face, their favourite expression being, "This gets on my nerves." Such hyper-aesthesia takes the form, for instance, of migraine with its over-sensitiveness to light, etc., when Madame wants to avoid an unpleasant discussion with her husband. In the sexual situation she is so sensitive that every approach hurts her, a defence which disappears when she is in harmony with the man. Others develop touchiness (as assistance!), not for defensive, but for aggressive purposes. If you refuse to comply with one of their wishes, they look so hurt as to make you feel you have committed a crime; and the next time, although you recognize the emotional blackmail, you do not dare refuse their demands.

The picture of hyper-aesthesia—the readiness to be hurt—would not be complete, without considering the projection of hurting. Every person who is easily offended, easily hurt, has an equally strong but inhibited inclination towards inflicting pain. This sometimes finds its outlet and aim in a round-about way. Melancholic characters, for instance, enjoy making other people feel miserable, and often admit that they mostly succeed in making others feel awkward, embarrassed and irritable.

The production of the opposite resistance, of de-sensitivization (hypo-aesthesia and anaesthesia) requires still more research work. Sometimes hypo-aesthesia is produced by prolonged medium-tensed muscular contractions, sometimes by concentrating on a "figure" different from that required by the situation (dummy).

A patient complained of lack of sensations during intercourse. Inquiries into details of his experiences revealed that during the act he "thought," instead of being concentrated on his feelings. Often in his phantasy he was busy reading a newspaper, a behaviour which analysis revealed to be a training against over-sensitiveness, against his ejaculatio praecox. By diverting his attention from his sensations to the newspaper he had conquered his complaint, but had changed hyper-aesthesia into anaesthesia, without healthy gratification being possible in either case.

De-sensitivization is often accompanied by a feeling of being wrapped in cotton wool, or by a mental black-out. Yet, whenever a patient maintained that he felt or thought nothing, I found that the black-out or anaesthesia was not complete, but that it was merely a hypo-aesthesia, a kind of dimming. Thoughts were present (but rather in the background), and so were feelings, although they were described as being of a stale or dull nature.

In a case described by Freud, the patient complained about a permanent veil, which was torn only during defaecation. I presume this "re-veilation" was identical with his feeling of the contact of the faeces with the wall of the anus, that is with the exit-contact. The absence of this contact constitutes an unguarded confluence between personality and world. *This confluence, the absence of the Ego-boundary, is essential for the development of projections.*

Small children shut their eyes tightly if they do not want to look. This is a plus-function, an activity. It is an additional muscular impulse preventing their curiosity from becoming effective. It appears that the veil of Freud's patient is similarly a cover, an additional function, a kind of senso-motoric hallucination. By properly describing and analysing such cover-functions, one can unmask their aim: the avoidance of some emotional experience. In cases of anal numbness I was given descriptions such as: "The faeces pass through a rubber tube"; or, "It is as if an air space exists"; or, "The faeces do not touch the wall."

Similar descriptions are given in cases of genital frigidity. Here, too, hallucinated layers are found side by side with the minus functions, like lack of concentration and of adequate figure-background formation.

Oral frigidity (numbness of taste, lack of appetite) plays a considerable part in the disturbance of the Ego-development. It prevents the experience of enjoyment as well as disgust, and it promotes the introjection of food.

X

PROJECTION

Whilst with the help of the existing analytical literature we were able to form a clear picture of the origin of introjection, we are still in the dark about the genesis of projection.

There exists a pre-different stage for which, to my knowledge, no name has yet been coined. One often observes a baby throwing its doll out of a pram. The doll stands for the child itself: "I want to be where the doll is." This emotional (ex-movere) stage differentiates later into *expression* and *projection*. A healthy mental metabolism requires development in the direction of expression and not projection. *The healthy character expresses* his emotions and ideas, *the paranoid character projects* them.

The importance of the subject of expression can hardly be over-estimated if one bears in mind two facts:

(1) It is incorrect to speak of the repression of instincts. Instincts can never be repressed—only their expressions can be.
(2) In addition to the inhibited expression of instincts (mainly in action) every neurosis shows difficulties in expressing the "Self" (mainly in words). Expression is replaced by play-acting, broadcasting, hypocrisy, self-consciousness and projecting.

Genuine expression is not deliberately created; it comes "from the heart," but it is consciously moulded. Every artist is an inventor, finding means and ways—sometimes new ways—of expressing himself.

Projection is essentially an unconscious phenomenon. The projecting person cannot satisfactorily distinguish between the inside and outside world. He visualizes in the outside world those parts of his own personality with which he refuses to identify himself. The organism experiences them as being outside the Ego-boundaries and reacts accordingly with aggression.[1]

[1] Certain complications are left out here for simplification. God, for instance, is a projection of man's omnipotence wishes, but by partial identification ("My" God) the aggression comes into play only against a foreign god or in situations where "God's will" is not accepted, as after disappointments.

People often are said to remember God only when they need Him. This is not a memory, but every time a new projection. When in a difficult situation they feel helpless and wish for power and magic resources, they project such omnipotence wishes, and the all-powerful God is re-created.

Feelings of guilt are unpleasant to bear; therefore children and adults with an insufficiently developed sense of responsibility are inclined to project any anticipated blame on to something else. A child who has hurt itself on a chair, blames the "naughty" chair. A man who ruins his business may throw the responsibility on to "bad times" or "fate"—some scapegoat or another will always be at hand.

These projections of guilt have the advantage of giving temporary relief, but they deprive the personality of the Ego-functions of contact, identification and responsibility.

In analysing patients who had previously been treated by other analysts I noticed that some of them showed an extraordinary number of projections. Repressed parts of their personalities had been made conscious, but the patients had not accepted the facts and functions brought to the surface. They were bad "chewers" and had never managed to assimilate the released material. This material had been ejected from the Unconscious directly to the world, without passing the Ego-boundaries. One case, by projecting his sexual impulses on to his friends, had almost developed a persecution mania. Another showed a marked increase of fear developed through projecting his aggression on to the world. By releasing the repressed material without assimilating it both cases went from the rain into the trough.

A mother told me that her child had experienced a nightmare. He woke up crying that a dog wanted to bite him. I found that in his attempt at playing "doggie" with his mother and eating her up he had met with a stern refusal, and he had been told not to be naughty. I made no attempt to explain to the child the meaning of the dog as totem animal and its rôle within the Oedipus-complex; I simply took it for granted that the child had projected its frustrated aggression on to the dog in the dream. Thereby his rôle of an active biter was changed into the fear of being bitten. I advised the mother to encourage both the dog-play and the child's aggression. The nightmare has not recurred.

A person who is inclined to project, resembles someone sitting in a house lined with mirrors. Wherever he looks he thinks he sees the world through the glass, whereas he actually sees only reflections of the un-accepted parts of his own personality.

Except in dreams and in a fully developed psychosis, one always finds the tendency to use an adequate object as a screen or receiver for the projection. The child with the nightmare would have developed a phobia of dogs, if he had not regained his aggressiveness. The frightfulness of the aggressor nations is increased by the same amount of aggression which the victim projects into them, and it is decreased to its actual level when the victim refuses to be intimidated and makes use of his own aggressiveness.

Not always is it the outside world, however, which serves as a screen for projections; they can also take place *within the personality*. There are people whose stern conscience cannot be explained merely by introjection. Parents who, according to the introjection-theory, reappear within the personality as conscience, may in reality be anything but stern. In one of my cases the parents had been extraordinarily sympathetic, but had killed their child's aggression by kindness. This patient suffered from severe feelings of guilt and intense reproaches from his conscience. He had projected his aggression—his tendency to reproach—into his conscience which he subsequently experienced as attacking him. As soon as he managed to be openly aggressive his conscience lost its grip on him, and his feelings of guilt disappeared. An over-stern conscience can be cured only when self *re*proach changes into object *ap*proach.

The Russian "saints" in pre-Soviet literature, by curbing their aggressiveness and renouncing sin increased their feelings of guilt. On the other hand, a child may have very intolerant parents, but if it keeps up its fighting spirit and does not project its own aggression into the parents or into its conscience, it will remain healthy.

Projections can attach themselves to the most unexpected objects and situations. One of my patients spent most of his time worrying about his genitals, and how to feel sensations in them. He often imagined that his penis had disappeared into his stomach, that it was not manly enough, or that it was weak. Whatever theme cropped up, he always returned to the subject of his penis. The analysis of his genital and oral difficulties brought improvement, but no solution. It then struck me that his Ego-functions were limited to complaining and to rare spells of crying and annoyance. Where were the remaining features of his personality? They were projected into his penis. He did not feel that he was running away from certain situations, but in such cases he had the feeling that his penis had disappeared into his stomach. *He* did not feel weak, his *genitals* were weak. Instead of attempting to overcome the dullness of his life, he permanently tried to arouse more sensations in his penis.

Such a case is certainly exceptional. What we see rather frequently, however, is *projection into the past*. Instead of expressing an emotion within the actual situation, the patient produces a memory. Instead of saying to the analyst, "you are talking a lot of bilge," he appears to be indifferent, but remembers suddenly a situation where he attacked a friend for talking "a lot of bilge." Such overlooking of projection into the past helps psycho-analysis on the one hand to maintain the dogma of the all-important past and, on the other hand, interferes with the clearing up of the actual conflicts.

Usually the bulk of unwanted material is projected on to the outside world. Sometimes it is very difficult indeed to discover projections, for instance in the case of the neurotic's need for affection, a phenomenon that has always proved a stumbling block in analytical theory and practice.

Karen Horney has recognized the important part that this character-feature plays in the neurotic of our time, and I have already explained that this need cannot be satisfied, because love, if and when offered, is not really accepted and assimilated.

Psycho-analysis and individual psychology (Adler) proclaim the dogma that the neurotic has remained more or less infantile. The need for affection is certainly present in every child, and the inability to love is frequently a characteristic of the neurotic; but the ability to love is by no means reserved for adults. The child hates and loves with an intensity which grown-ups can only envy. The tragedy of the neurotic is not that he has never *developed* love, nor that he has regressed into the state of a child—it lies in his *inhibition* to love and still more in his inability to express his love. If unaccepted love is followed by disappointment, the painful experience makes him shrink from yielding to his emotions. It is as if he had decided, "Let others do the loving; I won't run such a risk again." Every time he arouses love, however, the situation becomes precarious anew; he feels tempted to answer love with love, but he is ashamed of being ridiculous and romantic. He feels afraid of being taken advantage of or having to suffer rebukes. If, in addition to this, he is an oral character, the need for affection coincides with his general greed.

The neurotic projects the (inhibited) love, and consequently (in his expectations and phantasies) he conjures up visions of receiving just those affections which he suppresses in himself. In other words, he does not suffer from an inability to love, but from an inhibition—from the fear of loving too much.

Just as the neurotic's "need for affection" has its anchorage in the projection, so has the other symptom which classical psycho-analysis regards as neurotic symptom number one. I am referring to the castration-complex which is based on the fear that the genitals might be completely or partially destroyed. To prove the existence of such a complex, every part of the body is interpreted by the Freudians as penis. Even the demand of the mother for the child's stool is explained as a castration. Psycho-analysis, however, overlooks the decisive fact that with all the so-called penis-substitutes only one factor remains constant—namely that of damage: every disciplinary education threatens, and sometimes inflicts damage, be it to the penis, eyes, buttocks, brain or honour. The neurotic's recurring fear of suffering damage cannot be cured by squeezing every possible penis-symbol into the castration-complex, but rather by undoing the projections of the neurotic's aggression—of his unexpressed desire to threaten and to inflict damage.

A young man with a strong, though unhappy, mother-fixation, admitted that he shrank from sexual intercourse for fear something might happen to his penis inside the vagina. His dreams revealed that he was afraid of a vagina dentata. The female genital was a kind of shark to him, which would bite off his penis. This was apparently an unambiguous castration complex. He was an artist and showed an unusual abhorrence of any reviews of his work, because of the *sharp biting* criticism they might express. He avoided the threats to both his penis and to his narcissism.

Further symptoms brought the solution of his neurosis: he hardly ever used his front teeth and was afraid of hurting even a fly—two phenomena mostly found together. Biting and hurting were projected, but not only into the vagina, so that his fear of being hurt was not confined to the penis. To consider the penis as the only, or even the primary object, is in my opinion an arbitrary decision, and mistakes a symptom for a cause. Even if a neurotic of this type could be convinced that there is no danger in the vagina, his troubles would not be over, for his castration-complex is not the centre of his neurosis; it is but one result of his projected aggressiveness. He may become sexually potent, but the fear of damage (e.g. to his prestige) may nevertheless remain and he would merely search for another screen for his projections. Our patient's diffident attitude changed, after he had learned to use his aggression, to put his teeth into things and to get his share out of life. During the treatment I heard him express some very sharp criticism.

Projections are, in the strictest sense, hallucinations. The little boy's nightmare is such a projective hallucination, which in genuine paranoia is a central symptom. Where enough sense of reality remains, the hallucinations are rationalized; we may then speak of a paranoid character. Typical of it is the looking for "points," for realities which may serve as proof to the paranoid that he is not hallucinating. The morbidly jealous husband, for instance, will lie in wait and try to trap his wife in order to discover whether she smiles at anyone else; and if this happens, he interprets her smile in accordance with his preconceived ideas of jealousy.[1]

A man was haunted by the fear that one day he would be killed by a tile falling from a roof. He avoided going near the rows of houses, and by walking in the street took the increased risk of being run over. He could not, of course, be convinced that his chances of being killed by a tile were a million to one. One day he brought a newspaper cutting to me and triumphantly showed me that a man *had* been killed by a tile: "You see, I was right; such things *do* happen." He was looking for points and at last had found one. His fear was dissolved through undoing the projection of his particular urge to lean out of the window and to throw stones at those people who had treated him "unjustly."

Milder cases of paranoid characters show a certain selectivity which emphasizes some characteristics in a person, and scotomizes others. The attacked features correspond to the projections, to the alienated parts of the paranoid personality. Projections are thus very suitable means of

[1] Jealousy is always due to unexpressed, projected wishes.

avoiding the solution of the ambivalence attitude. By projecting one's own hostile attitude it is easy to be tolerant. Does one not deserve a pat on the back for being so good in the midst of such a bad world?

As an organismic conception cannot be satisfied with the inquiry into the mere psychological aspects, we may attempt to find what, on the somatic side, corresponds to the process of projection.

XI

PSEUDO-METABOLISM OF THE PARANOIC CHARACTER

Two figures may show, in a simple form, the activity of the alimentary tract of the organism: Fig. I illustrates the healthy food metabolism; Fig. II, a pathological phenomenon which resembles metabolism, but is actually a frustration, and may be called pseudo-metabolism.

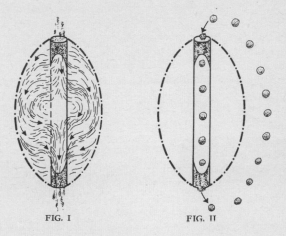

FIG. I   FIG. II

The alimentary tube is a skin separating the organism proper from the outside world (as does the epidermis). As long as the food is within the tube and has not penetrated its walls it is still isolated from the organism. In a sense it remains part of the outside world, as does the oxygen in the lungs before being absorbed through the alveoli. Both oxygen and food become part of the organism only after having been absorbed.

Without proper preparation (chewing, etc.) food does not become absorbable. People who do not chew properly may discover whole mealie-corns, berries and similar objects in their stools. Introjected material remains outside the organism proper, and is then correctly felt as something strange to the Self, something which provokes dental aggression or the desire to get rid of it. This material is defaecated not as waste matter, but as *projection*. It does not disappear from the projector's world, but only from his personality.

Under the influence of resistances the healthy state of eating and defaecating often changes into the pathological conditions of introjection and projection; with the help of sensoric resistances (hypo-aesthesia), os and anus become places of confluence instead of regulated communication.

When I first discovered cases in which the patient did not accept, but projected the material released by psycho-analysis from the Unconscious, I tried to puzzle out how this material could slip out without Ego-contact —without the patient becoming aware of this process. I found the solution in the structural identity of physical and mental processes. In all these cases there exists an anaesthesia, a frigidity of the anus. Thus the analytical material, like the faeces, does not (to use Federn's terminology) filter through the Ego-boundaries; or, as I would prefer to express it, the Ego is non-existent, not functioning. As there is a confluence between organism and world, it is not noticed that parts of the personality are leaving the system.

One result of the anaesthesia, which sometimes stretches far up the rectum, is that the feeling of the urge to defaecate is considerably reduced, an unsureness which manifests itself mostly in a permanent tightening of the constricting muscle of the anus and in chronic constipation. The control of defaecation is not functioning biologically; the anus is, for safety's sake, rigidly locked; the defaecation is a forced one and often piles develop. The passing of the faeces through the anus is not felt; it takes place without adequate sensations. Instead of full awareness, mind wandering —sometimes even a kind of trance—accompanies the defaecation.

In the healthy organism the mental and physical food is assimilated and transformed into energies, which are applied in activity; they appear as work and emotions. Indigestible material is discharged and discarded as waste; it is expressed, but not projected.

In pseudo-metabolism the material taken in is insufficiently assimilated and passes out of the personality more or less unused, carrying with it energies from the system. They slip out without having fulfilled their task in the organism. If the material were only discarded and treated as waste the harm done to the organism could be retrieved. To a considerable degree the loss could be compensated for by an increase in the quantity of food. (An "introjector" is greedy, and a certain amount of the swallowed food will always find its way into the tissues, in spite of the lack of oral destruction.) It appears, however, that *to the same degree as the powerful digestive instinct remains ungratified the organism craves to regain its own substance*. In a primitive way, we meet this tendency in the perversion of coprophagy and on a higher level in the aggressiveness of the paranoid against his projections.

*   *   *

To understand the pathology of the pseudo-metabolism (especially the paradoxical tendency of the paranoic character—that of being both hostile to, and fascinated by, his projections), one has to emphasize the part which repressed disgust plays in the process. Introjection is identical with the food too hastily passing the oral zone. If certain food were tasted, it would evoke disgust and vomiting; to avoid this, it is quickly swallowed and disgust repressed. The result is general oral anaesthesia and, exactly as in the anus, a place of confluence is created. (This oral anaesthesia has been known to medicine as a hysterical symptom for a long time.) Once the censor—the taste and feel of the food—is silenced, there is not much discrimination left. Physically (food) as well as mentally (knowledge) everything is indiscriminately swallowed. Hand in hand with this lack of differentiation goes lack of concentration—mind wandering and other neurasthenic symptoms.

If we look upon repressed memories as an accumulation of undigested morsels, we see two ways of getting rid of them—assimilation or ejection. To be assimilated, the material must be re-chewed, and to be re-chewed, it must be brought up. Disgust is the emotional component of vomiting. If this undigested material is not brought up (repeated) it passes in the opposite direction, is ejected.

Ejection is not felt as separation, once anal anaesthesia has *created* confluence: *ejection becomes projection*. The organism continues its attempts to attack and to destroy the newly projected material which attaches itself to suitable objects of the outer world. Whenever these objects become "figure," the organism answers with aggression—with hostility, vindictiveness and persecution.

This paranoic persecution is a very remarkable phenomenon. It is an attempt to establish the Ego-boundary which did not exist at the moment of projecting. But the attempt is bound to fail, as the paranoic wants to attack and treat as outside material that which is really a part of himself. He cannot leave the "project" alone because his aggression is fundamentally alimentary. However, as this aggression is not applied as dental aggression the destruction is unsuccessful and leads only to re-introjection. The digestive and re-digestive situation still remains unfinished—the enemy is incorporated, but not assimilated, and is later projected again and experienced as the persecutor.[1] And so on and on. Anaesthesia of both mouth and anus result in a lack of awareness: the feel of the food (tasting the flavour and realizing its structure), and the feel of defaecation have ceased to be Ego-functions.

As the unassimilated material is not merely ejected and discarded but projected into the world, it increasingly contains previously projected material, which again remains incompletely digested. A vicious circle is

[1] The persecuting of one's projections changes in the true paranoia by projection into the idea of "being persecuted."

started and established and the paranoid character, gradually losing contact with the real world, becomes isolated from his surroundings. He lives in an "imaginary" world. Of this he is usually unaware, for, owing to the failure of mouth and anus to regulate the communication, he remains in confluence with the projected world which he mistakes for the real one.[1]

The following example may illustrate the development of the projection/introjection cycle: A boy admires a great footballer. His enthusiasm is ridiculed; so he suppresses it and projects his admiration on to his sister by imagining her as the hero's admirer. Later he introjects the hero and wants to be admired himself. To gain this admiration he "shows off" by clowning and by bringing into play the rest of his childish repertoire. Instead of getting admiration he is scolded and laughed at by his sister. The boy becomes shy and has secret day-dreams of being an outstanding sportsman. He is now on the road to becoming a neurotic, but he is not yet a paranoic. This, however, may happen if at the same time he resents, begrudges the successes of his former hero who has, in his imagination, become his competitor. If he then projects the grudge and thereby experiences the belief that the world begrudges his (phantasied) merits, he creates a wall between himself and his environment; he becomes silent and secretive, or in turn irritable and explosive. The foundation of a paranoic character, perhaps even of a future paranoia, has been laid.

I have intentionally over-simplified the paranoic metabolism. There are many more places by way of which introjections and projections enter and leave the organism, but the frequency with which one finds alimentary disturbances connected with paranoid symptoms is so obvious that one feels justified in taking the pseudo-metabolism as a primary symptom.

In the sexual sphere we find, among other symptoms, jealousy and voyeurism. A young man was too shy to have intercourse with his fiancée but projected his ideas on to a friend and became jealous of him. It was easy to show him that he visualized exactly what he failed to express as his own wish. A re-identification cleared the situation quickly.

This was not so easy with another patient. Here the process had developed further. This man was married and after the projection he had introjected his imagined competitor. He behaved in sexual intercourse "as if" he were the other man. Not being in complete agreement with his biological needs, but being instead concentrated on a performance of imitating his friend, the contact with his wife was insufficient: the act remained unsatisfactory and fundamentally unfinished. This enhanced the vicious circle of projections and introjections.

In another case insufficient feel of the penis created confluence. In

[1] If at least the disgust were not repressed its powerful barrier would prevent the projections from being re-introjected and the vicious circle could be interrupted. Disgust is an Ego-boundary—though certainly not a pleasant one.

this instance the penis was projected on to the female and a lifelong search for a woman with a penis started. Here we have a real castration complex, or, rather, a hallucinatory castration corresponding to the absence of adequate sensations.

We have previously dealt with another aspect of the castration complex: namely, that projected aggression creates fear that some part of oneself (e.g. the penis) might be damaged. There is one complaint, however, which psycho-analysis also attributes to the castration complex but which cannot be explained by projected aggression. Many men believe that the loss of semen makes them weak or insane; others live in constant fear of losing their money and becoming poor. If an activity is projected, the Ego experiences itself as being passive; in the case of projected aggression, it experiences itself as being attacked. The loss of energy, however, is felt as a function of the own organism and not as the result of an attack.

The person who projects indeed loses energies, instead of applying and expressing them. The boy in the above example, instead of experiencing his enthusiasm (and with it an intense joy in living), goes to no end of trouble to induce people to become enthusiastic about his own person. By projecting his enthusiasm, he loses it; this is the first step in reducing the personality.

A paranoid patient complained that in spite of very reduced sexual activities he suffered continuous loss of energy. He had an ejaculatio praecox. He projected his semen, hardly felt the discharge and experienced nothing even approaching a genuine orgasm. Instead of a temporary confluence of his personality with his wife, instead of the oneness which characterizes sexual intercourse, there was always sexual over-excitement, but no personal contact.

It is true, in the moment of the orgasm there is a confluence, a oneness between the man and the woman so that world and individuality cease to exist. But this confluence is the climax of the rising curve of personal, skin, and finally, genital contact. The dissolving of the contact/isolation phenomenon into confluence is experienced as intense satisfaction.[1]

People with an ejaculatio praecox are characterized by an undeveloped contact zone and weak Ego-functions. They have as little genital contact possibilities as their food contact is impaired. As they demand the immediate effort-free flowing of the milk, so they let their semen flow, without passing and creating the contact boundary, e.g. without the experience of satisfaction. Ejaculatio praecox is characteristic of a person incapable of a concentrated effort. The *effort* is projected and is expected to be exerted by someone else instead. Such cases appear either infantile—dependant on a mother substitute—or as a boss having employees and servants to do the work for them. Both (sometimes the two attitudes are found in the same person) are lost if they have to stand on their own feet.

[1] A well-known example is the sweet reconciliation after a quarrel.

Whilst in the example of ejaculatio praecox the specific effort is projected and only an unspecific excitement (irritation) remains as expression of the personality, we find also the reverse: the frigid personality who projects his *excitement*, but exerts a most extraordinarily concentrated but fruitless (dummy) effort. In the sexual situation these frigid characters avoid the necessary discharge and expression of intense excitement, but they do anything to excite their partner. They themselves remain empty, dissatisfied, disappointed, or at best they enjoy a poor substitute, a sadistic pleasure in having achieved their aim of exciting the partner while remaining unmoved themselves. Their frigidity is a fortification which they try to penetrate, but their sexual as well as their oral gratification is nearly as insufficient as in the case of ejaculatio praecox. They tire themselves out to such an extent that after intercourse they are not happy but just exhausted. Both types, the ejaculatio praecox and retardata, never achieve a finished situation—a proper balance as required by the organism.

The neurotic who is in permanent need of affection and appreciation is in a similar situation. Even if he obtains the desired love, he does not get the expected satisfaction. His pseudo-metabolism is usually rather simple; he is greedy for appreciation, but once he gets it (praise or criticism) he either refuses it or introjects—swallows it indiscriminately. He does not derive the benefit of the gift, he does not assimilate but he projects the appreciation, and continues the vicious circle. Loss of energies by projection, that is by lack of assimilation, brings about the atrophy of the paranoic character's personality.

XII

MEGALOMANIA–OUTCAST COMPLEX

As the various introjection/projection cycles in the paranoid character occur simultaneously they have to be isolated for the purpose of analysis. One of these cycles deserves special interest. It is present in every paranoid and is, in a milder form, frequently encountered in everyday life. An appropriate name for this cycle would be megalomania-outcast complex, or, to use more familiar words, superiority-inferiority complex. Of this one half, the inferiority complex, has become the public favourite No. 1.

Whilst A. Adler, the father of the "inferiority feeling," maintains that its source is a childhood trauma based on some somatic inferiority, W. Reich sees in it a symptom of sexual impotence. Both of them, however, overlook the fact that the inferiority feelings appear in situations where arrogant, etc., people do not succeed in keeping up their superiority pose.

In this chapter I intend describing a peculiar relationship between inferiority-feeling and a special evaluation derived from the evaluation of the faeces. Those cases which suffer more severely from inferiority-feelings experience themselves as outcasts, as not being accepted by the rest of the world. At other times they show arrogance—megalomaniac phantasies (often concealed in day-dreams), in which they are kings, leaders, the best cricket players, etc., and thus entitled to look down upon their fellow men. In the proper paranoia these phantasies become convictions.

We have dealt with one root of such phantasies, the projections which change admiration into an obsessional wish to be admired. Even if these wishes cannot be satisfied, the imagined wish-fulfilment shows a narcissistic aim and gain, namely, to be "top dog," to be better, stronger or more beautiful than others, or at least than the competitor. Being on top the day-dreamer can despise and deprecate the world; he can look down on his fellow creatures. A boy dreamt his father—a very impressive personality—was a little dwarf.

The vicious circle continues: "The bigger you are, the harder you fall." Despising is projected on to others and the day-dreamer feels himself despised, rejected—an outcast. He soon introjects the despiser and treats others as outcasts.

Retroflection is a complication of this cycle worth mentioning: in certain cases megalomania and outcast periods coincide; the paranoic's character is then split in two; he retroflects his contempt and despises "himself" for characteristics or actions—he is despiser and despised at the same time. The greater the difficulty he has in accepting his real self, the greater is the urge to justify himself by demanding the impossible of himself and his environment. During the period of projection he imagines that demands are continuously being made upon him. One of my patients could not bear one empty hour in her life—she had to stuff her time-table as she stuffed her stomach; but as soon as she made her appointments they became a demand upon her, a duty worrying her to death.

Often one finds a difficulty in accepting compliments, affection, presents, etc. In their outcast periods the *inability* of such people *to accept* signs of love is projected, and they feel themselves not acceptable, unworthy, and nothing can convince them of the contrary. If this is retroflected, they cannot accept themselves as they really are. They do not like their own odour, cannot stand the sight of themselves, and so on.

The outcast-megalomania complex differs from the more comprehensive phenomenon of pseudo-metabolism by being charged with evaluations which are more or less identical with the common outlook in regard to the faeces. In the psycho-analytical interpretation faeces stand mostly as a symbol for something valuable, for a child (resemblance to the birth situation) or for money (expression by its opposite). These interpretations may be correct for the baby situation. At that time the faeces are often considered by mother and child as a present, but soon during the training in cleanliness, the child learns to despise them and to introject the disgust which the environment displays towards them.

For the adult of our time faeces have the unambiguous, symbolic meaning of something filthy, disgusting, intolerable—something that should not exist at all. "You are a piece of dirt—a piece of shit," is an extremely grave insult. This symbolic meaning of something filthy, disgusting, intolerable is the basis of the "outcast" or inferiority feeling. *In the period of introjection—of identification with the faeces—the paranoid character feels himself as dirt; in times of projection—of alienation—he thinks himself superior and looks upon the world as dirt.*

A reminder of the faecal origin of introjections is the bad ("dirty") taste paranoic characters often feel in their mouth, and they are only too willing to consider many things and actions as "bad taste." Bad smell from the mouth might really be present, as according to my observation every paranoid character shows disturbances of the alimentary functions. In the case of a stomach neurosis one can always look out for accompanying paranoid features.

When during the analysis a paranoid character begins to face the projections as being the despised parts of his own personality, he experiences disgust and a strong urge to vomit. This is a good sign. It indicates the re-establishment of censor and Ego-boundaries. The projections are not blindly introjected any more. When the taste is re-established, the disgust (aroused by the faecal origin of the projections) will come to the surface. Without the reappearance of disgust the analysis of any alimentary or paranoid neurosis is hopeless.

*　　　*　　　*

Psycho-analysis has already recognized that most neuroses have a psychotic nucleus. In obsessional neurosis the paranoic nucleus has up till now been regarded as being insensitive to treatment. This nucleus, however, can be dissolved if we pay sufficient attention to its alimentary component.

We find all kinds of intermediate forms between the paranoic and the obsessional character, but there are certain decisive differences. The paranoic functions are mostly unconscious and the Ego-functions are deeply disturbed; in the obsessional process the Ego-functions are *qualitatively* exaggerated (nearly solidified) though *quantitatively* diminished. Furthermore in obsessional neurosis numbness plays a far lesser part, the dominating factor being the actual conscious avoidance of contact. Undoing the "feel" of being dirty is mostly attempted by continual washing and avoiding contact with dirt. Thus the feeling of being dirty is projected to a far lesser degree than by the paranoid. In the oral attitude of the obsessional neurotic we find less complete introjection (than in the case of the paranoid), but more actual avoidance of biting and hurting. We find, too, a rigidity in the muscles (mainly of the jaws). It seems as though the obsessional neurotic attempts, in biting, to avoid the contact of the upper and lower front teeth, thus establishing an oral confluence. In contrast to the paranoid he often uses his molars, but he is incapable of making a "clean cut"; he is afraid of hurting directly, and accumulates a tremendous amount of aggression (resentment). Therefore hurting and killing play a predominant part in his obsessional thoughts.

The danger that these phantasies of killing may be transformed into action does not exist at the obsessional end, but increases towards the paranoic end of the scale of intermediate stages (cf. the excellent studies of paranoics in the film *Rage in Heaven*, and Cronin's novel, *Hatter's Castle*).

Both obsessional neurosis and paranoia are characterized by a strong leaning towards confluence. Of this the paranoic is not aware, but the obsessional character lives in permanent fear of losing his individuality and self-control. He prevents the danger of sliding into a paranoic confluence by establishing rigid boundaries. His defence—like the Maginot Line—suffers from lack of mobility. The holding on to such rigid boundaries gives him a false sense of security, similar to that which the

French people had experienced; they were insufficiently aware of the existing confluence via the Low Countries (as conventional boundaries do not exist for Hitler), and of the necessity of elastic defence boundaries. The Maginot Line became a dummy—an indestructible, but rigid, and therefore unadaptable, object.

Further investigations will throw more light on the relationship between obsessional neurosis and paranoia. One thing seems certain: both ill-nesses, unlike hysteria and neurasthenia, show very little inclination to remissions or spontaneous cure, but rather a tendency to go from bad to worse. This is not surprising if one remembers the vicious circle of the paranoic pseudo-metabolism and the increasing avoidance of the obses-sional character, both of which progressively disintegrate the personality. In their *advanced* stages both types have lost the ability to smile—to appreciate humour. They are always deadly serious.

The discovery of the paranoic nucleus in the obsessional neurosis entails one danger. One might be tempted to make a short cut and treat the core alone. This would be a bad mistake and would only increase the dummy activities and the suffering of the obsessional character. One has therefore to sharpen the blunted aggressiveness. For this purpose one can use a symptom which I always found present in this type and which has the advantage of being a contact phenomenon, although often dis-torted by projection. The obsessional character likes to hurt and embarrass people by making fools of them, an attitude which at times is cleverly hidden (for instance in making people feel stupid, impotent or confused) but in the early stage is expressed in a very primitive way. A quite intel-ligent young man asked his father, who had a university degree, silly questions like: "Daddy, you are so clever, I am sure you can tell me how much is three times four?" If, however, the obsessional characters project their fooling, they don't even derive pleasure from it, but live in permanent fear and under the illusion of being made a fool of.

Treatment of obsessional neurosis must prevent a further spreading of avoidances of aggressiveness and instigate its direct expression. Once this is achieved the treatment coincides with that of the paranoic character, in whom we have to stop the vicious progress of the projection/intro-jection circle and to reverse the development by re-establishing the healthy functioning of the Ego.

It does not matter where one first interrupts the vicious circle, provided one works holistically, keeps its structure in mind and attends thoroughly and completely to all three essential points:

(1) The thorough destruction and tasting of physical and mental food as preparation for its assimilation; special attention to be given to the unearthing of repressed disgust and the chewing up of intro-jections.

(2) The feel of the defaecation-function, and the development of the ability to stand embarrassment and shame. Learning to recognize and to assimilate projections.

(3) The undoing of retroflections.

We have, by now, dealt with all the points of the above prescription except for the "ability to stand embarrassment and shame" (in point 2), which requires some more attention.

XIII

EMOTIONAL RESISTANCES

Corresponding to body, mind and soul as three aspects of the human organism, there is a differentiation between somatic, intellectual and emotional resistances. Such classification of resistances is, of course, an artificial one. In every case all three aspects will be present, but in varying degree and composition. Mostly, however, one aspect will be predominant and will afford a more convenient approach than the others.

Previous chapters have dealt with the senso-motoric (somatic) resistances. Intellectual resistances are justifications, rationalizations, verbal demands of the conscience, and the censor, the importance of all of which has been demonstrated by Freud. But in spite of stressing in the basic psycho-analytical rule the importance of embarrassment, his theoretical interests lay more with the details of the intellectual than with those of the emotional resistances. Even to-day the emotional resistances—except hostility—have still not been approached by psycho-analysis with the degree of interest they deserve.

We may superficially classify emotions as complete and incomplete, ¶ and ‡, positive and negative.

Among *incomplete emotions* we find worrying and sadness as representative examples. Sadness, for instance, can last for hours and days if it does not gather enough momentum for discharge in an outburst of crying which will restore the organismic equilibrium.

Worrying is related to grumbling and nagging, and corresponds to the nibbling of food. The worrying person does not take full action, his aggression is partly repressed and returns as nagging and worrying. It suffers the usual fate of repressed aggression—it is either projected and thus reversed to passivity ("I am *worried* by this or that," "The idea of having to go to that dance *worries* me all the time"), or retroflected ("I am *worrying myself to death*").

A mother's annoyance with her daughter for being out late will, if unexpressed, turn into worrying or into phantasies of accidents. If she explodes, once the daughter is home, the situation will be finished; but if she does not dare to do so, or if she has to keep up a mask of friendliness and love, she will have to pay for this hypocrisy with insomnia or at least with nightmares.

A boy stops worrying his mother as soon as he has got his sweets, as soon as action has been taken. Among adult "worriers" there are always people who do not take action themselves but expect others to do it for them. The obsessional character's inability to take action subjects him to continuous worrying; the paranoid's permanent irritability is due to unrecognized and unfinished attempts at re-hashing his projections. A patient of mine, an obsessional-paranoid type with predominant obsessional features, worried for weeks about a tiny stain on his coat. He did not remove this speck, as he did not want to touch dirt. He felt like nagging his wife to remove the speck for him, but he suppressed that urge, too, and went on worrying himself and his wife subvocally. An imperfect situation indeed, while to finish the situation, to remove the speck, would have taken him only a few minutes.

The emotion corresponding to unfinishable situations is *resentment*, the understanding of which is not possible before the significance of the hanging-on attitude has been grasped. The hanger-on cannot let go, resign and turn to a more promising occupation or person. At the same time, he cannot successfully deal with the one on which he has his fixation: by intensifying the "hanging-on bite" he tries to get more and more out of an already exhausted relationship, thus not getting any more satisfaction, but exhausting himself and increasing his resentment. This in turn promotes an even stronger hanging-on attitude, and so on *ad infinitum* in an ever increasing vicious circle.

He does not want to realize the uselessness of his endeavours as, on the other hand, he cannot recognize his potentialities of turning to new fields of occupation (dental impotence). The "resenter" projects his dental potency into the fixation object and endows it in this way with indomitable power to which the "resenter" himself has to submit. Through the projection he has lost his own power of meeting it adequately. He can neither refuse nor accept what the fixation object does or says. Though he cannot accept, he will find himself harping on what has been said; "nagging," but not chewing and digesting it. Would the "resenter" assimilate the situation, he would have to let go, to give up the fixation object, to finish the situation by going through the emotional upheaval of the mourning labour in order to achieve the emotional zero point of resignation and freedom.

The need of the organism to finish emotional situations is best demonstrated by comparison with the processes of excretion. One can retain urine for quite a few hours, but one cannot urinate for longer than a minute. The holding-in of emotions leads to an emotional poisoning, just as retention of urine causes uraemia. People are poisoned with bitterness against the whole world if they fail to discharge their fury against a particular object.

Again I have to give warning against the idea that emotions are mysterious energies. They are always connected with somatic occurrences to such an extent indeed that often the unfinished emotion and unfinished action are hardly differentiated. Likewise, the term "katharsis" or "emotional discharge" is an expression to be used temporarily till we know more about the functions involved in this process.

*   *   *

¶ and ‡ emotions are either *auto*plastic or *allo*plastic. The alloplastic ‡ takes the form of object destruction (pleasure from crisp food, running amok, etc.); the autoplastic destruction is resignation, mourning labour, accompanied, if successful, by crying. Suppression of crying is harmful, as it prevents the organism from adjusting itself to loss or frustration. When someone hurts you, crying—not necessarily in public—is the curative process. The educational principle "a boy does not cry" promotes paranoic aggression. Even sergeants sometimes say, "Don't hit back; cry!"

The ancient Greeks were by no means ashamed of crying, yet Achilles was a pretty "tough guy." In modern literature, especially Russian and Chinese, one finds many references to the man who weeps. Parallel with their greater emotional independence goes the ability for independent action (Guerilla warfare).

A differentiation of ‡ has, it seems to me, taken place: alloplastic destruction appears to be more of a physical, autoplastic more of a chemical nature. Autoplastic destruction turned outwards appears as impotent rage, or verbal vindictiveness. It is more like spitting than biting and is of little value to the organism.

*   *   *

To understand "positive" and "negative" emotions we have to recall the dialectical law that quantity changes into quality.

Every emotion, every sensation changes from pleasantness into unpleasantness, when its tension or intensity increases beyond a certain limit. A hot bath may at first be pleasant, but the higher the temperature is raised, the more unpleasant it becomes, until a point is reached where we are burnt and life is endangered. To most people tea has an unpleasant bitter taste, but by adding one or two spoons of sugar, the taste becomes pleasant; by adding more and more sugar it becomes nauseatingly sweet, undrinkable for most people. Children like to be hugged, but they will not like it if you "squeeze the life" out of them. Under pathological conditions pride can change into shame, appetite into disgust, love into hatred. Children pass readily from laughing into crying. Enthusiasm and apathy, elation and depression are some more examples of emotional opposites.

The unpleasant character of negative emotions entails the wish to avoid the emotions themselves which, however, cannot change back into their pleasant opposites if we do not allow—by discharge—their change from over-tension to a bearable tension, and further on to the organismic zero-point.

Emotions can be controlled, but it is very doubtful whether they can be repressed and pushed into the Unconscious. Under favourable conditions they are discharged in minute quantities (annoyance, for instance, as sulking); in less favourable conditions they are either projected, or else their control requires a permanent watchfulness.

The inability to face unpleasant situations mobilizes the Quislings of the organism: embarrassment and shame.

Shyness is the pre-different stage of shame, the counter-pole of which is pride. In these emotions—as in self-consciousness—the personality tends to become the figure against the background of its environment. If the child's attempt to express its achievement receives interest, praise or encouragement, its development will be furthered; but if reasonable appreciation is withheld, praise and limelight become more important than the actual *doing* of things. The child, instead of concentrating on an *object* becomes *self*-centred. Starve a child of sensible praise, and it will acquire a permanent—often unsatiable—greed for it. Expression turns into exhibition, but his attempts to show off are mostly discouraged. The achievement itself is overlooked while his exhibitionism is condemned and suppressed. Suppression then turns exhibition into its negative, into inhibition; instead of "getting it out" the child "keeps it in" (*ex*-habere and *in*-habere).

If the child's genuine expressions are deprecated, pride turns into shame. Although in shame the inclination to become background, to disappear, is felt it is not successful; the isolation from the environment is done symbolically; the face and other parts are covered (with blushing, or by the hands), the child turns away, but in a kind of fascination remains rooted to the spot. The physiological aspect is especially interesting. Corresponding to the intense feeling of exposure the blood rushes into the actually exposed parts (cheeks, neck, etc.) instead of into those parts through the activity of which the feeling of shame arose (brain: numbness, inability to think, light-headedness; muscles: awkwardness, inability to move; genitals: deadness, frigidity in place of sensations and erection).

As our expressions are manifold we can feel ashamed of nearly everything. Imagine the embarrassment of a typical peasant girl, dressed in her Sunday best, who is superciliously scrutinized by a fashionable lady. With genuine *naïveté* and without the wish to be foreground-figure she would not even experience self-consciousness.

It makes all the difference to a child who has built a castle in the garden, whether the mother is interested and appreciative, or whether she shouts, "Look how dirty you are! What a mess you have made! You really ought to be ashamed of yourself!" This last oft-heard reproach is of particular consequence in education, in so far as it does not confine the blame to any particular activity or situation, but deprecates and stigmatizes the *whole* personality.

I have called shame and embarrassment Quislings of the organism. Instead of assisting in the healthy functioning of the organism, they obstruct and arrest it. Shame and embarrassment (and disgust) are such unpleasant emotions that we try to avoid experiencing them. They are the primary tools of repressions, the "means whereby" neurosis is produced.[1] As the Quislings identify themselves with the enemy and not with their own people, so shame, embarrassment, self-consciousness and fear restrict the individual's expressions. Expressions change into repressions.

The value of adhering to the basic analytical rule now becomes evident. Endurance of embarrassment brings the repressed material to the surface, leads to confidence and contact, and helps the patient to accept previously refused material via the amazingly relieving discovery that the facts behind the embarrassment may not be so incriminating after all, and may even be accepted with interest by the analyst. But if the patient suppresses his embarrassment instead of expressing it, he will develop a brazen, impudent attitude, and will "show off" (without genuine confidence). Brazenness produces loss of contact. Giving way to embarrassment (repression) leads to hypocrisy and feelings of guilt. Therefore the analyst must not fail to impress upon the patient that under no circumstances should he force himself to say anything at the cost of suppressing embarrassment, shame, fear or disgust. The danger of repressing either the resisting emotions or the actions which would produce the unpleasant emotion has always to be kept in mind, and likewise the demand that *for an analysis we need the complete situation; resisting emotions plus resisted actions.*

Taking agoraphobia as an example, we see that our patients either avoid crossing a street, and allow their fear to dictate their action or, rather, their non-action; or else, if their environment or conscience insists on self-control, they will suppress their fear. They can only do so by getting tense and numb, thus complicating their neurotic attitude still further.

A successful treatment of phobia requires the endurance of *both* the fear and the attempt at action. I have developed a curative method comparable with the "approach" in aviation. The flying pupil makes several approaches until the situation is favourable for landing. Similarly every attempt the patient makes at crossing the street will bring a piece of resistance to the surface, a piece which has to be analysed and changed into an adequate Ego-function, until the balance is in favour of the crossing. Let us assume the agoraphobia results from an unconscious

[1] They, in turn, have at their disposal the muscular system.

suicide wish. The decreased awareness resulting from the numbness can only increase the patient's chances of getting killed, if he forces the crossing. If we leave his fear principally intact and make him realize at first that he is not afraid of the street itself but of the vehicles, and if we allow him his exaggerated fear of the vehicles, we have already built a bridge to normality. Later we will probably find behind his fear of being killed the wish to kill somebody else, and we may find that wish to be so strong that his fear is apparently justified.

One of the most interesting neuroses is what one might call a "paradoxical neurosis," the outcome of a resistance against the resistance. Thus, with repressed shame we get an impudent (pudere = being ashamed) cheeky (cheeks not blushing) character. Repression of disgust does not lead to the restoration of appetite but to greediness and stuffing.

Certain perversions owe their paradoxical aspect to an endeavour to master emotional resistances. The masochist, although consciously seeking pain, is a person afraid of pain, and in spite of all his training he will never be able to stand more than a certain amount of it. The exhibitionist is permanently busy with suppressing his shame. The voyeur (peeping Tom) has an unconscious aversion to seeing what he feels an urge to look at.

One of Freud's definitions of neurosis is that it is a repressed perversion. Just the opposite is the case. A perversion is a neurosis because and as long as its content remains an unfinished situation. The voyeur does not accept what he sees and he has to repeat his peeping again and again. Once he is convinced that what he sees is correct his curiosity is gratified and thus nullified.

Common to all these cases is the fact that the suppression of the emotional resistances absorbs most of the subject's energy and interest in life. Their endeavours in the long run are as exhausting and useless as the attempt to keep a ball under water by permanently counteracting its tendency to rise. Shame, disgust, embarrassment and fear must be allowed to break surface, to become conscious.

The awareness of, and the ability to endure, unwanted emotions are the conditio sine qua non for a successful cure; these emotions will be discharged once they have become Ego-functions. This process, and not the process of remembering, forms the *via regia* to health.

The ability to stand unpleasant emotions is required not only from the patient but even more from the therapist. The psycho-analytical method still suffers from the personal difficulty of its founder: Freud's inability to stand his own feeling of embarrassment. In personal contact— as I have experienced myself and heard from others—he suppressed his embarrassment by impoliteness, even downright rudeness. In analysis— as he himself admitted—being under the patient's eye made him feel uncomfortable and embarrassed; he avoided the unpleasant tension by arranging the analytical situation in such a way as not to be exposed to the patient's stare.

That this arrangement could become a dogma strictly adhered to by psycho-analysis, is no wonder; who would not like to be spared embarrassment? Yet apart from the consequences for the analyst, it proves a definite handicap for the analytical treatment, as it makes it easy for the patient, who cannot see the analyst looking at him, to scotomize the fact that he is under observation himself, to avoid the awareness of embarrassment and shame, and with it a healthier Ego-development.

*　　　*　　　*

More important than all these emotional resistances is the unemotional resistance which we call "force of habit." Neither the libidinal cathexis nor the death-instinct, neither the conditioning nor the engram theory, reveals anything of its true conditions. The dummy attitude and the fear of the unknown explains a little of the reluctance to change, but the inertia and the true nature of habit remains the darkest riddle of all. For practical purposes we might be satisfied with this knowledge: habits are economical devices which relieve the tasks of the Ego-functions, as concentration is possible only on one item at a time. In the healthy organism habits are co-operative, aimed at the maintenance of Holism. Under certain conditions, for instance with advancing age or changing environment, habits become inadequate. Instead of assisting Holism, they disturb it, leading to disharmony and conflict. In such cases de-automatization is required—a contrasting of unwanted habits with the training in desirable attitudes.

F. M. Alexander's approach to this question is most interesting. He is in favour of "inhibition" before acting. (The experience of this inhibition is identical with Friedlaender's "Creative Zero-point.") This is not the place to deal with his neglect of the organismic drive, and the factors which determine the "forgetting to remember" (e.g. unconscious sabotage, fear of changes). What I want to point out is that his "inhibition" brings about the de-automatization of habits, the chance to feel the drive behind the habit.

Let us take as an example a person who shows the habit of jumping up and walking about during a conversation. By remembering to inhibit this habit he may be able to overcome it, but the essential drive of his getting up remains untouched. He might be habitually confused or panicky but he is not aware of more than a slight nervousness. His getting up and walking away from the people with whom he deals, his withdrawing into a shell, is his only way of sorting out his ideas. Another possibility is that in the course of conversation he might have become annoyed. Instead of expressing this he tries to run away. Again, he knows nothing of this drive except that he feels restless.

By inhibiting his impulse, however, by keeping it in suspense, he becomes aware of the "naked" impulse.[1] I maintain that very little good is achieved by neglecting the meaning of his impulse and reconditioning him, if at the same time we do not deal with his powerful internal drive. Encouraging his expression is, and always will remain, the best and simplest way to do this. If he were to ask his associates to wait for a moment because he is confused or if he gave vent to his annoyance, he would change an unpleasant habit into an adequate mastery of the situation.

Those, however, are details. They do not detract in the slightest from the value of Alexander's contention that one should come to a standstill before rushing into action or thinking. By mere reconditioning he minimizes (but without completely avoiding) the danger of enhancing a paranoic attitude. People who break habits and have not the faculty for "sublimation," let alone the power of expression, will invariably project the impulses which originally led to the formation of their habits and will be left not happier, but emptier.

Alexander is mostly interested in, and deals with, over-tense people; his "inhibition" coincides with the releasing of the hanging-on bite (Verbissenheit), and if he succeeds in replacing this infantile attitude by conscious planning he certainly achieves a fundamental change. He correctly stresses the difficulty which his pupils have in bringing about changes. Fortunately not the whole of mankind is fixed in the hanging-on attitude; fortunately there are a number of chewers left, people who are willing and capable of bringing about changes within themselves and without.

*　　*　　*

Alexander's method of "inhibiting the wrong attitude" and concentrating on the correct one is as insufficient and one-sided as is Freud's approach, which concentrates mainly on the analysis of undesirable attitudes. A combination, a synchronization of analysis and reconditioning, is required. Destruction and construction are mere aspects of the basically indivisible process of organismic reorganization.

[1] In this respect Freud's technique resembles that of Alexander, in that it carries out treatment under frustration—a very "active" technique strongly interfering with the patient's spontaneous impulses.

PART THREE

CONCENTRATION—THERAPY

I

THE TECHNIQUE

The practical application of scientific discoveries demands the development of a new technique. The fact that the French people neglected to keep pace with the new technique of modern warfare inaugurated by the invention of tanks and aeroplanes was one important factor contributing to their defeat.

The invention of a new drug like "M & B 693" *simplified* the treatment of many diseases. The discovery of the microbes, on the other hand, led to the development of a special antiseptic technique making operations more and more *complicated*.

The wide application of "M & B" became possible only through the classification of diseases according to their bacteriological origin. This re-classification brought a simplification which would have been impossible only a century ago. Who would have thought at that time that such heterogenous illnesses as gonorrhea and pneumonia could be related to each other (the germs of both belonging to the cocci-family)?

Theories are wholes, unifications of numerous facts. Sometimes a simple theory has to be corrected when new factors, not fitting into the original conception, are discovered. Sometimes so many additions have to be provided that we come to a confusing complexity instead of to a working hypothesis. When such a situation arises we have to pause and seek a re-orientation, look for new common factors that can simplify the scientific outlook.

We find an example in the "transference" theory. As long as the conception of "libido" occupied its all-important place in psycho-analysis, transference was identical with being fond of the analyst. When, in the patient's hostile attitude towards the analyst, aggression was admitted, one spoke of "negative transference." Again, after it was realized that no patient could be as frank as was hitherto expected, and the analysis of resistances received more attention, the "latent negative transference" came into existence. And a further development in psycho-analysis, if it adheres to the "transference," may make it necessary to add even more "handles" to the latent negative transference.

The new technique developed in this book is theoretically simple: its aim is to regain the "feel of ourselves," but the achievement of this aim is sometimes very difficult. If you are "wrongly" conditioned, if you have "wrong" habits, it will be much more difficult to rectify this state of affairs than to acquire new habits. I can recommend the books of F. M. Alexander to those who want to realize how strong an acquired habit, or, as we could call it, a fixed "gestalt," can become. The acquisition of a new technique, even without considering the undoing of wrong attitudes, is by no means easy. You have only to remember how long, for instance, it took to acquire the technique of writing, how painfully every letter had to be produced and reproduced over and over again, how long it was before you succeeded in combining these letters into words, until you were able to write fluently. Only when you look upon the acquisition of the new technique, which I want to demonstrate, with the full awareness of the difficulties looming ahead, shall I be able to assist you in acquiring the alphabet of "feeling" yourself.

I use the term "alphabet" intentionally, as it is not necessary to adhere to the sequence as set out in the following chapters. You might pick and choose according to your inclination and taste—at least in the beginning. Once, however, you start to feel some benefit and once you begin to gain confidence in this method, undertake the process of reconditioning as far as possible in the order presented.

Our technique is not an intellectual procedure, though we cannot completely disregard the intellect. It resembles the Yoga technique though its aim is completely different. In Yoga the *deadening* of the organism for the sake of developing other faculties plays a prominent part, whereas our aim is to waken the organism to a fuller life.

By assuming that we are "Time-Space events" within the changing fields of our existence, I am also in accordance with the present trend of science. Just as Einstein achieved a new scientific insight by taking the human self into account, so we can gain new psychological insight by realizing the relativity of human behaviour, of "right" and "wrong," of "good" and bad"; by replacing these terms by "familiar" and "strange"; and, finally, by operating with the Ego-functions "identification" and "alienation." Every bit of Ego-consciousness, far from making us more selfish (as popular conception assumes), will make us more understanding and more objective.

II

CONCENTRATION AND NEURASTHENIA

Before we begin with our technical ABC we have to introduce one more theoretical aspect. It has long been realized that the essential element in every progress, in every success, is concentration. You may have all the talents, all the facilities in the world, but without concentration these are valueless. (Schiller: Genius is concentration, *Genie ist Fleiss*.)

It has further been realized that concentration has something to do with interest and attention, the three conceptions often being used as synonyms. Do these expressions reveal anything? *Interest* means to be in a situation; *concentration* means to get right into the centre (nucleus, essence) of a situation; and *attention* means that a tension is directed towards an object. There are no magic roots in these expressions. They are simple descriptions of a state, an action and a direction. Common to all three terms is the fact that they are different expressions of the figure-background phenomenon. The healthy figure should be strong and relatively stationary, neither jumpy, as in the case of association mentality (neurasthenia, many psychoses, scatterbrains), nor rigid (obsessions, perversions, fixed ideas). These deviations from the healthy zero-point have lately been successfully studied by Experimental Psychology. It has been found that a normal perseveration index exists, and that too high or too low perseveration figures are indicative of mental disturbances.

For nearly everybody concentration has still a magic reference, best expressed by Freud's idea of libidinal cathexis. Concentration is not a movable substance, but a function. It is a mere Ego-function in the case of negative artificial concentration. It is a function of the Unconscious in fixations or in "Imago" concentration. The harmonious function of both Ego and Unconscious is the basis for the "positive," biologically correct concentration.

While the unconscious concentration, the domain of classical psychoanalysis, need not be dealt with in this chapter, we have to draw the critical attention to the "popular," the one-sided outlook on concentration. Most people mean by concentration a deliberate effort. Actually this is the "negative," inadvisable type of concentration.

The perfect concentration is an harmonious process of conscious and unconscious co-operation. Concentration in the popular sense is a pure

Ego-function, not supported by spontaneous interest. It is identification with duty, conscience or ideals, and is characterized by intense muscular contractions, by irritability, and by such an amount of strain that it leads to fatigue and promotes neurasthenia or even nervous breakdowns. It is artificial and negative, as it lacks natural (organismic) support. An artificial wall is built up to keep out everything which might attract interest, which tends to become figure instead of remaining background.

We find two kinds of unsound concentration: the one just described, and the conscious obsessional concentration. In the obsessional concentration the compelling[1] is projected, and the person in question lives as if he were forced, compelled to do things against which he protests, and which he would like to reject as strange and senseless. In the negative concentration, however, the compelling is not projected but retroflected, and he compels himself to attend to matters in which he is not sufficiently interested. More than on his task he is concentrated on the defence against any disturbance (noises, etc.). He contracts his muscles, knits his eyebrows, tightens his mouth, clamps his jaws and holds his breath in order to keep down his temper (unconsciously directed against the very work he is doing)—a temper which is ready to explode at any moment against any interference. The more unconscious attraction he feels for the disturber, the more ready is he to "bite his ruddy neck off," which indicates the appetite, the dental nature of his aggression.

If you have understood the hanging-on and dummy attitudes you will recognize them in those two kinds of concentration. In the negative concentration you hang on to your work with clenched jaws; in the obsessional concentration you persist in a dummy attitude without benefit or change. On the ice-rink I met a man who practised the same figures for two years. He was always eager to take advice, but he never put the advice into practice, he never changed. He could not bear any deviation from that which felt right and familiar to him. The fear of the unknown made him stick to his petrified pattern.

Correct concentration is best described by the word fascination; here the object occupies the foreground without any effort, the rest of the world disappears, time and surroundings cease to exist; no internal conflict or protest against the concentration arises. Such concentration is easily found in children, and often in adults when engaged in some interesting work or hobby. As every part of the personality is temporarily co-ordinated and subordinated to one purpose only, it is not difficult to realize that such an attitude is the basis of every development. If, to quote Freud, compulsion changes into volition, the most important stepping stone to a healthy and successful life is laid.

*　　　*　　　*

[1] The obsessional character is an inhibited slave driver.

We have put down avoidance as the main characteristic of neurosis, and it is obvious that its correct opposite is concentration. But, of course, it is the concentration on the object which according to the structure of the situation demands to become figure. In plain words: we have to face facts. Psycho-therapy means: assisting the patient in facing those facts which he hides from himself.

Psycho-analysis describes the process in this way: free associations will automatically lead to unconscious problems on account of their magnetic attraction; or, the pressure of the instincts is strong enough to reach the surface, though often distortedly, and on by-paths.

Gestalt-psychology would probably formulate: the hidden gestalt is so strong that it must show in the foreground, mostly in the shape of a symptom or other expression in disguise.

We must not lose the thread leading from the symptom to the hidden *gestalt*. The method of free associations is unreliable and lends itself easily to all kinds of avoidances. By concentration on the symptom we remain in the field (though on the periphery) of the repressed gestalt. By persevering with such concentration we work towards the centre of the field or "complex"; during this process we encounter and reorganize the specific avoidances, e.g. resistances.

The avoidance of the biologically required gestalt goes always hand in hand with concentration on objects of heterogenous spheres (detraction of mind, dummy). Through avoiding the natural figure-background formation the negative, forced concentration leads to neurosis or, in an acute situation, to neurasthenia, of which the lack of power of concentration has always been recognized as a prominent symptom. Here are two examples of how—through the neglect of the principle of organismic self-regulation—one-sided concentration must turn into its opposite, into mental instability.

An extremely conscientious officer was much concerned with the fact that he had repeated breakdowns, which gained him the reputation of shrinking from his duties. He struck me as a sincere person, and I believed him when he told me that he simply could not go on with his work after three or four months. What happened was this: during each day he had to deal with quite a number of problems, many of which could not be brought to a conclusion the same day. They represented a number of unfinished situations. Before going to bed he read some fantastic story and slept badly, as the unfinished situations disturbed his sleep and he started next morning with increased fatigue. This reduced his capacity, and more tasks remained unfinished. Increased night worries, increased fatigue and further diminishing of working power started and continued the vicious circle, until his lack of ability to concentrate forced him to stop altogether. When I met him, he was in a state of exhaustion; his work, piled up to an unconquerable mountain, left him with a feeling of utter impotence; he felt like howling from despair. The solution of his difficulty was found in the decrease of the number of problems he had to tackle, to finish as many as possible during the day, and to dispose of all unfinished problems before going to bed. After having learned that the crux of his trouble was simply due to unfinished situations, he learned to confine his work problems to office hours, not to start a fresh task before he had finished the task at hand, and to play in his leisure hours. By drawing this balance he not only worked better, but regained his enjoyment of life.

The second case is still simpler. A boy, working for his matric, complained that he could not concentrate on his studies. All kinds of day-dreams interfered and distracted his attention. He adopted my advice to separate his day-dreams from his studies. As soon as a day-dream appeared he allowed himself ten minutes or so for day-dreaming and then returned to his work. In the beginning even this was not easy. He was so used to the internal conflict that no sooner had he started day-dreaming, than sentences and pictures of his text-books intruded. He then followed up this material till a day-dream reappeared. By not resisting either call he learned to sort out the two spheres and was soon in the position to cope with his studies without effort.

Positive concentration complies with the laws of holism in every respect. Not only are all functions put to one purpose—in negative concentration only a part is put to its purpose—but we are also capable of concentrating fully only on those objects which mean the completion of an incomplete whole.

*   *   *

In addition to lack of concentration there are two other important symptoms of neurasthenia to be mentioned. One is headaches, backaches and the whole scale of fatigue symptoms all based on mal-co-ordination of the motoric system. These will be dealt with in the chapter on Body Concentration. The other symptom is fed-up-ness with life, lack of interest, and increasing dissatisfaction with everybody. This symptom is the expression of disgust with life. The disgust, I admit, is often not felt as such, but appears frequently as neurasthenic dyspepsia and lack of appetite.

By concentrating on our meals we achieve several aims at once. We learn the art of concentrating; we cure nervous dyspepsia; we develop a taste of our own; we develop intelligence and individuality. Although the chances are small that a more severe neurosis could be cured by following the advice given in this book (the resistances against persevering with the exercises probably being too great), anybody having a tendency towards neurasthenia can convince himself of the effectiveness of the method.

But how do we get out of the dilemma if we have no power of concentration and if at the same time we must not force ourselves to concentrate? The solution lies in the trial-and-error method. Without forcing himself, the baby tries again and again to master the difficult mechanism of walking until it has achieved the proper co-ordination of his motoric system. In adult life we find a good example in the flying pupil. A great part of his training to fly is taken up by approaches. Sometimes he overshoots the landing ground and sometimes he glides in too early. To force himself to do a landing would in either case be foolish if not dangerous. Trial-and-error is the approach which I advise the reader to follow, as it is the only one that can lead to success. Do not mind the failures, as every approach will bring to the surface a piece of resistance which can be worked through and will give rise to a better understanding and assimilation. The perseverance in the approaches, in spite of many failures, will, in itself, be a great contribution to the development of a healthy and comprehensive personality. If in addition you can learn to analyse, to understand the sense of your "wrong" attitudes instead of condemning them, you are bound to win in the end.

III

CONCENTRATING ON EATING

The exercises in this chapter are the quintessence of this book. Give this chapter preference to every other exercise, especially if you feel like sneering at me for harping too much on the subject of correct eating. I do so because it is of vital importance in achieving an intelligent harmonious personality. It is the "means whereby" of the removal of the bottle-neck of mental inhibitions. If you find yourself belittling the importance of the chapters on the hunger instinct and especially if you feel like skipping them, you can take this as an indication that you have dental inhibitions and deep-seated neurotic attitudes.

Let me once more explain in brief the fundamental difference between the pre-dental and dental stages. The suckling is actively concentrated on one action only—the hanging-on bite. This hanging-on bite means the creation of a vacuum which is similar to that of a rubber cap when pressed against a window. There is no need to hold it there as long as the suction action continues. After the preliminary hanging-on bite the conscious activity of the baby ceases. The suckling, to keep up the vacuum continues with unconscious, subcortical movements. During this time the baby becomes more and more drowsy until, finally, it falls asleep. We interpret the "smile" of the just-fed baby as an expression of happiness, but it is merely complete relaxation, the collapse of the hanging-on bite motoric.

From this picture we must draw two conclusions. Firstly, the suckling's feeding rhythm with its decreasing tension shows a curve completely different from the curve of sexual gratification with its increasing tension and sharp decline—a fact which provides one more proof against the libido-theory.

The second conclusion, which interests us more in this connection, is the fact that the suckling needs only a short spell of concentration while the adult, in his need for coping with solid food, has to concentrate during the entire eating process. The proper assimilation of solid food requires the continuous and conscious concentration on the destruction, the taste and the "feel" of the permanently changing ingested material.

It is no use attempting to correct one's eating until this fundamental difference is completely understood. This should not be difficult as at some time you must have seen a greedy, impatient eater behaving like a suckling displaying real interest in the food only *before* the meal; as soon as he sits down at the table, his behaviour shows the characteristics of the hanging-on bite; he concentrates only on the first taste and bites; then, like the suckling, he falls into a state of trance, at least as far as the eating process is concerned, his interest being invested in thinking, day-dreaming, talking or reading. The solid food goes down his throat "as if" it were a drink, and his inability to bring about a change in the structure and taste of his food (just as in drinking no change in structure or taste takes place) becomes reflected in his basic attitude towards life. He is afraid, or incapable of bringing about changes in himself or his environment, even when desirable. He cannot say "No" as he is afraid benevolence might change into antagonism. He sticks to worn out customs in preference to replacing them with better institutions, and he is afraid of the risk which a change-over, even in a proposition with better prospects, might involve.

He will never gain independence, the confluence with his environment[1] being as desirable to him as the confluence with its mother is to the drinking suckling. The feeling of individuality which demands the awareness of separating boundaries has not been achieved. Or else, an artificial wall, represented by the tightening of the mouth, the refusal to have any contact with the world at all, has been built, leading to loneliness, lack of interest and contact, misanthropy and boredom. Both phenomena, the complete confluence (lack of individuality) and complete resistance against the confluence (pretence of an individuality) can be found as extremes in the symptoms of automatism and negativism in dementia praecox.[2] In the first phase, the patient follows automatically every command given, and in the latter does just the opposite to what he has been told. In less extreme cases we find over-obedience and defiance.

What methods have we at our disposal to sail through the Scylla of confluence and the Charybdis of seclusion? How can we achieve that change which makes such substance of the outside world as we require our own, without becoming Nazi-like destructionists? How do we set out to achieve the transition from the pre-dental to the dental stage?

The answer seems simple: we have to use our teeth. Fletcher has given the prescription to chew every morsel thirty or forty times. But Fletcher's method is obsessional, and a person without obsessional inclinations cannot stand such monotonous counting and will soon drop

[1] The so-called herd or mass instinct is a phenomenon of confluence.
[2] Dementia praecox is essentially a disturbance of the Ego-boundary function and of the holistic structure of the personality. Sometimes it is possible to re-establish the holistic function through shock-treatment, which makes the disintegrated parts of the patient rally and join in the services of the instinct of self-preservation—for the purpose of "survival."

it, whilst an obsessional character will welcome it, without deriving much benefit from it. It would provide him with another dummy, another excuse to concentrate on a meaningless action. His interest would be invested in a continuation of his queer behaviour and not in the biological function required to bring about the liquifaction and other changes of solid food. Could you imagine a ruminating cow counting every one of her jaw movements and deciding that thirty chews is the exact number required to finish each mouthful?

No. We have to set about it in a different way, and the beginning will be most difficult. We have to keep our mind on the eating; *we have to be fully aware of the fact that we are eating*. This sounds simple, perhaps even silly. You think, of course, that you are aware of your eating. But are you? Or do you read, talk, day-dream or worry while eating? How often is your mind full of anxiety that you might miss the bus, or be late for work or for a theatre appointment? How often do you, while eating, speculate on the outcome of affairs that you have to attend to? How often do you swallow the newspaper with your meals?

Once you have decided to become aware of your eating, you will begin to make astounding discoveries. At first it will be extremely difficult to keep your mind fully on the process of eating, even for a short time. Within a few seconds you will probably find that your mind has wandered away, and you are anywhere but at the table, consuming food. Do not force yourself to concentrate, but call yourself back each time you notice that you are slipping away from the concentration, and slowly you will learn to concentrate for ten or twenty seconds and then up to a minute or even longer.

Whilst you are prolonging the duration of your ability to concentrate, start to develop another attitude—that of being satisfied with pure observation without premature interference. After what you have already learned I feel sure you will be impatient to improve your biting and chewing, but such a premature interference will disturb and spoil a sound development. It will serve no other purpose than to hide from yourself the basic reluctance to chew. Not until you have fully felt the gulping down of undestroyed bits and pieces, not before you realize that you are drinking solid food instead of eating it, should you set out to remedy it, otherwise it would mean senseless blind obedience, and not insight into one of the most important biological processes.

Without fully realizing the familiar, but "wrong," attitude—in this case greed and impatience—you cannot prevent it from returning as soon as your mind slips away. You have to make the impatience conscious, then change impatience into annoyance, after that into dental aggression, and finally to consolidate it as interest in the working through of every task—in a patient but energetic chewing up of your physical and mental food.

Should you, after a while, still experience difficulty in concentration, apply the description technique. Analyse (I do not mean psycho-analyse) your experiences. Describe all the details of what you feel and taste: hot and cold, bitter and sweet, spicy and insipid, soft and hard. But not nice and nasty, appetizing and revolting, tasty and unpalatable. In other words, develop your *appreciation of facts in contrast to their evaluation*.

Last, but not least, concentrate on the structure of the food, and *censor every undestroyed morsel*, which seeks to escape the grinding mill of your molars. Do not rest till you have reconditioned yourself to the perfect "censor" who should feel in his throat every morsel which is not liquified and who should automatically push it back into his mouth for complete destruction. By this time you should have at your disposal the means to master the art of eating. The knowledge of the details and the full awareness of the eating process will work together to bring about the required change in your food. Good taste will develop, and you will stop introjecting your physical and, likewise, your mental food.

A few remarks might serve to drive home still more the advantages gained from proper eating. The stomach and intestines are a mere skin, and the food (as for example, a piece of solid meat on your plate) has to penetrate this internal skin. This can never take place without complete liquifaction. The juices provided by the glands of your mouth, stomach, etc., will not flow without sufficient movements of your jaw, and they cannot mix with the food if the food is not properly minced.

Above all, avoid the danger of introjection, avoid the swallowing of mental and physical morsels which are bound to remain foreign bodies in your system. To understand and assimilate the world you have to make full use of your teeth. Learn to cut right through until the front teeth meet. If you are in the habit of tearing and nibbling, get out of it. If you tear your food apart instead of biting through it, you remain in a state of confluence instead of contact; the mental gap—the door between the outside and inside world—remains open. This concerns especially those people who cannot make a clean cut, who cannot bite off their share of it. They cannot "parti"cipate ("*teil*" *nehmen*), take their part.

If you are afraid to hurt people, to attack them, to say "No" when the situation demands it, you should attend to the following exercise: imagine yourself biting a piece of flesh out of someone's body. Can you imagine biting it clean off or do your teeth only make an impression, as if you were biting on rubber? If, in your imagination, you are able to bite right through, can you experience the proper "feel" of the flesh on your teeth? You might condemn such an exercise as vicious and cruel, but this cruelty is just as much part and parcel of your organism as it is of the animal's in its struggle for life. Your biological aggressiveness has to find outlets somewhere and somehow; even behind the mask of the mildest person, a person with a sweet, forgiving character, there lurks a latent aggressive nature which must come out in one way or another, as projection or as moralizing or as killing with kindness.

What, if you come to think of it, has mankind gained by repressing the individual biological aggressiveness? Look at the ingenious means of destruction and the amount of suffering in the present war. Is that not proof enough of the fact that just through the vicious circle of pseudo-metabolism aggressiveness has developed to the present paranoic stage of wholesale destruction?

The more we allow ourselves to expend cruelty and lust for destruction in the biologically correct place—that is, the teeth—the less danger will there be of aggression finding its outlet as a character feature. Those pathological fears we might harbour, too, will greatly diminish; for, the more the aggression is invested in biting and chewing, the less aggression will be left for projection. The result will inevitably be a decrease in the number of fears (phobias).

A person who has aggressiveness at his disposal must not be confused with the man who is permanently irritable, who grumbles and grouses day in and day out, and who at the same time is incapable of tackling and finishing his problems. Permanent irritability is one more example of an incomplete situation, of half-hearted and wrongly applied aggression. Such a man is a "nagger" and not a "biter." Related to the latter is the "confluence" type. With these types one always finds the gap between the front teeth. Such a person either walks about with his mouth half open or, as over-compensation, tightly clenched. He is specially afraid of being an individual or, alternatively, he is concentrated on proving to himself and the world that he is an individual, that he has an opinion of his own, even if it is only one which is permanently in opposition to everything. I knew a man who, out of opposition to his bourgeois family, became a Communist. He then joined a party which, though Communist in principle, was in opposition to the accepted Communist doctrines. He soon found faults with this party too, and became a fascist. "Mary, Mary, quite contrary."

For those who find fault with their individuality, there is an exercise improving the contact zone (Federn's Ego-boundary). Let the teeth of the upper and lower jaw just lightly touch each other. Neither contract the jaw muscles hard, nor relax so much that the lower jaw drops; there should be neither hyper- nor hypo-tonus in the muscles concerned. In the beginning you might feel a slight, or even a marked, trembling (chattering of the teeth as in cold weather or in fear). In that case change the unconscious tremor to conscious small, quick biting movements, and then try again.

Once you have started to recondition your mode of eating, there is a little exercise which is of special value in curing impatience and muddled thinking. Train yourself to interrupt the continuous flow of food. Many people push new food into the mouth *before* they have cleared and liquified the previous mouthful. This attitude is another symptom of treating solid food as a liquid. If you exaggerate the healthy attitude, if you learn to keep your mouth empty between the bites for a few seconds, you will soon find yourself capable of finishing all the big and small items of your life; your mental stomach—your brain—will be in much better order. Hence, much of your messy and incoherent thinking will disappear and you will find no difficulty in clarifying your ideas and concepts. This applies not only to your thinking, but to your general activities as well. If you belong to those who start on a new job before finishing the one at hand, if you frequently find yourself landing in a mess, then the above exercise is exactly what you need.

If you have succeeded in putting the foregoing exercises into practice you will have achieved a great deal. You will have found that you have often come across resistances, such as excuses, listlessness, lack of time, and so on, but with some determination and perseverance, these exercises lie within the orbit of everyone's possibilities. A much greater resistance is bound to be encountered when we approach the exercises dealing with disgust. These, however, should not be attempted before the previous exercises have become more or less automatic.

*   *   *

The ambivalence of our attitude towards food in particular, and the world in general, is so deeply rooted that most of us still have the childish attitudes of thinking that everything is either "poofy" or "m-m-m." I am amazed to find how many people use, as their immediate reaction towards every piece of music they hear, or every cinema picture they see, every person they meet, the expressions "awful" or "marvellous." In most cases their effort goes in the direction of refining their critical abilities instead of deepening their experiences. Some people admit not being able to sit through a screen performance without keeping up a running commentary, without continuously saying to themselves "Oh, that's fine" or "How stupid," etc., their whole interest being concentrated on evaluating and not on being moved. With this type of individual, I invariably find that 90 per cent of their thinking consists of prejudices. They can be characterized as having a selectivity paranoia. In order to overcome such an attitude it is necessary to cure their oral frigidity by bringing their repressed disgust to the surface and disposing of it. They eat with their judgment and not with their palate.

In the tasting exercises you will have noticed that it is much easier to concentrate on foods which you like than on those which you dislike or which are foreign to you. You will also have experienced, to a certain extent, that the limit of your taste has widened and, once you have overcome the effort of concentration, that you enjoy your food more than you did before. (If the exercises are correctly carried out the whole process should now be effortless.) Very few people are aware of their oral frigidity. Not only has the real gourmet, lingering over and enjoying every course of his dinner, become a rarity, but our general attitude towards the consumption of food has become more and more barbarous. The numbness of the palate is over-compensated by all kinds of stimulating spices, and by all kinds of perverted behaviour. One patient of mine could not enjoy soup unless it was burning hot, because otherwise the taste seemed insipid to her.

The sound sense of the animal which will not touch food which is too hot or too cold has been completely lost by many people. This attitude is displayed not only towards food but towards other spheres of pleasure as well, leading to degeneration all along the line. In the dance hall the music must be hot, the partner exciting, when gambling the stakes must be high, and in the sartorial world everything not in the latest style is completely worthless. In these circles, where the language used consists of strings of superlatives, the state of intelligence is correspondingly low. We find all kinds of stimulants in different classes of society, and these stimulants, to retain their effect, have to be administered in increasing doses. There is the habit of drinking, for example, common to all classes. The drunkard never uses his teeth and palate properly. If he did—if he were a real "biteling"—he would not need to take to the bottle. To cure a drunkard it is necessary to undo the retroflection of self-destruction and bring the pleasure of destruction back to the teeth.

In severe cases of oral frigidity the food exists only as long as it is on the plate. Once it is in the mouth it is not felt, much less tasted. This is, of course, an extreme case of introjection. Such behaviour goes hand-in-hand with heavy drinking, intense use of spices, and stuffing oneself without ever reaching real satisfaction; periods of irresistible greed alternate with rigid food discipline. The picture is completed on the mental side by a perpetual greed for affection, power, success and thrills, which, however, never yield any genuine pleasure or satisfaction.

Although it is easy to make people understand the importance of analysing anxiety, fear or embarrassment, it is an arduous task to drive home the significance of realizing and analysing the powerful emotion (or sensation) of *disgust*. To obtain a clear picture we have to distinguish not less than four layers involved in its development. The basic layer is the healthy, natural, undistorted appetite with all its tensions and gratifications which might be interfered with in two ways: an original and intense appetite may be condemned for being directed towards "poofy" things, or the child is supposed to ingest things against which its organism protests violently. This protest, the disgust, provides the second layer. Once the disgust has developed, objections against it are raised by many parents. Disgust and vomiting are regarded as naughtiness and the child who dares to bring up its spinach or castor oil is threatened with punishment. Thus the third layer, the oral frigidity, is established in order to avoid disgust, vomiting and the threatened punishment. Afterwards, to get some kind of pseudo taste from the food, the numbness is covered by a fourth layer, the layer of artificial stimulation.

The crux of the analysis of disgust is the same as that of embarrassment. Generally, either disgust dominates the situation, in which case you refuse to approach the object of disgust, or else the determination to incorporate something which would normally evoke disgust gives the ruling: you repress the disgust, and numb your taste and smell. The task at hand is to stand disgust, not to repress it and, at the same time, not to shrink from the object of disgust, not to avoid contact with persons, foods, smells or other things which are revolting to you. To achieve the analysis of oral frigidity, you must learn to become fully aware of the experience of disgust, even if it means vomiting or going through great unpleasantness. But do not attempt the unearthing and cure of disgust, before you can fully concentrate on your ordinary meals. Even if the disgust is only half discharged, if you feel it as a sudden spell of coughing or as a bilious sensation, it will help tremendously in overcoming an indifference towards food and the world in general. Whatever your inclinations towards your environment may be, you will always find them identical with the degree of your appetite or disgust. Those who can be disgusted with people and their actions are certainly more alive than those who accept anything with a dull and bored mental palate.

As the physical and mental intake obey the same laws, your attitude towards mental food will change with your progress of the preceding exercises. Psychological examinations of patients with stomach diseases as well as my general psycho-analytical observations have proved this over and over again. Approach mental food from the point of view of assimilation. Distinguish between sloppy, sweetish literature and solid material that can contribute to the growth of your personality. But do not overlook the danger that "highbrow" literature will be nothing but an unnecessary burden if it is merely introjected—if it remains a foreign body in your system. One sentence properly chewed and assimilated is of greater value than a whole book which is merely introjected. If you want to improve your mentality, settle down to the study of semantics, the best antidote against the frigidity of the mental palate. Learn to assimilate the nucleus of words—the sense, the meaning of your language.

IV

VISUALIZATION

If a pair of scales is off balance, you have, in order to restore the balance, to add weight to the lighter scale. This is what I try to do with this book. Often I might appear to be just as one-sided as the theories which I criticize. I have, however, endeavoured to keep the complete organismic structure in mind and to throw my weight into the neglected scale. I consider the analysis of the hunger instinct as a step-child of psycho-analysis without underestimating the importance of the analysis of the sex instinct. I stress the importance of the active behaviour of our sense-mind as counterweight to the mechanistic passive concept. In reality there is never such a thing as an individual or an environment. They both form an inseparable unit in which, for instance, stimulus and readiness or ability to be stimulated cannot be separated. The rays of light do exist—but there must be an organismic situation (interest) for which they can exist.

Although everybody will be willing to realize that our organism is very active in the consumption and assimilation of our food, the corresponding activity of our senses is less readily recognized. We are so used to thinking in terms of the reflex arc theory, we take so much for granted that some outside stimulus makes our organism react in a kind of mechanical way that it requires an effort to realize that perception is an activity, and not a mere passive attitude. Neither does food flow into our system of its free will, nor do the acoustic waves of a symphony concert.

In the latter case we have to go through a good deal of activity in order to bring our organism into the desired acoustic field. We have to get tickets, take ourselves to the concert hall, and during the performance itself our activity goes on unceasingly. Do not imagine that the hundreds of people in the audience conceive the same music; they do not even perceive the same sounds. A passage which means chaos to one listener is a clear "gestalt" to another. The bassoon which one attentive listener discovers beside the double bass, does not even strike the ears of the untrained person. How much of the acoustic waves you will take in, depends on many factors: on your musical approach, on your emotional identification, training, and, most of all, on your power of concentration.

If you are tired, if the listening involves too much strain or if for other reasons the orchestra cannot hold your interest, your mind slips away, loses contact with the performance. If you find yourself in that state, if you notice that the music has completely ceased to be figure and that you have not the slightest idea what has been played, then you will become convinced of two things: of the importance of the figure-background phenomenon and its connection with concentration, and of the amount of activity involved in the use of your senses.

We are assisted in our delusions about the passivity of the senses by our knowledge of the photographic camera, and we are only too ready to assume that our organism simply takes pictures and that the rays of light impress themselves on the plate while the pictures are storing themselves away somewhere in the brain. We forget that every photographer has to invest a great deal of activity before he manages to take a single picture. We forget what an amount of labour is condensed into a single photographic plate and that our organism has to be a continuous working chemical plant and a continual photographer. We also do not sufficiently realize that the photographer's work is determined by his interest (hobby, livelihood or learning).

The senses in man have developed from mere signallers to organs of the "mental stomach" and of a second and third human world. On the second plane (the world of imagination) plans and simplifications, intake and assimilation play the decisive part. We have already dealt with memories as undigested morsels and with hallucinations and the mistaking of the imaginary field for the real one. The third plane is the world of evaluations (M. Scheler). In this chapter we shall be concerned with the way in which to organize the use of our senses for the greatest benefit of the whole organism.

The best way to approach this problem is through our ability of visualization. Most of our mentality consists of pictures and words. The unconscious has a greater affinity to pictures, the conscious mind to words. In order to achieve a good harmony between Ego and Unconscious we should have the greatest possible control over our visualization, a control which is clearly lacking in day-dreams. Day-dreams are often so much beyond the influence of conscious control that many people only know of the fact that they are day-dreaming without having any trace left except the feeling that they were in a trance, that they were somewhere else. On the other hand, any conscious effort to visualize things is an impossibility for many people. Every conscious effort to get a picture in their mind is either frustrated (the mind is a blank) or we encounter a jumble of meaningless pictures, for instance, before falling asleep.

The greatest difficulty is, of course, encountered by people who apparently have no visualization at all. This is a symptom of a severe neurotic disturbance and is outside the scope of self-treatment. Here we can only hint at the unconscious habit of excluding pictures with the help of intense contractions of different eye muscles. With the relaxation of these contractions, pictures will re-appear. (This will be dealt with more extensively in the chapter on Body Concentration.) Behind this visualization deficiency one often finds a fear of looking at things which one wants to avoid or which might evoke emotions or memories of any kind. Sometimes a refusal to gratify one's "peeping" propensities may have spread, so that all looking becomes included in this taboo. People who look at things without seeing them, will find the same deficiency when turning their gaze inwards, when calling up mental pictures, while those who employ their observation, who look at things squarely and with recognition, will have an equally alert internal eye, making visualization comparatively easy. People whose minds are full of words or resentment or day-dreams generally do not look at the world at all, but merely stare at or look through things without a real interest in their environment. If we do not create, or rather *re-create* the world with our eyes, creation cannot take place within the personality.

Let us assume that you belong to the majority of people who can visualize things. Find out how your internal vision works. Close your eyes and watch whatever picture might appear on the screen of your mind. Here, again, you might find a tendency to flight, a desire to resist the picture that presents itself. Or else there may be a jumble of pictures, or you may find yourself jumping from one to another, unable to sustain any one of them for more than a split second. This jumping about from one picture to another characterizes the person, who, in life, too, is jumpy, restless, unable to concentrate.

The first step necessary to remedy this is to realize that the *pictures* do not jump, but that *you* are jumping from one picture to another. Try to become fully aware of your jumping about, and soon you will notice tiny movements in your eyes every time you turn your glance from one picture to another. Allow this restlessness in your eyes and vision to go on. Try not to interfere, not to resist your unsteadiness, until you have a clear conception of the nervousness of your eye balls. Do not push the responsibility on the pictures and do not go ahead until you properly realize that it is *you* who is wandering, not the pictures. And then find out what makes you jumpy. Is it shyness, impatience, lack of interest, fear, etc.? (This analysis is important, in order to increase the Ego-functions.) Only after you are fully aware of your emotional attitude towards your internal pictures, can you begin with the analysis of senso-motoric resistances. If an image, after staying for a few seconds, becomes blurred, or if you are mentally jumping away to another picture, you should find out what things you are trying to avoid in connection with the visualized image. Do not be satisfied to call the jumping away an association. We do not want associates, we do not want the next best thing, but the person or thing itself. Concentrate again and again on the same image till the reason and purpose of avoidance "jumps" into your awareness. When, without interfering, you have discovered what is getting between you and your pictures, go into reverse: be bold and persevering and interested so that *you* stop jumping about and look the pictures squarely in the face.

When you have mastered this exercise, or if you are not a jumper at all but can see scenes and hold a picture at least for a few seconds, then the task is much simpler. It is sufficient if, out of a jumble of pictures, you can find one or two which you can look at for several seconds. The greatest benefit is derived from static images which appear like those projected by a magic lantern or from the analysis of dreams which often repeat themselves. These are introjected pictures, undigested morsels in your mental stomach. Having found your picture, do two things: first, ascertain your emotional reaction towards it. Do you like or dislike the person or thing seen, or do you feel indifferent? Do you experience any resistance towards this picture? If you do, express it. Be abusive if you do not like it, and if the vision is of someone or something you love do not be too shy to say so. If you are alone, express (and this means discharge, get rid of) your resistance aloud, and as realistically as possible.

An organism, remember, responds to a situation. Your reaction to this artificial picture-situation is more or less coinciding with your real behaviour. By enticing pictures into the psycho-analytical laboratory you get a good substitute for the external reality. In many cases it is the best possible preparation for the real approach. People with contact difficulties invariably tend to visualize inanimate things, or paintings or photographs or busts of people instead of the living persons themselves. This is not necessarily—as Freudism maintains—the *symbolic expression* of unconscious death-wishes, but a *projection* covering up the lameness and fear of reaction—the emotional deadness of the patient himself. Should you, therefore, find yourself selecting inanimate objects and pictures, realize that you want to avoid the living objects and, with this, your emotional reactions.

Try these concentration exercises first on everyday events. Perhaps you are taking driving lessons. If you rely exclusively upon these lessons your progress will be much slower than if you practise in imagination what you have been taught, adhering to all the details. In your phantasy go for a long drive with yourself at the wheel, remembering and adhering to all the rules you have been taught: you will be amazed at the growth of your confidence and competence. If you are learning shorthand, put the thoughts that crowd in your mind into symbols, especially just before going to sleep; visualize in signs the words you speak, and speed and accuracy must ensue. It requires at least as much concentration to do things correctly in your mind as with your muscles, with the added advantage that, while during the actual driving or shorthand lesson you may be distracted by other things without noticing them, you cannot possibly practise anything in phantasy without investing all your interest, thereby checking up your power of concentration. You have, however, to observe every possible detail; one cannot drive a car or write shorthand in "outline."

When you have gained confidence in your power of conscious imagination, and after you have managed to hold an image for some time, enlarge on the detail description. Very good material is often offered by dreams, which always contain a great deal of unassimilated material. (That is why most of them are so incomprehensible.) Take the single items in turn, but return again and again to the whole dream. According to Freud the first essential in the unravelling of a dream is to attend to each individual item, independently of the context as a whole. I call this: tearing the dream apart, using your mental front teeth to cut it into bits and pieces. The second part, the chewing up, the dissolving of morsels and the setting free of resistances, is done by Freud through the medium of free associations. I have shown the danger of these free associations leading to free dissociations, and therefore I prefer the method of chewing up, contacting the dream morsels. The resistance, the avoidance of the contact, emerges more clearly. This chewing up is done by detail description. You cannot possibly describe anything in detail without concentrating on it.

While the repression of a detail makes the screen memories and the dreams unintelligible, the detail description of dream morsels and the blotted out details will bring about their assimilation and understanding. Just as in the detective story the good detective distinguishes himself by observing the details which others miss, so the revelation of details completes the dream or picture, and solves a problem which would otherwise remain baffling.

Detail description is, however, only a "means whereby." It is like the mason's scaffold which is removed once the house is completed. By translating our observations into words we use description as a means whereby we keep our attention focussed on details, which, through the process of chewing up, undergo a development. The picture itself might change, other pictures and memories, belonging to the same sphere, might appear, but it is essential not to wander from the central picture until it is completely assimilated, understood and dissolved.

On account of an outward similarity it will in the beginning be very difficult to see the decisive difference between the material which concentration yields on the one hand and associations on the other. The psycho-analyst will probably bring forward, as proof for the association technique, Freud's experiments to recover forgotten names. I maintain that names come to the surface not through associations, but through concentration. If you go on associating you will not find the forgotten name, but there is such a fascination (the highest form of concentration) in the existence of a blind spot that you will return to it again and again. Few unfinished situations exert such a pressure to finish them as do forgotten names.

Concentration therapy provides a shorter and superior way to "emotional revival" than either ordinary conversational talk or the technique of free associations. A man who, for instance, speaks rather disparagingly of his father when asked to visualize him and to concentrate on the details of his appearance, might suddenly burst into tears. He will be surprised by his sudden emotional outburst and amazed that he still has so much feeling left for the old man. The cathartic value of concentrating on the image of a person or event to whom or which one has an emotional relationship is nearly that of hypno- or narco-analysis with the additional benefit that it strengthens the conscious personality.

A more difficult, but very valuable step in obtaining a four-dimensional mental life, a life re-creating the outside reality, is the training of the other senses—like hearing, smelling and tasting. To achieve this four-dimensional plastic mentality you have to make your imaginary contact as complete as possible, and by this I mean doing more than just visualizing pictures. If you visualize a landscape you can describe all the details: the trees, the meadows, the shadows, the grazing cattle, the fragrant flowers. But you must do more. You must walk in it, climb the trees, dig the rich brown earth, smell the blossoms, sit on the shadowed grass, listen to the birds singing, throw stones into the stream, watch the bees about their busy-ness! Give free range to every possible impulse, chiefly those which (like tumbling a girl beneath a hedge, or stealing fruit from the apple orchard, or urinating into the ditch) in reality would cause you embarrassment, but which occur to you in phantasy.

This senso-motoric approach, especially that of touching, gives you the proper feel of things and introduces experience of the four dimensions. It will develop your sense of actuality, and will help to bring about that eidetic memory (identity of perception and visualization) which in dreams themselves is always present.

V

SENSE OF ACTUALITY

Thinking in four dimensions in accordance with the outside world, coupled with the ability to distinguish between internal and external reality, is a basic requirement of mental hygiene. In our training we were up till now concerned with isolated exercises only; we started with two-dimensional pictures and added the third (depth) and even the fourth dimension (duration or extension in time). The experience of this time factor is necessary if we want to have a fuller life, e.g. more comprehensive experience. Self-realization is only possible if "time-space awareness" penetrates every corner of our existence; fundamentally it is the sense of actuality, the appreciation of the identity of reality and present.

This sense of actuality must not be confused with Freud's "sense of reality." Freud contrasted the "impulsive" biological behaviour with the need for sublimation and postponement of gratification as demanded, by society. But to call the ability to stand suspense before attaining pleasure the "principle of reality" is not correct. Pains and pleasures and a hundred other experiences are just as much reality as are environment and the ability to stand suspense. Even the hallucinations in delirium tremens are psychological realities, though the victim is incapable of distinguishing between internal and environmental fields.

The ever-moving reality of the present can be compared with a railway, the rails presenting the duration and the running train the actuality. The ever-changing scenery outside and our internal experiences (thoughts, hunger, impatience, etc.) would then symbolize "life."

Sense of actuality means nothing else but the appreciation that every occurrence takes place in the "present." I have found a great number of people, mostly "hanging-on" characters, who have the greatest difficulty in grasping that *this ever-changing something, elusive and unsubstantial, is the only existing reality*. They want to hang on to what they have. They want to freeze the fluid present, to make a permanency out of it. They become confused when the reality of one moment is no more a reality in the very next second. They are inclined, rather than to live the present, to preserve it by taking photos. They adhere to worn-out customs. They have great difficulty in switching from one situation to another. When awake, they cannot go to bed; when in bed, they cannot get up. When consulting a doctor, they cannot finish the interview, and find dozens of reasons and questions to prolong their visit.

The anticipatory character—described in Part One—has somewhat less difficulty in regaining the sense of actuality. He is apparently more trained in thinking in terms of time.

*   *   *

Most human contact is made through the instrument of language. This fine tool is generally so badly used, words contain such multiple meanings, that already an understanding of everyday events becomes difficult. When A uses a word he might mean something quite different from what B understands. The revolutionary science of semantics—the meaning of the meaning—will, I hope, provide a remedy for this Babylonian confusion. Language is not a mere conglomeration, but an organization of meanings, and its skeleton is grammar. Mental and emotional disorder produces both distortion of meaning and wrong application of grammar. Grasping the meaning of certain parts of grammar will considerably assist you in the undoing of neurotic avoidances.

Following Russell, we may distinguish three possibilities in language:

(1) Expressive speaking by which, as the name indicates, we express ourselves and—through emotional discharge—bring about a change within ourselves (*auto*plastic action).
(2) Purposive or suggestive speaking, which intends to bring about a change in the mind of someone else (*allo*plastic action).
(3) Descriptive speaking.

The three different kinds of language have their specific relation to time. The relation of expression is, although causal, that with the present; the urge which causes the expression must still be present, otherwise expression changes into description or play-acting.

Suggestive speaking tends towards the future. Propaganda, for instance, aims at bringing about desired changes in other people.[1] Without such an alloplastic aim the whole technique of advertising and salesmanship becomes senseless.

The importance of differentiating between autoplastic and alloplastic behaviour may be demonstrated by two examples of crying. If a child cries genuinely, his crying is caused by a hurt and is more in the nature of a reaction than of an action (autoplastic behaviour). If, however, a spoilt woman starts to cry in order to move her husband to pity because "she has nothing to wear," then we see the purpose of her crying—the action of her behaviour; indeed, in this case, we speak of "acting." Her purpose is to bring about a change in his heart or his purse (alloplastic action).

[1] Auto-suggestion (retroflected suggestion) is an apparent exception.

Description has the strongest connection with the present. A picture, a situation, must be present either objectively or in imagination, otherwise it is not possible to describe it; and for description we need words into which we translate things or images, and from which we re-create the image we are refering to. Thus the double translation will easily lead to misunderstanding as soon as words with ambiguous meanings are used.

While most animals possess the ability to *impress* and *express*, there is nothing equivalent to *description* in animal kingdom. Description is the recreation of occurrences. Before the time of photography, verbal description provided the principal means by which men could convey facts to each other. The importance of an adequate description is fully recognized by science. An occurrence, in order to be describable, must fulfil three conditions: it must be existent, present (in environment or mind), and real (materially or mentally). The three terms, "existent," "present," and "real," can be condensed into one word: "actual."

By describing experiences in detail you develop a capacity for observation and a sense of actuality at the same time. Throughout the theoretical part of this book I have been laying the utmost stress on this sense of actuality—on the importance of realizing that there is no other reality than the present.

How can this sense of actuality be developed? To begin with, you must realize in what tense you live. Are you in contact with the present? Are you awake to the reality of your surroundings, or do you wander off into the past or future? In order to get the full benefit from the exercise of realizing tenses, you have to take stock of how much of your time is spent in attending to actual reality and how much in remembering or anticipating. At the same time realize that the actual process of remembering or anticipating always proceeds from the present moment, and that, though you are either looking backwards or forwards, you always do this from the bearing of the present. Once you have fully found your bearings in the present you will soon learn to realize yourself as a "time-space event." Train your sense of actuality by watching your inclination to slide off into the past or future. At the same time find out if you upset your balance by *avoiding* to look into either past or future.

The flight into the past is mostly characteristic of people who need scapegoats. These people fail to realize that, despite what has happened in the past, their present life is their own, and that it is now their own responsibility to remedy their shortcomings, whatever they may be. Whenever these people who hang on to the past encounter difficulties, they spend all their energy in complaining, or in finding "causes" outside themselves. "Reasons are as cheap as raspberries." As this search cannot be successful they become more and more depressed and querulous and develop all kinds of illnesses and tricks in order to get sympathy from others. They may go so far as to use the pattern of the entirely helpless child. Psycho-analysis calls such an attitude "regression," but this regression is in most cases merely a trick and not an unconscious event (cf. Burlap, in Huxley's *Point Counter Point*).

Psycho-analysis, after having made a general law out of the tautological platitude that every phenomenon has its origin in its history, applied it on every possible occasion. Freud's conception of regression is a typical example. When the neurotic encounters difficulties in life, he regresses, so Freud maintains, to certain stages in childhood, a regression which can almost be measured in years. What happens, in my opinion, is rarely an historical regression; it is the mere fact that the patient's true self, his "weaknesses," become more clearly visible. His pretences, over-compensations and such achievements which have not become an integral part of his personality, are being thrown overboard. The anxious person who generally manages to appear cool, calm and collected is, in times of stress, more concentrated on his problems than on keeping up appearances. He does not regress to the state of his childhood anxiety. His nucleus, his true self, was never anything else but excitable; his under-development has never ceased to exist. He has fallen back to his true self, perhaps to his constitutional nature, but not to his childhood. If an over-polite patient during a psycho-analytical treatment becomes abusive and flies into a rage, every analyst will welcome this behaviour as a discharge of suppressed emotion. The patient behaving like a naughty child changes from latent to open hostility, thus revealing for a moment his true self (like Beckmesser in the *Mastersingers*). But the fact that children, too, have fits of temper and use "bad" language cannot be taken as proof that such behaviour in itself is infantile.

So much for indulging in the past. It is from the aspect of futuristic thinking that we can derive even greater practical knowledge about ourselves, once we realize the fundamental mistake of failing to distinguish between planning and dreaming. Much futuristic thinking consists in day-dreaming of all sorts. In extreme cases people might show symptoms of being in a state of trance, coming back from excursions into the Unconscious with feelings of surprise or terror at finding themselves standing before the mirror with raised shaving brush and noticing that for the last two minutes they had been completely unaware of their surroundings—that their Ego had ceased to function. The day-dreamer runs away from the present in his attempt to compensate for frustrations. He does not realize that his dreams never lead to the restoration of his organismic balance. He does not realize that they merely cover up a frustration, just as a morphia injection covers up, but does not cure, a painful disease.

If you are "broke" you can easily get away from the realization of the truth by day-dreaming of winning a sweepstake, whereas in reality you would be quite satisfied with a five-pound note. Sex starvation might make you have day-dreams about being in love with a famous film star, whereas in reality you could be quite satisfied with your nice neighbour. Indulgence in day-dreaming, the expectation, the hope that it might come true, leads to ever greater disappointments in actual life. These disappointments will increase the day-dreaming and so start a vicious circle.

I have shown in the chapter on Organismic Balance that an organismic minus produces a mental +, but in the case of day-dreaming you produce a mental + + +. Does it help you to day-dream about a million dollars? To pay off the small debts that worry you, you would require much less. The whims of a film star would probably make you very unhappy, if you were married to her.

What you can learn from day-dreams is the direction of your needs. If you want to fly from New York to Montreal (this means nearly due north) you take your bearings from a magnetic needle which has the North Pole as its aim. But you do not identify yourself with this goal, you do not fly to the North Pole itself, you abstract only the *direction* from the needle's behaviour. In the same way take only the direction from your day-dreams, using them as a help to understand where your needs lie—money or love or whatever it may be. The day-dreams serve the good purpose to show the aim, the direction of your ambitions, but with that their usefulness is exhausted. If you invest too much time and energy in wishful thinking, you achieve a pseudo-happiness for which you have to pay heavily with disappointments and the weakening of the Ego-functions. In order to cure such disfunction, you must learn to re-organize your energies, to face the unpleasant situations which you imagine you cannot tolerate, and which you try to overcome by day-dreaming. Be unhappy about the unpleasantness; and, if experienced and expressed fully, the unhappiness itself will be of benefit. Then take steps in the direction indicated by your day-dreams; set about actually building these "castles in the air" which so intrigue you, but build them on solid ground. Do not be content with taking non-existing jumps into a non-existent paradise, but do something to link those dreams with reality. Translate the "impossible" into the "possible." If you day-dream about becoming a famous author, the probability is that you have latent talents in this direction which should be cultivated. If you imagine yourself a great lover, you obviously have amorous abilities; unhitch them from the film star, where they can never be fulfilled, and you will soon find someone worthy of your attentions. If your day-dreams are of painting or engineering or acquiring wealth, do something about it; follow their direction even though you will have to lower your standard.

One has, however, to differentiate between the day-dream which pictures the ideal *situation* and the day-dream which glorifies an *ideal*. This form of idealism forms a part of the megalomania-outcast complex, and is a very important sign of our paranoic civilization. About the detrimental influence of idealism I shall say a few words in the last chapter of this book. For the time being understand one point: sense of actuality means the experience of this very second—not the experience of what did happen even only one minute ago!

VI

INTERNAL SILENCE

Experiments have shown that a chimpanzee and a human child show little difference in their intelligence from birth to that time when the human child learns to understand and use words. The unification of diverse concrete events by abstract terms and the simplification brought about by the use of word-symbols gave man his first and decisive superiority over the animals. Like many other tools, however, the word has turned against man. As the powder of Chinese fireworks has turned into gunpowder, as the transport plane has become the bomber, so has the word turned from a means of expression and conveyance to a deadly weapon directed against our natural selves and has become more a tool of concealing than revealing.

Words can hardly ever equal genuine feeling, which has nothing to do with hazy emotions or mysticism. Bergson has reinstated the term "intuition" for that deepest knowledge of our existence which stretches beyond images and words. Words have become part of our daily routine as much as have other commodities of life: food, shelter, transport or money. But imagine yourself transplanted to a lonely island! Your outlook will change completely; everything will adopt a different meaning. The things around you will take on a much deeper significance, while language, and especially abstract language, will lose its importance. Every word you use will need to have its precise referent. The biological will overshadow the intellectual existence.

In warfare already, although the soldier is as far as possible provided with the necessities of life, the biological self asserts itself, and the intellect—at least that part which has no contact with the soldier's foremost needs—is thrown overboard. Every return to the deeper layers of our existence will bring about a re-orientation of the intellect[1] and its representative: language. There is one way by which we can contact the deeper layers of our existence, rejuvenate our thinking and gain "intuition" (harmony of thinking and being): internal silence.[2] Before you can master

[1] Intellect is always bound up with words—intelligence is not!

[2] After having finished this book I came across Korzybski's *Science and Sanity*. Although he represents a far deeper semantic analysis than I have ever attempted, and although his *structural differential* provides an apparently very effective

the art of internal silence, however, you have to practise the "listening" to your thoughts.

Verbal thinking and speaking have, as previously shown, a pre-differential state: verbal thinking is a kind of imaginary talking. Similarly there exists a pre-differential state which differentiates into speaking and listening and which corresponds on the acoustic level to the eidetic attitude in the visual sphere. If you can succeed in regaining this speaking/listening unity, you can tremendously increase the knowledge and awareness of what and how you think.

As an initial exercise read aloud or recite anything you like, and listen to your manner of speaking; but you must neither criticize nor change your speech. The secret of success is the same as in every concentration exercise: not to make any special effort except that you should become aware of one specific action. Once you notice in the training situation that you can hear yourself, listen occasionally to your voice when in company.

After that make an earnest attempt to become aware of your so-called thinking. This exercise must be carried out at first in solitude. When you try to listen to your thinking you will in the beginning probably not succeed. You will become confused like the famous centipede, and your internal talking will stop under scrutiny. But as soon as you relax your attention, your internal "babbling" (called "thinking") will start again. Repeat this attempt over and over, especially when your thinking is a genuine subvocal speaking—when you would use sentences like: "I say to myself," or when you prepare to meet somebody and rehearse in your mind what you are going to say. Persist until you get the "feel" of your thinking, the *identity of listening and talking*. When this happens you will notice two more phenomena. Your thinking will become much more expressive, and at the same time that part of your thinking which is not a genuine expression will begin to disintegrate. Your obsessional internal talking will break up, and you might feel like nearly going insane when you hear bits and pieces of your incoherent language floating about, senseless phrases coming into your mind and waiting to be rehashed. Few actions will develop the sense of actuality to such an extent as will the listening to your thinking, especially when you experience the reorganization of your thinking and the rediscovery of the language as a tool of meaning and expression.

Such reorganization of thinking is absolutely necessary for people

method for experiencing the unspeakable level, I consider the method set out in this chapter to be simpler and more practicable than his.

Nobody can read his book without deriving the greatest benefit from it. Later on I hope to be able to deal extensively with his magnificent approach to the psycho-"logical" problem. At present I have only to state that my attitude differs considerably from his wholesale condemnation of identification (see the chapter on Ego-functions) and that I consider the figure-background concept to be preferable to the abstraction theory.

who have difficulty in making genuine contact. This applies to timid, awkward or stammering people as much as it does to persons of the opposite nature, persons who always have to take the floor, who cannot stop talking, who bubble over whenever they meet anybody, and who cannot take in anything that anyone says, any more than they themselves can contribute anything useful, interesting or amusing.

With the improvement of the "feel," a deeper knowledge, a "psycho-analysis" of the characteristics of your personality will follow. You will discover your Self in the monotony, the lecturing, the broadcasting, the wailing or the boasting of your internal voice. Once you have recognized your specific characteristic, take it as an expression of your whole personality, and try to discover the same attitude in your other actions and behaviour.

Learn to value each word, learn to chew up, to taste, to experience the power which is hidden in the "logos" of every word. Winston Churchill is said to have been at one time an awkward, diffident speaker. Now he tastes every word, every sentence he utters. The result is a powerful, penetrating speech in which every word carries its weight. He has the "feel" of his thoughts and this leads to forceful expression. It would be blasphemous to apply the same word "talking" to the verbal effusions of some babbling society lady, who is hiding beneath a torrent of words the fact that she has nothing to convey.

After you have mastered the internal listening, you can proceed to the decisive exercise: that of training in internal silence. External silence already is a situation which many people cannot tolerate. When they are in company they feel they must talk and, if there is a silence for a few minutes, they feel embarrassed and search their minds for a topic with which to break it. In a situation which calls for silence—a beautiful mountain view or the roar of the sea—they must go on chattering. They have lost contact with Nature to such an extent that they have to cling to talk as their only means of some kind of contact.

It is much more difficult, even for people who are not chatter-boxes, to cope with internal silence. Internal silence must not be mistaken for a blank mind (trance, *petit mal*, cessation of all mental functions). In this exercise we are exclusively concerned with the mastery of only one mental function: subvocal talking. Try to keep internally silent, to suppress your verbal thinking, yet to stay awake. In the beginning you will find this very difficult, and you will realize the obsessional character of your internal talking. You will notice, despite an earnest attempt to comply with this exercise, that only for the first few moments will you be able to keep your mind empty of words. Without noticing it, your attention will slacken and you will produce verbal thoughts again. If you are persistent, you will learn to prolong the silence, and you will thus make room for the fuller play of your senses. You will visualize things or perceive your subtler "body"-sensations more clearly. Once you succeed in keeping this internal silence for a minute or so, the energies, or, rather, activities which were replaced by talking, will come up from the deeper biological layers—your biological Self will stir under its covering crust of words.

Try, then, to apply this newly-gained power of concentration towards the outside world. I recommend listening to music. Nowhere else can you check up so effectively on your power of concentration. In full concentration there is no room for both listening to the music and thinking or dreaming.

If you listen to music you will have the advantage of remaining in the acoustic field. After you have gained full command over the acoustic concentration you can proceed to the final exercise to fill your mind with the experiences of the other senses. Look, for instance, at a picture which attracts your interest, or a flower garden, or a sunset, or even your own room. Try to take in all the details without internal broadcast or verbal description. Silently, without verbiage, learn to appreciate what interests or attracts you.

Perhaps the most valuable outcome of the training in internal silence is the achievement of a state beyond evaluation (beyond good and bad), e.g. a genuine appreciation of reactions and facts.

VII

FIRST PERSON SINGULAR

During our visualization exercises we discovered that, by switching our mentality from "the pictures coming into our minds" to "ourselves looking at pictures," we improve our Ego-functions. We turn from a passive to a more active attitude. Such an activity corresponds to the general active, centrifugal character of the organismic behaviour, which is much more pronounced than reflex-theory and religion make us believe. I have previously shown that *the Ego is a symbol for the fact of identification*; thus if we do not identify ourselves with our external or internal visualization, we deprive ourselves of a vital function.

Usually only such pictures as are connected with our problems, with unfinished situations and organismic needs, will appear in our mind. In addition to those images which signal genuine requirements our internal bioscope contains many pictures which we, originally, conjured up either as illustrations of our ideals, or as resistances—as a counterweight against condemned emotions. Once we realize fully that none of these pictures—even the day-dream—appears without good purpose, we should be ready to take more responsibility for the "working of our mind."

As a general rule we can say that these pictures which we deliberately conjure up are resistances and not expressions of a primary need. But even so it is advisable to identify ourselves with every picture and to say: "I see such and such a person in my mind." The avoidance of responsibility and the avoidance of the Ego-language are closely related. As responsibility is so often connected with blame, shame and punishment, it is small wonder that people shrink frequently from responsibility and disown their actions and thoughts.

When the Army Medical Officer comes across a doubtful illness, he lands himself in a conflict largely due to his unsureness and his inability to decide where to look for responsibility. Should he look for causes or for purposes? The malingerer, for instance, produces the "cause" for his illness and the Army Medical Officer runs after the cause. Headaches, backaches, amnesia and dyspepsia are more or less easily produced, but if these are not sufficient proofs the malingerer calls back a former illness, not in a mechanical regression, but for the purpose of producing a cause, an historical fact which will give him former doctors as witnesses. Only if the Medical Officer is the winner in the battle of wits, does he dare to say that the patient's "I" and not his "It" is responsible for his illness. Only then does he recognize the *purpose* and not the *cause*.

In our society it is often very difficult to apply the Ego-language. Assuming you have had a late night and do not feel like getting up. You are late at the office. Will you say to the boss, "I did not want to get up," or will you shield behind a tram that did not arrive, a lift which did not work, a headache which might or might not be present? Just imagine the upheaval were you to tell him the truth. The situation, however, is different when you can be truthful, be it with yourself or your friends. But even if you imagine that you are strictly truthful with yourself, you still might be mistaken. How often are you annoyed that "the tram just went off," instead of admitting that, by dawdling, you missed it?

It is even more difficult to realize that you yourself produce all the neurotic symptoms, and not a mysterious "It" or "libido", that—as I have mentioned before and am going to show in greater detail later on—you contract your muscles and thus produce your anxiety, frigidity, headaches, and so on.

The importance of this conception can hardly be over-emphasized. Without taking full responsibility, without rechanging neurotic symptoms into conscious Ego-functions, no cure is possible. We might not go to such extremes as the obsessional character who maintains that "there was a thought in my brain," instead of saying, "I thought this and that"—although very few of us, indeed, are completely free from such manner of speech. Most people on being tackled about a dream will admit, "I" dreamt this last night; but when they have killed somebody in their dream they deny that they themselves imagined the killing, and they refuse responsibility for their dreams.

Every time you do apply the proper Ego-language, you express yourself. You assist in the development of your personality. Therefore, at first you must realize if and when you are shrinking from the use of the "I." Later translate the "It" language into "I" language, first silently and eventually aloud. You will readily realize the difference between the two kinds of speech when you hear somebody saying: "The cup slipped out of my hand" instead of "*I* dropped the cup" "My hand slipped" instead of "*I* gave him a slap," or "I have such a bad memory" instead of "*I* forgot" or even more truthfully, "*I* did not want to remember, *I* did not want to be bothered." Are you in the habit of blaming Fate, Circumstances or Illness, etc., for the mistakes you make in life? Are you shielding behind an "It" similar to that in Freud's mocking remark: "Insecurity and darkness robbed me of my watch"?

If you put "*It* is raining" and "*It* occurred to me, that . . ." on the same plane, your ability to differentiate between inside and outside world does not look too perfect.

Many intellectuals look enthusiastically to Groddeck's theory of the Id. After they had dethroned God and Fate, but were not yet strong enough to take sufficient responsibility themselves, they found the necessary support in the conception of the Id. They needed a *prima causa* and found a solution by transferring God from his heaven into their own system. Their "Id" concept showed a striking resemblance to Jung's mysterious *Collective Unconscious* and impeded rather than developed their Ego-functions.

Just as Freud introjected Rank's Birth Trauma to fill a gap in his historic explanation of anxiety, so did he with the acceptance of Groddeck's "It" or "Id" (both being synonyms). The "Id" fitted nicely into Freud's scheme of "Super-Ego," "I" and "Id"—but brought about a confusion: the organismic needs and the repressed parts of the personality are placed into the same pigeon-hole, a conception inherited from the Christian hostility against the body.

Adler shows good insight into the part which the conscious personality plays in the training of the production of symptoms. On the other hand, Freud has shown how hypocritical our conscious mind is. The Ego-language is not always an expression of organismic needs. If you cannot sleep you will have the greatest difficulty in realizing that "you" as representative of the organism do not want to sleep, that "you" want to sleep only as representative of habit and hypochondria. Of course, you could say, "I want to sleep, but my 'Unconscious' does not want to sleep." But what difference is there between such an expression and a statement that "Darkness and Insecurity steal watches"?

The Ego's meaning is that of a symbol and not of a substance. As the Ego indicates the acceptance of, and identification with, certain parts of the personality, we can make use of the Ego-language for the purpose of assimilating disowned parts of ourselves. These disowned parts are either repressed or projected. The "It" language is a mild form of projection and results, like any other projection, in a change from an active into a passive attitude, from responsibility into fatalism.

Thus, although the expression "I thought" looks, at first glance, like an irrelevant change from "a thought occurred to me," I must deliberately point out in a pedantic manner that this is not so. Though the difference between the two modes of expression looks insignificant, its rectification will have the most profound repercussions on the whole personality. It is fundamentally identical with Freud's remark that with the cure compulsion changes into volition.

In order to bring about a proper Ego-language we have to adhere to the basic rule of concentration therapy: never attempt a change before you are fully aware of all the details of the *incorrect* attitude. Observe at first the use of the "It" language in others as well as in yourself. Resist a premature change, and you will make most valuable observations.

You will discover a great deal about the motives of avoidance: feelings of guilt, shame, self-consciousness and embarrassment.

As the most important step translate (as far as that is possible) the "It" language into the Ego-language. A very valuable help is the expression "I produce"—leaving, for the time being, in abeyance the way in which you produce, say, a headache. And last, but not least, *apply* the Ego-language. Learn to speak and not only to write "I" with a capital letter. In trying to do this you will find, in the beginning, a great amount of difficulty mainly in connection with the just mentioned disagreeable emotions. *Correct Ego-language*, e.g. correct identification, *is the basis of self-expression and confidence.* How important a part self-expression plays in the prevention and cure of neurosis, should be known to you by now.

There is, however, one exception to the rule. Just as metabolism is fundamentally different from pseudo-metabolism, so the genuine Ego-language differs from a "Pseudo-Ego-language." I am referring to those little overtures with which many people embroider their speech: "I thought," "I mean," "I feel." These overtures are not expressions, but avoidances of emotions; they are mostly inhibitions in making contact—avoidance of the correct use of "You." "I think you are cross with me" is emotionally much weaker than "Are you cross with me?"

In these cases not the "I" but the "You" is avoided. The speech is as much censored and reshaped as in the "It" language. In both cases freedom from self-consciousness is very dearly bought. It is paid for with the deterioration of the personality.

VIII

UNDOING OF RETROFLECTIONS

I am writing on a table. This table consists, according to the present standards of physical science, overwhelmingly of space filled with billions of racing electrons. Yet I behave "as if" the table was solid. Scientifically the table has a different meaning from the practical one. With me in my occupational field it "is" a solid piece of furniture. A similar discrepancy between appearance and fact exists in the case of the Ego. I could have started this chapter like this: F. Perls identifying himself with an urge to convey certain facts. . . . Instead of this long-winded sentence I use the symbol "I," knowing well that, had not the major part of his personality identified itself with the urge to write, he would not have produced this book.

Identification is mostly an unconscious process. Conscious identification occurs in conflicts, for instance between ideal and organismic need. Conscious identification ("I") if it encounters resistances creates volition ("shall not"), mostly in the form of interference against environment or organic self-regulation (retroflected interference). Volition thus probably originates from "negation."

If a child shuts "his" eyes when soap gets into them, this appears from the linguistic point of view to be a retroflection. But it is not. It is merely a reaction—a reflex, but not a retroflex. The eyes shut without any conscious Ego-function. This child, however, might identify himself not with his organism but with some Roman Ideal, like Mucius Scaevola, and decide not to close his eyes in spite of an intense burning. Negations of such kind are the basis of "will power." In this case an active part of the child's personality interferes with another one which thus becomes passive and suffering.

A genuine retroflection is always based upon such a split personality and is composed of an active (A) and a passive (P) part. Sometimes A and sometimes P will be in the forefront. "I get annoyed with myself" has more active character, "I deceive myself" more passive character. In the latter instance not the deceiving but the wish to be deceived—the unwillingness to see the truth—is the essential factor.

The main characteristics of the four principal inhibitions are these:

(1) In *repression*, the material as well as the Ego-functions are distorted or have disappeared. Classical analysis has dealt so extensively

with this phenomenon that we can neglect it in this book, except that we must draw attention to the great part retroflection plays in producing and keeping up repressions.

(2) In *introjection*, the material remains essentially intact, but has changed from the environmental to the internal field. *Passivity becomes activity.* (The nurse hits the child. Child introjects, plays nurse and hits another child.) The Ego-functions become *hyper*trophied and pretentious ("as if" functions).

(3) In *projection*, the material, completely unchanged, slips from the internal into the environmental field. *Activity becomes passivity.* (The child wants to hit the nurse. Child projects and expects the nurse to hit him.) The Ego-functions become *hypo*trophied and hallucinatory.

(4) In *retroflection*,[1] relatively little material is lost and the Ego-functions remain largely intact; but the Self is substituted for an object with the purpose of avoiding apparently dangerous contacts.

This loss of contact with the environment often leads to catastrophic results. The emotional discharge is inadequate, and, if aggression is retroflected, the expressions and functions of the subdued parts P become impaired. But the therapy of retroflections is simpler than the therapy of either repressions or projections, as a mere change of direction is required and the conflicts leading to retroflection lie partly on the surface. Furthermore, the process of retroflection is intelligible, whilst in the case of repression, we have often to be satisfied with the mere fact, without knowing exactly how repressions occur.[2] In retroflection, however, we can always deal with a conscious part (Ego or A) of the personality, which directs its activities against another part (remaining "Self" or P), even if the accent lies on P. Even if you intend to teach yourself chemistry you will at times prefer to be taught.

In the following example of flagellantism—the tendency to beat oneself—one can appreciate the importance of the accent being on A or P.[3]

---

[1] I was tempted to use for this phenomenon the term "introversion," but this would lead to confusions with Jung's character classification. Jung uses the opposites "introversion" and "extraversion" to indicate two more or less normal types. Introversion-extraversion are not correct dialectical opposites. The healthy personality is normally directed towards the world—is extraverted. The dialectical deviations from the normal are the melancholic-introverted and the super-extraverted paranoid types. No wonder that the term "introvert" has found its way into medicine and literature, whilst the expression "extravert" has been entirely neglected as being meaningless, and is not even mentioned in the average encyclopaedias.

[2] We neither know how the "libido" is undertaking its journeys through the organism nor have we yet the slightest idea how, in the topographical concept, the transfer from one system into another takes place. As long as these suppositions have not been demonstrated we have to regard them as speculations and not as "hard facts."

[3] Freud is not always clear in his appreciation of activity and passivity. The psycho-analyst asks of the patient that he lie on a couch in a "passive" state and

(A) A boy liked to play at being a coachman. In his games with his playmates he was always the driver and enjoyed whipping his friends, who invariably had to be the horses. When he was on his own he often continued the game, but had to whip himself, being driver and horse at the same time.

(P) Another boy, while doing homework, hit his knuckles very hard whenever he made a mistake. He did this in anticipation of being hit by the teacher.

Reich and others have interpreted moral masochism as the policy of the minor evil, of bribery. A great deal of self-imposed suffering has to be explained this way: "Look, God, I am punishing myself (with fasting and sacrifices); so you cannot be so cruel as to punish me in addition."

As the organism is primarily active, the last example already shows that for the more passive retroflection a certain amount of projection is required. At least some of the believer's cruelty and lust to punish must have been projected on to God.[1] In some instances A has been so completely projected that only a hint of the original activity remains visible. In self-pity, for instance, the pity for other people can hardly be traced; the retroflection in this case means: If nobody is sorry for me, I have to be sorry for myself.

The example of the suicide wish is very instructive. Here again the mixture of retroflection and projection shows the over-balancing of part P. A girl has been deserted by her lover, she considers suicide. The situation is simple as far as part A is concerned. Her first reaction is: "I shall kill him because he left me. If I can't have him nobody else shall." (As usual in these cases the aggression does not get into the chewing up and digesting of the unpleasant event.) But then her aggression turns into suffering: "I can't live without him, life is too painful. I want to escape, die." The wish to kill has turned into the wish to die.

"Life is painful, fate is cruel." The aggression which, in the act of suicide, turns against P is projected; not she, but fate (or the beloved) is cruel. Furthermore, her condemnation of him is projected into her

---

allow his thoughts to appear in his conscious mind. The psycho-analyst means, however, that the patient should lie in a state of indifference, in an inactive—or impassive—state. If we admit that Freud demands remembering instead of acting, and becomes very indignant when a patient becomes active, we realize that Freud unconsciously (in spite of his angry condemnation of active therapy) distributes the rôles in the analytical situation in such a way that the analyst takes the active and the patient the passive part—another relic of the hypnotical situation.

Expression by activity and acting is emphasized by two branches of psycho-analysis: Child-analysis, and the technique of Moreno who treats psycho-neuroses by urging the patients to write, produce and act their own plays as a means of self-expression and self-realization.

[1] Parallel with Christ's milder character, his God is mild in contrast to Moses' and his God's vindictiveness. The Christian Church, however, makes up for this negligence of human nature by projecting cruelty into a Devil and a Hell.

conscience. "If I kill him I'll be guilty of murder." This anticipation of punishment is, as already mentioned, the root of moral masochism. "Before they punish me, I'd rather do it myself." Finally, the panic, the danger of being killed, deprives her of the last vestige of reason, and suicide emerges as the triumphant solution which apparently gratifies all her revenge wishes. "If I kill myself he'll suffer for the rest of his life. He (projecting her own unhappiness) can never be happy any more; and he will be sorry for what he has done to me." After all the ramifications, the original wish to destroy him is gratified—but only in her fantasy. What price revenge?

Compared with this complicated process, the knowledge of the uncomplicated retroflection is theoretically simple and sufficient for practical purposes; but if we want to apply this knowledge in treatment we are bound to come up against the brick wall of moral resistances. I have hardly found anyone yet who did not feel that the undoing of retroflection went against his principles. We are bound to encounter such remarks as: "It is not fair," or "I'd rather do this to myself than to anybody else," "I would feel guilty if I did that." If we simplify the retroflection into the picture of a ball bouncing back from a wall, we must realize that without a wall the ball would not bounce back, but would fly straight forward. If a man urinates too close to a tree he is bound to soil his clothes. Without the wall of conscience, embarrassment, moralistic taboos and fear of consequences, retroflection would not exist. Activities would contact the world and we would not have to undertake the task of straightening out the bent arrow.

Similar to the cure of insomnia, the cure of pathological retroflections is essentially a semantic procedure. Once you understand fully the meaning of "retroflection," the main task is accomplished. Exercises are of importance only as far as they assist you towards becoming aware of the structure of retroflections. Here are three exercises to this effect:

First notice that whenever you use the word "myself," you might be retroflecting some activity. The same applies to a noun in connection with "self," for instance, self-reproach.

As a second step, find out if the retroflection is more of an A or of a P nature, if self-reproach stands more for reproaching somebody, or of being reproached.

Thirdly, meditate on what reasons you can give—"why" you should not retroflect. Find the rationalization which probably is covering up a resistance.

From the practical point of view the most important retroflections are: hatred directed against the self, narcissism, and self-control. Self-destruction is, of course, the most dangerous of all retroflections. Its minor brother is the tendency to repress (repression is retroflected oppression).

*   *   *

The ability to suppress one's emotions and other expressions is called self-control. By idealization, self-control is split off from its social sense and often becomes a virtue cultivated for its own sake. Self-control thus changes into over-control. The tendency to domineer others is in such cases retroflected and is applied, often with great brutality, against their own organismic needs. People with too much self-discipline are inhibited disciplinarians and bullies. I have still to see a case of nervous breakdown which is not due to over-control, and to its aggravation by the nagging of friends to "pull yourself together."

Most people understand by self-control both the repression of spontaneous needs and the compulsion to do things without that important ego-function—*interest*.

The example of a motor car suggests itself. The motor car has many controls. The brakes are only one of them, and the crudest at that. The better the driver understands how to handle all the controls, the more efficiently will the car function. But if he drives with the brakes permanently on, the wear and tear on brake *and* engine will be enormous; the performance of the car will deteriorate, and sooner or later there will be a breakdown. The better a driver understands a car's potentialities, the better can he control it and the less will he mis-handle it. The over-controlled person behaves in exactly the same way as the ignorant driver. He knows no other means of control than the brakes—than repressions.

The cure of a nervous breakdown (the result of over-control) has first of all to effect the undoing of the retroflection. The self-controlled person always has dictatorial tendencies. By leaving himself alone and ordering other people about, he gives his Self a breathing space, and allows his organismic needs to express themselves. He must learn to understand his requirements and to identify himself with them, and not only with the demands of environment and conscience. Only when he learns to strike the balance between egoism and altruism—between identification with his own and other people's requirements—will he find peace of mind. The harmonious functioning of individual and society depends upon: "Thou shalt love thy neighbour as thyself." Not less, but also not more.

Retroflection remains an ego-function, while in repressions and projections the ego-function is obliterated. As I pointed out before, the ego, by retroflecting, merely replaces an outside object by the self. The woman who controls her crying, and interferes with the biological adjustment to a painful situation, generally shows a tendency to interfere with others, and to condemn those who "let themselves go."

Let us assume, a girl with a puritanical outlook on life represses her delight in dancing. Every time she hears dance music she stifles rhythmic movements in her legs, and becomes clumsy and awkward. To be cured, she must first of all realize that her puritanical outlook is mainly a "means whereby" she suppresses both her own pleasure and that of others. Once she has realized the pleasure she derives from interfering with other people, she will leave herself alone and will interfere rather with people who try to prevent *her* from dancing.

A very interesting example of retroflection, which sheds light on the *inferiority complex*, is given by Karen Horney in *The Neurotic Personality of Our Time*. A beautiful girl with pathological inferiority feelings, on entering a ballroom, sees her plain-looking competitor and shrinks from competing with her, thinking, "How can I, an ugly duckling, dare come here?" I, personally, do not regard this as a feeling of inferiority but as one of arrogance concealed behind retroflection. We see the situation in its proper perspective if we imagine her, instead of talking to herself, addressing the other girl: "How dare you, you ugly duckling, come here." The girl in question is inclined to deprecate people, but retroflects the sneering on to herself.

This last case is a retroflected reproach. If our beauty would tackle the plain girl instead of herself, she would make a great step forwards in the cure of her neurosis. She would change her inferiority complex—her self-*re*proach into an object-*ap*proach.

Such an approach is often difficult, as it is loaded with self-consciousness, embarrassment and fear. My advice, therefore, is: the undoing of such embarrassing retroflections should, at first, be carried out in phantasy only. Although the discharge cannot be satisfactory, we may achieve several aims with this exercise: (*a*) we may change the direction and give P a chance to come to the surface; (*b*) we may recognize many danger signals as mere blinds; (*c*) we may increase the amount of free aggression which, in turn, can be applied for assimilation. This temporary setting free of aggression is a phenomenon for which psycho-analysis uses the name "transitory symptom."

Your possibilities of approach and contact will show a decisive improvement if you undo the retroflection of your "thinking." "I said to myself," What for? If you can say it, you must know it. So what sense is there in conveying a message to yourself? Such talking to himself is found in every child; later on when his talking becomes silent, we call it "thinking." If you examine your thinking, you will notice that you give yourself explanations, you broadcast what you experience, you rehearse what you intend to say in a difficult situation. In your imagination you mean to explain, broadcast, complain to other people. My advice is to apply as an exercise the re-direction of all your thinking (first in your phantasy and then, if possible, in actuality) to a living person. This is a simple and efficient way to make good contact.

Assuming you are in company racking your brains for something to say, thinking to yourself, "I must find a theme to start a conversation," then you can simply change the direction of your sentence and order the company: "You must find a topic to start a conversation." The contact is established and the torturing silence broken.

Introspection is another retroflection and is very often found in people who are interested in psychology. It is the tendency to observe oneself, to study oneself instead of observing and studying other people, a state of brooding inactivity, which is in direct conflict with that senso-motoric awareness mentioned before in this book (and with the cultivation of which I will deal later). That the undoing of self-observation is not easy will be gathered from the following example. A patient told me: "Yesterday I had more pluck. I answered my wife more energetically than usual, and when I observed myself I could not find any unpleasant reactions." What he had really observed was not himself, but her, because he was still afraid of his own courage and consequently felt relieved that he saw no unfavourable reactions in her. People repress their object-observation and change it into self-observation in the desire to avoid unpleasantness, embarrassment and fear, not wanting to be taken as impolite and inquisitive.

Introspection is different from hypochrondia in so far as in introspection the accent is on A while in hypochrondia it is on P. Thus the hypochondriac's tendency to make passive contact reveals itself by his readiness to see a doctor.

Many years ago Stekel had already realized that masturbation is often a substitute for homosexuality; although the homosexual's problem is much more complicated, a great amount of retroflection is certainly present. A masturbation-fixation has the meaning of playing with one's penis because another is not available or else is taboo. The accent can likewise be either on A or P.

In a situation like the last one, the avoidance of contact is easily appreciated, but in no case does the retroflection absorb all activity. We are never so self-centred that we do not interfere with others, although we might do a great deal of self-interference or self-correction or self-control or self-education. Sometimes even the self-reproach is so thinly veiled that we hardly discern anything but the direct reproach. The woman who complains, "Why must *I* have such a naughty child?" or "Why must *my* husband always be so late?" does not mean to criticize herself, but the mischievous child or the unpunctual husband.

The most damaging retroflection is the one of destruction and vindictiveness. The admission that one feels revengeful is so much in conflict with one's ideals that a frank, straightforward tendency to retaliate is seldom encountered. Up to the time of puberty it seems to be more or less admitted, but most adults display their pleasure in vindictiveness vicariously by reading crime stories, or following court proceedings, or indulging in righteousness, or pushing the execution of their revenge on to God or fate. Admittedly, revengefulness is not one of the pleasant characteristics of humanity, but being vindictive at one's own expense not only develops hypocrisy, in the guise of pity, but produces inhibitions which leave situations incomplete; whilst retaliation, whether it takes the form of gratitude or revenge, definitely closes an account.

IX

BODY CONCENTRATION

I was treating a young man supposed to be suffering from a neurosis of the heart. I told him that he really suffered from an anxiety neurosis, and he laughed.

"But, doctor, I am not an anxious person; I can even see myself in a burning 'plane without feeling the slightest anxiety!"

"Indeed," I replied. "And can you also *feel* yourself in the 'plane? If so, describe in detail what you experience."

"Oh, no, doctor," he gasped, "I couldn't possibly."

He began to breathe heavily, his face flushed, and he displayed all the symptoms of an acute anxiety attack. I had succeeded for a few moments in making him feel himself, instead of merely visualizing himself as he wanted to be.

How did he manage to be so unaware of his anxiety? He abstracted from the complete situation, which included anxiety, the mere picture of himself, and he did this by avoiding the feel of himself. The moment he felt himself, his anxiety came to the surface. He, as an observer, had shown me not his real self but the hero he would have liked to be.

I could have brought forward interpretations based on the libido-theory. I could have interpreted the aeroplane as a phallus symbol, the burning as the fire of love, and the image of himself as the potent conqueror. This interpretation would have been correct, but I realized that his *primary* difficulty was in "avoidance"; he avoided physical sensations in many spheres, not only, and not primarily, in the sexual. His ideal was victory over the body. This ascetic attitude resulted in an intellectual hypertrophy and a sensoric hypotrophy.

By immobilizing our motoric system, we immobilize at the same time our sensations; we can re-mobilize both by proper concentration. By re-establishing the differentiated movements of our "body" we dissolve the rigid personality's numbness and awkwardness, and we reinstate the motoric Ego-functions. To feed a person suffering from too much intellect and too little feeling with still more intellect, e.g. interpretations, is a technical mistake. To dissolve a neurotic symptom in one's organism one needs the awareness of the symptom in all its complexity, not intellectual introspection and explanations; just as to dissolve a piece of sugar one needs water, not philosophy.

Our aim is—through concentration—to re-establish the Ego-functions, to dissolve the rigidity of the "body" and the petrified Ego, the "character." This development must at first move in the direction of a regression. We want to halt the progress of a neurosis and of the characterological ossification and, at the same time, regress to the biological layers of our existence. The more remote we are from our biological self during working hours, the more urgent becomes the cry for holidays. We all require —at least occasionally—a respite from the stress which profession and society lay upon us, a regression to our natural self. Every night we return to such an animalistic state and over week-ends we return to "nature."

The neurotic symptom is always a sign that the biological self wants attention. It indicates that you have lost the intuition (in the sense of Bergson)—the contact between your deliberate and spontaneous Self. To regain this contact you have first of all to refrain from asking irrelevant questions, like the eternal "Why?" and replace them by relevant ones, "How?" "When?" "Where?" and "What for?" Instead of producing causes and explanations, which may or may not be correct, you must want to establish facts. Through full contact with a neurotic symptom you will be in the position to dissolve it. To acquire the correct technique of concentration on the "body," the description technique is especially useful. In the beginning you will feel a strong reluctance to go into details, but if you keep to the details without faltering you are bound to come across specific resistances, and eventually to self-explanatory, self-evident solutions. Express the resistances but keep on the detail description. Later on apply the perfected technique, the silent concentration; but for the time being keep up the verbal description as an excellent aid in keeping your attention on the symptom.

The theory of somatic concentration is very simple. We repress vital functions (vegetative energy, as Reich calls their sum) by muscular contractions. The civil war raging in the neurotic organism is mostly waged between the motoric system and unaccepted organismic energies which strive for expression and gratification. The motoric system has to a great extent lost its function as a working, active, world-bound system and, by retroflection, has become the jailer rather than the assistant of important biological needs. Every dissolved symptom means setting free both policeman *and* the prisoner—motoric *and* "vegetative" energies— for the common struggle of life.

If we call the contractions of the muscular system "repressors," then the remedy for repressions obviously appears to be relaxation. Unfortunately deliberate relaxation—even if carried out as thoroughly as Jacobson prescribes it in *You Must Relax*—is insufficient. It has the same disadvantage as have superficial resolutions; though you might be able to relax if you concentrate on relaxation, in any state of excitement the "muscular armour" is bound to return. Moreover, Jacobson, like F. M. Alexander, neglects the meaning of contractions as repressors.

By mere concentration on muscular relaxation the repressed biological functions (which are feared, despised, not admissible into consciousness) are bound to come to the surface before the patient has been warned and before he is properly prepared to deal with them. If, however, some-one is undergoing psycho-analytical treatment (even of the old type) he will assist it considerably by training himself in Jacobson's method at the same time. More repressed material will come to the surface and can be dealt with in the analytical session.[1]

If properly understood, relaxation can be a help in acute emergency. Sometimes on the screen and in cheap literature you hear the expression, "Relax, sister!" addressed to somebody over-tensed and over-excited. Relaxing in this case means letting go of the hanging-on attitude ("Verbissenheit"), getting one's bearings, switching from the blind emotional to the rational aspect, recovering one's senses. In such cases relaxation, even as a short interruption of the tension, can work wonders.

Two more shortcomings of Jacobson's method should be mentioned: Relaxation becomes a task and, as long as you are undertaking a task, "you" (the personality) cannot relax. In a state of complete relaxation the figure-background formation takes care of itself; but during an exercise a conscious (though under favourable conditions small) effort for the figure-background formation is required. We must also not overlook the fact that the tonus of a healthy, motoric system is neither hyper- nor hypo-tonic; it is elastic, alert. Relaxation, if carried out according to Jacobson's instructions, might lead to a state of flaccid paralysis—to a hypo-tonus. But it certainly has its merits; it increases the sense of motoric awareness. It makes one realize the existence of contractions.

And now to the exercises.

(1) Do not attempt any special analytical concentration-exercises before you are perfectly clear about the difference between forced concentration (hanging-on bite) and concentrated interest. If you cannot hold your interest, without an effort, on any senso-motoric phenomenon (a picture

[1] A perfect relaxation can be achieved in Narco-analysis. Under sodium pentothal the repressing motoric system, the self-control, becomes un-tensed, and pent-up emotion is released. The motoric resistances, however, are not analysed and re-organized. An improved method uses a weak mixture of nitrous oxygen (e.g. Minet's machine). This technique has several advantages: (1) The patient handles the apparatus himself. (2) He is conscious all the time. (3) He becomes acquainted with the "feel" of relaxation. (4) He experiences intense "physical" sensations. Hidden neurotic symptoms, such as anxiety, the feeling of bursting, vertigo, etc., come to the fore. (5) He is capable of describing his experiences to the analyst, thus assisting him to peel off the "armour" layer by layer. (6) No special Anaesthetist is required. The method of inhaling is simpler than that of intravenous injection, and toxic implications do not arise. Very few contra-indications exist from the Physician's point of view.

in your mind, an itch on the skin, a pain in the neck, a problem to be solved), then there is something fundamentally wrong in your mental make-up.

This does not apply to the concentration on the outside world. There you cannot rely on the organismic selection; there you might want to concentrate on items which do not evoke your natural interest but are selected by duty, snobbery, conventions, etc.

If you have understood the organismic balance as set out in the theoretical part of this book you will realize that the external figure-background formation follows primarily the internal urges, and once the internal concentration is achieved, the external one will follow suit. There is no objection to concentrating on external fascinating objects and in describing their details. This will convince you of the ease which characterizes healthy concentration and which you must know if you want to avoid the pathological, the forced concentration. Whenever you find yourself getting all tense with "wrong" concentration, remember: "Relax, sister!" Let go and get unconcentrated even to the degree of indulging in free associations. After this make another approach.

(2) There is no need to create special conditions for concentration exercises. After a short while you should be able to do them everywhere and whenever there is no need to keep contact with your environment. Eventually there should be a continuous self- and object-awareness as long as you stay awake. In the beginning, however, it is advisable to assist the direction of interest by selecting a quiet place. An easy chair or a couch will be of help to you at the start. In psycho-analysis I have dispensed with the classical arrangement.[1] I sit face to face with the

[1] Here the patient lies on a couch and the psycho-analyst sits behind him like an invisible God above the clouds, who must not be seen just as the pious Jew must not form an image of God, or as the Roman Catholic believer must not see his father-confessor.

How can a patient ever form a contact with reality if the analytical situation is kept on such a mystical level? The patient has nothing to go by but the analyst's voice, and sometimes not even that. I once had an analyst who did not open his mouth for weeks; to indicate that the session was finished he merely scraped the floor with his foot. His few remarks during the many months I spent with him were sometimes ingenious interpretations of my Unconscious, but at that time I was far from being able to accept them. At other times they were mere projections which I was likewise incapable of recognizing as such. Only after I had heard, many years later, that he was suffering from paranoia, the truth struck me forcibly. I stopped blaming myself for my inability to understand and to appreciate his remarks and directed the blame on to his inability to make himself understood and to appreciate my situation.

Change the psycho-analyst from the awe-inspiring image to a human being on the same level as the patient. Stop interpreting the patient's fear and protest as "God transference!" As long as the analyst goes on behaving as a priest with all the rites of the fixed analytical position and obsessional timing (an interview must by hook or crook last exactly fifty-five minutes), the patient must correctly

patient, but I still let him lie on the couch for the purpose of internal concentration exercises, thus providing adequate situations for both the external (overcoming of self-consciousness, facing the "enemy") and internal concentration.

(3) All balance exercises are useful. Gymnastics as long as they cultivate body-awareness and not the "he-man" stuff, sport as long as it is not one-sided and the slave of ambition, develops such holistic feeling. In walking, feel yourself walking and interrupt the "thinking" as often as possible. Above all, when you have nothing to do, just be satisfied with being aware of your body as a whole.

(4) If you cannot feel the whole of your body, let your attention travel from one part of it to another, chiefly selecting those parts which for you exist only dimly. But do not yet attempt concentration on the scotomized parts—on those parts which apparently do not exist in your consciousness at all. Occasionally, during your daily routine work become "body" conscious; open a door consciously, yet exactly as you do it always, without any particular emphasis or change of your usual attitude. Do not set out to open that door (or whatever conscious movement you want to perform) in an especially graceful or he-mannish way. This would only make you self-conscious, not body-conscious. There is a story of a centipede who was asked which leg he moved first and how he managed to walk with all his legs at the same time. When he tried to do it deliberately he got so confused that he could not walk at all. Instead of merely becoming aware of his movements, he interfered with them.

(5) In executing these exercises one has to remember what has been said before about "jumping" when observing mental pictures. Jumping from one part to another does not constitute good contact, although it is better than forcing your attention on to one single part, by which process you may succeed merely in squeezing a symptom away. You will experience this squeezing away as the disappearance of the symptom. If you feel an unpleasant itch, and it disappears while you are concentrating on it, you might feel highly satisfied, while in reality it has only been driven underground and has not vented its voice in the language of the organismic needs. It will probably come back once you have relaxed the squeezing grip.

If you are a "jumper," go from one sensation to another, and each time be satisfied in extending the contact from a fraction of a second to several seconds. You will then soon be able to select a symptom at will and analyse it. Many a symptom—those with minor resistances—will interest and even fascinate you. The revelation of its sense will come as a real "eye-opener." But if the sensation or symptom should disappear

interpret the analyst as a religious object, and no suggestions that this is a transference-phenomenon will silence his reactions as a believer or dissenter in the psycho-analytical religion.

without development, without having revealed its sense, you might recall it either by working on it from memory, or, still better, by attending to the means whereby it is repressed—to the muscular contractions.

(6) Once you can keep your mind for some time on one place, you may start with the attempt to realize the muscular concentrations involved in the "negative" concentration. The hanging-on "bite" is the pattern from which all the repressing contractions are formed. The hanging-on "attitude" is the exhausting negative concentration in a nutshell. It is the basis for awkwardness, mal-co-ordination and many unpleasant neurotic symptoms. You cannot achieve any natural contact by forcing yourself to concentrate. Your ability to direct your attention must be very feeble indeed if you have to play the corpse, hardly daring to move a muscle, or if you have to be constantly on the alert waiting to jump at anybody's throat who may willingly or unwillingly disturb your so-called concentration. How exhausting it must be for you to achieve anything in life if the basis of achievement, the concentration, is so artificial and expensive. I have elsewhere denoted "fascination" as the highest form of concentration. Up till now, however, you had to deal with so many resistances that you could hardly expect to be fascinated. This will come after constant repetition has made you realize how to change unpleasant sensations into pleasant ones. Therefore, once you have learned the feel of your muscular contractions, try to get them under your control for the purpose of releasing the repressed organismic functions and increasing your motoric agility. Once you have reached that point you will gain confidence in these exercises. You will then feel the first waves of fascination. Your activity and memory as well as your ability to get a quick grasp of situations will improve steadily and this will accumulate until you have achieved a good "feel of yourself." All these exercises will then become obsolete.

(7) To get your over-tense muscles under control you have to change spasms into Ego-functions. These contractions can appear anywhere. They can appear as writer's cramp in your arm and hand or as stammering in your speech. In anxiety-fits you find your chest muscles becoming stiff; in sexual inhibitions the small of the back becomes rigid. Disturbances of contact will appear as tightness in the muscles of the jaw and the arms.

Begin with concentration on the eye muscles, as we have already started with them in the chapter on visualization. There is no need to know the muscles involved, let alone their Latin names. When originally these muscles became contracted and nervy, you did something with them without knowing their anatomy and names. Once upon a time, before it became a habit, "you" contracted every one of the now cramped muscles intentionally; when you wanted to chase away some sensation, emotion or picture out of consciousness, you retroflected your motoric functions as a means of squeezing away what you did not want to feel.

You did this with a deliberate effort well known to you, an effort similar to your muscular activity when you have to keep down, for instance, an urge to urinate.

It is difficult to determine how far the influence of conscious Ego-control reaches. In the course of evolution, many of the lower centres of the organism have become autonomous and beyond the reach of conscious control.[1] The system of striped muscles, however, is within the range of conscious control. It is, for instance, being used for the purpose of repressing. To undo repressions you have to re-establish conscious command of your motoric system.

Wherever you encounter over-tenseness, cramps, spasms, contractions in your system, proceed in the following manner:

(a) Get the proper "feel." Do not attempt any dissolving before you can keep your mind for at least ten to fifteen seconds on the spot.

(b) Watch for the slightest development, like an increase or a decrease in tension, numbness or itching. Very promising is the appearance of a slight flutter or tremor or an "electric" sensation. Every change indicates that contact is made between conscious and unconscious instances.

(c) Be satisfied at first to describe the contraction in the "It" language, like: "There is a tension round my right eye," or "the eyeballs are very restless."

(d) Make an attempt to change the contractions into "Ego-functions," but without additional activity. Feel that "you" are knitting the forehead muscles or straining the eyes, or whatever is being done by you. If you are not successful, turn to exercise (e).

(e) If you have to avoid the responsibility for "your" contractions of the muscles, the change-over from the "It" to the "Ego"-function will be difficult. In this case it is helpful to take refuge in auto-suggestion. Repeat a sentence like this: "Although I do not feel I am contracting the muscles I know that subconsciously I am doing it. Therefore I imagine or I believe I am doing it." This auto-suggestion might be helpful as you tell yourself—in contrast to Coué's method[2]—the truth, the reality.

(f) Take over the control: relax and tighten up, by a fraction (!) of an inch, the muscle in question.

(g) Find out the purpose of your contracting. Find out what you are

---

[1] An "indirect" influence can be achieved, for instance, by a vivid imagination. A good actor, by putting himself into the imagined field of action and identifying himself with the person in question, can produce emotions which by direct conscious effort would not appear. (Hamlet admires this ability—contrasting it with his own emotional lameness.)

[2] Coué's method is based upon self-deception, not upon self-realization.

resisting; express the resistance: "I don't want to see my grand-mother," or "I'll be damned if I am going to cry."

(*h*) With the expression of the resistance, you have done all that is required. But persevere. Other resistances will come out and make conscious the conflict between repressor and repressed. Every picture admitted, every tear shed, puts a bit of energy at the disposal of your conscious personality.

*   *   *

The opposite to the contraction, the flaccid paralysis as a resistance, has been very little examined. Theoretically, the hypo-tonus should not play any part as a resistance; and as far as I can see, it does not occur in retroflection, in the repression of unaccepted parts of the personality. It occurs, however, in projections. It is a symptom of confluence and depression. It occurs as what one would describe as a jellyfish existence—as a technique of non-resistance. Such people are smooth and slippery as an eel. With them you feel as if you are striking into an empty space. They favour expressions like: "You can do to me what you like," or "It does not matter anyhow." In its extreme form the flaccid paralysis occurs as playing possum or as fainting. It is an atavistic behaviour, but can be useful to the homo sapiens of to-day for avoiding unpleasant situations.

*   *   *

The concentration technique is extremely simple in regard to sensoric resistances as long as some sensations are present. Only an intellectual effort is required to concentrate on hyper-aesthesia or pains. Pains demand so much attention that they are the most impressive figure-background formation. As W. Busch expressed it:

> "Only in the molar's hole
> Is the suff'rer's mind and soul."

You have to stand and express the pain, to concentrate with interest and without shouting for relief. It is often necessary to go "through" hell, but not "around" it. Pain is the organism's main signal for concentration. The diseased organ originally wants attention, not morphia. Although in a number of organic diseases the cure will be assisted by crying, hyperaemia (resulting from correct concentration) etc., it is not advisable to rely in any way on it. On the contrary! Wherever there is the slightest suspicion of an organic disease, the physician must be consulted. Many medical men have nowadays sufficient knowledge of medical psychology to enable them to decide whether an illness should be approached from the physical or mental direction, or from both. Concentration is in any case a better approach than the methods of Coué or

Christian Science, which only deny and scotomize an existing reality. Analytical concentration is certainly the method in question for all "nervous" pains, and those illnesses which are symptomatic of an unconscious suicide wish.

A simple way to convince oneself of the effectiveness of concentration is: attention to tiredness. If you feel tired and you have not the time to sleep, lie down and concentrate for ten minutes on the symptoms of feeling tired. Your eyes might be smarting, your limbs might be heavy and your head aching. Watch the development of these phenomena in a kind of dozing state and you will be surprised, after only a short period of practice, how refreshed you will feel when you rise. You must not fall asleep, but must retain that middle state between awareness and sleep.

A very arduous task, equal in difficulty only to the training in Internal Silence, is the attention to a mental scotoma. You have probably had the experience of searching for something only to be told that it was lying right in front of you. It was there but for you it was not there. You had a blind spot as far as that thing was concerned. The recovery is a release of tension—a discovery and surprise, which took the mental cover off. In many neurotic and especially hysterical symptoms such scotomization (mostly in the form of anaesthesia), plays a predominant part. Most cases of nervous sexual impotency, for instance, are not caused by, but are identical with, scotomization of the genital sensations.

Previously I have warned you against a premature attempt to deal with a scotoma, but by now you should be advanced enough to attend to it. If, by letting your attention wander through your body, you discover places which you cannot feel at all, find out at first the boundaries between felt and unfelt parts. After that, keep your attention on the unfelt region. This requires a considerable capacity for concentration. Eventually you will find that there is some particular feel—a hypo-aesthesia like a numbness or a dullness, a veil or a cloud. Feel this "as if" experience like a reality, until one day you can almost literally lift the veil; at that moment the biological sensations and images will come out into the open, at first for a fraction of a second only, but later increasing their duration, and finally assuming their proper place in the functioning of the personality.

In the theoretical part I have pointed out that the scotoma is mostly coupled with projections. The image, sensation or impulse disappears from the internal field and reappears in the environmental field. Therefore, if we tackle simultaneously with the scotoma the question of projection, we increase the internal push and assist considerably in the stabilization of the personality.

X

THE ASSIMILATION OF PROJECTIONS

Where and whenever anybody—from the apparently healthy individual to the advanced paranoic—is projecting, he will be only too ready to rationalize and justify his projections. For many people it is almost impossible to conceive that, for example, even the idea of a personal God is a projection, a mere hallucination.

The symptom of that patient who suffered agony from fear that one day a tile would fall on him dissolved as could be expected: It indicated an unfinished situation, the completion of which was kept in abeyance by the projection of the falling stone. He harboured the desire to throw a stone at an enemy, and changed this persecutory *activity* into the *passivity* of being haunted by the fear of a falling stone. This example shows that, although he projected his death wishes to spare himself feelings of guilt (in his conscious mind he ceased to be a potential murderer), he failed to achieve his purpose, which was to diminish his suffering. On the contrary, by reacting *as if* the projection were a reality, he suffered more agony than all the guilt feelings could have produced.

By projecting we change the whole "environmental field." After we have, for instance, projected our omnipotence wishes we act "as if" the omnipotent god was a reality who could perform all the miracles which we would like to be able to perform ourselves. This god might become such a reality that we change our whole behaviour and character lest we be punished by this creation of our imagination.[1] This reactive change coincides with another one, which occurs dialectically and simultaneously. Not only the "environmental field" but also the "intra-organismic field" changes. In the latter "omnipotence" changes into "impotence." Even this is not quite correct for both changes are isolated in this description, whereas actually only one change takes place involving the aspects of the "environmental—intra-organismic field." If you pour water from a jug into a glass, the emptying of the jug and the filling of the glass occur simultaneously.

Very disturbing is the patient's reaction upon his projections in the analytical situation, where projected *interference* creates a grave obstacle in the understanding between analyst and patient. What mostly happens in the analytical situation (and, of course, in all the other corresponding

[1] The creation itself is likewise projected. God becomes a creator.

situations of everyday life) is this: the psycho-analyst finds something that he wants to bring home to the patient. He points out a certain behaviour, say biting of the nails. Let us assume that this habit was condemned by our patient, but that his attempt to repress it was unsuccessful; he only scotomized it; it became an unconscious habit. The analyst's aim is to make this specific attitude a figure to be concentrated upon and to be dealt with. He wants to add consciousness in order to facilitate the clearing up of that specific attitude. The patient, however, mistakes the analytical, scientific attitude for a moralistic one through projecting his own inclination to moralize, to condemn and to interfere into the analyst. As he himself disapproves of nail-biting so he imagines the analyst does the same. He then reacts to his projection "as if" the analyst, and not he himself is disapproving. He is ashamed and therefore interferes with himself, and aims at repressing or hiding his unpleasant behaviour instead of discussing it openly. The result is that instead of expressing and disposing of the unwanted feature he drives it again underground. Many weeks might pass before it reappears. As a counter measure to this danger of re-suppressing W. Reich has developed the technique of concentrating continuously on the patient's central character-feature—an excellent approach and certainly more fertile than the technique of indiscriminate interpretations.

Although Freud has discovered the great part which projections play in some psychoses, they were rather neglected in neurosis. The psychoanalytical interest being more centred in repression, insufficient attention was paid to projection and retroflection, with the result that the psychotic nucleus of the neurosis often remained untouched. Only lately has the projection mechanism come more into the limelight, especially through Anna Freud, Annie Reich, etc., though still not sufficiently, and still overshadowed by the transference analysis.

The transference conception apparently effected a tremendous simplification of psycho-analytical treatment. By following the prescription to interpret everything that happened in the analytical situation as transference, psycho-analysis expected, after finding the original pattern, a neurosis to dissolve. A number of patterns are repeated since early childhood, but psycho-analysis looks far too much upon them as senseless, mechanical repetitions and not as unfinished problems which demand completion, in the analytical situation as well as everywhere else. In addition there remain sufficient problems of everyday life to be dealt with, not necessarily arising from childhood traumas but from constitution or social conditions. Special attention should be paid to the process of projection, which in itself is not a transference but a "screen" phenomenon. The film of a movie picture is not taken out of the projector and *transferred* on to the screen but remains in the machine and is merely projected.

The orthodox psycho-analyst will agree with me when I introduced another formula for the termination of the analytical cure by maintaining that not only has the psycho-analyst to understand the patient but the patient has to understand the psycho-analyst. He has to see the human being and not a screen upon which he projects his "transferences" and the hidden parts of his self. Only when he has succeeded in penetrating the veil woven out of hallucinations, evaluations, transferences and fixations, has he learned to see things as they are: he comes to his senses by applying his sense. He achieves genuine contact with reality in lieu of a pseudo-contact with his projections.

The obstacles which the orthodox analyst creates are several. Every personal contact with the patient is taboo, as it might disturb the "transference." Many projections are treated not as such but as transference phenomena, and the analysis of the paranoic nucleus cannot be effected.

How does this mistake arise?

The patient often sees something in the analyst which bears a resemblance to important persons of his childhood, but seldom is the image picture of the analyst identical with the original image, which has since gone through the procedure of pseudo-metabolism and possibly other changes. Every analyst has experienced that the "transferred" image changes in the course of the analysis, and that now this and then that feature of the image comes to the foreground. One could compare the so-called transference situation with a river. The history of a river shows its origin in one or several springs. Is, however, the water of the river still identical with that of the springs? Has it not on its way absorbed many chemicals and organic matter? Has not such a change occurred that the drinking of the two waters might mean all the difference between health and illness?

The following is typical of the way in which a "transference" is dissolved, and how, in most cases, "transference" turns out to be anything but a simple transfer from the image of the original person on to the analyst: let us say, the patient sees in the analyst a hard person lacking understanding, just as—so he maintains—his father was. Later it appears that his father was not so hard after all. So we have to correct the transference mechanism. We have to concede that he could not simply have transferred the father-image on to the analyst. What he had seen in the analyst was what he *imagined* his father was. As a child he had projected his own intolerance into the father. Later (perhaps for the purpose of ruling small sisters) he had introjected, copied this, his own image of his father, and finally disagreeing with "being like father" projected again. As usual, he will react in the analysis to his projections and attribute his own fears and restrictions to the sternness of the analyst. The whole complicated process, both aspects—the cruel father and the cruel analyst—boil down to the simple fact of projection of the unadmitted cruelty in the patient's own personality. In other words: dealing with the transference means an unnecessary complication—means a waste of time. If I can draw water from the tap in my room, it is unnecessary to go down to the well.

As usual, we shall achieve our task in steps, and the first one is the *awareness* of projections. Just as you were astonished when I mentioned that you were not aware of the fact that you are not concentrated on your meals so you will now deny the fact that you are a "projector." But make an earnest endeavour and search if you are really free from projecting. Projections can occur everywhere. I have previously pointed out the intra-organismic projection of aggression on to the conscience. I have also mentioned the case where Ego-functions were projected into the genitals.

The intra-organismic projections together with a dummy attitude are safeguards against the paranoic projection, and often enough one sees how the obsessional character develops the unending struggle between persecutor and victim within himself. A demand on the part of the conscience is answered by a determined attempt on the part of the remaining personality to obey, but this is soon followed up by defying the conscience. Increased feelings of guilt result, superimposed by ever heavier demands from the conscience, and so on *ad infinitum*.[1]

There is one sphere in which it is not difficult to discover the projections—the world of dreams. There are at least two kinds of dreams, pleasant and unpleasant. The pleasant dreams are direct or indirect completions of incomplete situations: they coincide with the wish fulfilment in Freud's terminology. The unpleasant dreams invariably contain projections, their best known prototype being the nightmare. The person or animal which dominates the nightmare is always an unwanted part of yourself. If you dream you are being bitten by a poisonous snake it might be correct to interpret the snake as an aggressive phallus symbol, but it is more useful to search for the poisonous snake hidden in your own character. Whenever the dental aggression is not expressed, but projected, you will find yourself, in your dreams, chased by dogs, lions and other animals symbolic of biting. Projected wishes to be a burglar, a killer, a policeman or other puerile ideals will appear in the dream, as fear of being assaulted or arrested.

The projective nature of dream parts is easier to grasp than most other projections; whilst in the ordinary projection parts of the outside world are mistaken for what actually is intra-organismic, we find in the dream

[1] An important difference between the paranoic and the obsessional character is this: while the obsessional character shows definite restrictions in his sphere of activity, and while his conflicts take place within the organismic field, the paranoic develops an over-activity, but directed only towards and taking place within a pseudo-world. Being unable to distinguish between the real and projective world he will try to solve his *internal* conflicts in the *environmental* field. Restrictions of object contact is present in both types.

a zero-point—the knowledge that a dream takes place within our organism, but has at the same time the quality of taking place in the outside world.

*   *   *

After the first step of realizing the existence of projections and the second one of recognizing them as belonging to your own personality, you have to assimilate them. This assimilation is the very cure for all paranoic tendencies. If you merely introject the "project," you only increase the danger of becoming a paranoic. Therefore you must get to the nucleus—to the sense of every projection. If you feel persecuted by a policeman and you merely introject him, you then imagine you are a cop or you want to become one. A proper assimilation, on the other hand, will show that you want to watch or punish a certain person. If you maintain that you are a bear you will be certified as insane, but it is quite a different matter, if you express the sense of this identification and say that you are as hungry as a bear. Someone projected the wish to bully his wife and dreamt that he was being chased by a bull.

The first step might be an interesting intellectual pastime—namely, to accept that under certain conditions you would like to be a burglar or a policeman; but the actual re-identification with the persecutor might be difficult. The resistance which introduced the projection will be encountered as soon as you try to think out all the consequences of being the bogey yourself. It is not easy to admit, when you have frightening dreams, that you find a fiendish delight in frightening other people, or that you are a poisonous snake or a man-eater.

The dream drawings on the following pages are very instructive. The dreamer had a severe psycho-neurosis. He had religious ideals of being mild, unselfish. He was unable to hit back when attacked. His aggression was largely projected. The result: an anxiety neurosis, exemplified by the nightmare of the first picture. The aggressor—the train—is not even visible. In the second picture we find the solution: consciously he identifies himself with the victim. He suffers all the tortures which the other man (symbolizing his own projected aggressiveness) inflicts upon him. Actually he had a very strong, though repressed, sadistic streak in him.

The difficulty in undoing religious projections lies in the embarrassment to own up to certain omnipotence ideas, as, for instance, Heine has expressed it:

> "And if I were the Mighty God
> and sitting in the sky . . ."

We do not often imagine we are God, but there are very few who do not occasionally say: "If I were a dictator then . . ."

In people and certainly in every neurotic there is one character difficulty

241

where the undoing of projections is especially helpful. This is the need for affection, admiration and love, and concerns foremost the narcissistic character—that type which K. Horney has described in great detail. This type does not express affection, etc., but projects and wants it over and over again.

There is one decisive difference between projected aggression and

NIGHTMARE

projected love. If you are afraid to express "I hate you," you will soon imagine yourself being hated by the world, and likewise if you are too shy to say "I love you," you will find yourself expecting love from the world. The difference is, of course, that we would prefer to be persecuted by love rather than by hate. To change the narcissistic attitude into one of object relationship is not as difficult as in the case of the projected aggression. At least we are spared the working through of ideological resistances, as love is the religious favourite number one.

To put into practice what we have just learned we had best turn to our day-dreams. Assuming that you see yourself admired for your skill in sports, or decorated for some heroic deed, or spoiled and mothered by the girl of your choice, make an earnest attempt to reverse the situation

TORTURE

and look for instances where you could allow yourself to admire a sports-man, become enthusiastic about a hero, or spoil and mother someone else. Not only will you develop a more active and adult attitude by undoing these projections, but you will also achieve that position in which you can finish situations and restore the organismic balance which is and remains disturbed by affection which tends to overflow but cannot find an outlet. Projected affection, as pointed out previously, produces the insatiable greed for affection.

The greatest difficulty which is encountered in dealing with projections is their affinity to objects of the outside world. The more reasoning power someone has, the more he is afraid of "imagining" things. He will therefore rationalize the projections, justify them by finding proofs and correlations in the outside world. As in this case projective activity and figure-background formation (interests) coincide, he will develop an uncanny ability to discover the objects which correspond to the projection.

Often a mere selectivity of certain aspects and scotomization of others (monovalent attitude) is sufficient to bring about a paranoic distortion. In this case we can speak of "Selective Paranoia," which is about the worst possible solution of the ambivalence conflict. If you look for points you can always find them. You can misinterpret things, you can value one side of a person's character and under-estimate another to suit your purpose. You can make a mountain out of a molehill, and see the mote in your neighbour's eye while overlooking the beam in your own.

The suspicious man should suspect himself, the victimized one certainly victimizes his environment. If you feel unjustly treated, you can be sure that you are the last one who is fair in his dealings with others. Take the instance of a jealous husband! When he projects his own wish to be unfaithful he will interpret the harmless friendly smile of his wife for another man as a love approach. He suffers and insists that she should not make any advances, he goes to great pains to detect the smallest signs to justify his imagined suspicions, but all the time he fails to look into himself. In general it can be said that whenever you feel jealous, suspicious, unjustly treated, victimized or querulous, you can lay heavy odds that you are projecting, perhaps even that you are a paranoid character.

Against all this unpleasantness of the paranoid behaviour stands one great advantage. Once you have recognized the projective mechanism, it is simple to gain tremendous knowledge of yourself. In *repression* important parts of the personality disappear from sight and can only be regained after working through the big walls of resistance, and even then, as I have often experienced when taking over half-finished analyses, the released parts may still not become incorporated into the conscious personality, but are often projected.

Once you can read the book of projections, once you understand the meaning of *Tat twam asi* (You are I), you have the opportunity of enlarging tremendously the sphere of your personality. Valuable as it is, however, to recognize and assimilate as many projections as possible, it would be an unending Sisyphus task as long as the *tendency* to project remains; for the disposal of this tendency two more steps are required.

The first is to remove the anal and oral frigidity in order to establish the proper boundary between personality and outside world. This task requires a more extensive treatment. It has been dealt with in previous chapters, and will be further elaborated in the next one.

The second step is to learn to express yourself fully. Previously I pointed out that an unnamed pre-different state exists of projection and expression, and the fate of a personality depends largely upon whether the development takes the course of projecting or expressing. People who can express themselves are not paranoic, and the paranoics do not express themselves adequately.

The apparent exceptions to this rule are the fits of temper, the waves of aggression of the paranoic character. These waves are not genuine expression: they are misdirected hostility which can be very dangerous.[1] Owing to the wrong direction they do not bring the specific conflict to a conclusion. They are, on the surface, aggressive defences against the paranoic's own projections and, on the biological level, attempts of re-incorporation. Whenever the paranoic character feels guilty and is too embarrassed to stand and to express the feeling of being in the wrong, he immediately tries to project the guilt, to moralize and victimize the environment (cf. Anna Freud's example of the boy who came home late).

A clear indication of inhibited expression is the use of the "It" language, and also the application of overtures which change expressions into statements which put any clear-cut emotions in a haze. Such overtures are "I think," "You see," "I wonder," "It seems to me," and so on. Try to speak without these fringes and you will immediately come up against resistances, embarrassment, attempts to change the wording, or to keep silent altogether.

If you want to learn self-expression, express yourself first in phantasy as soon as you feel a resistance. In the chapter on visualization I stressed the importance of detailed description, but I stressed at the same time the fact that description is only an intermediate stage, a scaffold to be removed once the house is built. This time visualize a person against whom you feel a grudge. Tell him exactly what you think of him. Let yourself go; be as emotional as you can; break his bloody neck; swear at him as you have never sworn before. Do not be afraid that this will become your character. On the contrary, this imaginary work will discharge much hostility, especially in cases of latent hostility, as, for instance, in a strained or estranged marriage. It often works wonders! Instead of forcing yourself to be nice and to hide your irritability behind a mask of politeness, you clear the air. Often, however, this imaginary action will be insufficient, especially if in your phantasy you push aside the fear you would experience when facing your enemy.

After you have calmed down take the next, the most important step: realize that all the time you have fought your own self only—remember the mote and the beam. Never mind feeling ashamed of having been so "silly." If it resulted in your assimilating your projections it was worth it.

[1] The killing of a million Jews does not help the Hitlerites to dispose in the least of those of their own characteristics which they project into the Jewish race.

A few examples might serve to illustrate projective behaviour.

There are two excellent films presenting two different themes of projection. One deals with projected aggression of a fully developed case of paranoia: *Rage in Heaven*. In the other, the *Chocolate Soldier*, the projective mechanism is less obvious; in this film love is projected. The hero cannot express the love he feels for his wife and is irritable and grumpy. He projects his loving activities on to a competitor, the Russian singer, whom he creates and plays as having all the characteristics which he is incapable of expressing. Only after he has learned to express himself through this medium of his creation, the need to project collapses, and he becomes himself the lover. No more jealousy, suspicion or irritability.

A lady left in her testament the following wish: her gold-fish had to be looked after, but it had to wear a dress. Here we see a double projection. No normal human being would see anything indecent in a gold-fish. She projected her wish to swim in the nude on to the fish, but also her defence, her shame. Therefore this poor creature had to suffer a dress, even after her death.

More complicated but rather amusing is the story of a Chinese, as related by Arthur Schmidt. A Chinese visits an acquaintance of his. He is asked to wait in a room which has a beam across the ceiling. Upon the beam stands a jar of oil. A rat, disturbed by the visitor, runs across the beam and knocks the jar over. The jar hits the guest rather painfully and the oil stains his precious garment. The victim is red with rage when his host enters. After exchanging the usual formal greetings the visitor says: "When I entered your honourable apartment and seated myself below your honourable beam, I frightened your honourable rat, which took flight and dropped your honourable oil jar upon my despicable clothes. This is the cause of my unsightly appearance in your honourable presence."

XI

UNDOING OF A NEGATION (CONSTIPATION)

Few of Freud's remarks have impressed me as deeply as his answer to the reproach that he was turning everything upside down. He denied it: "If people are standing on their heads, then it is necessary to turn them upside down—to put them on their feet again."

In this book we call such a reversal "undoing" ("re"-adjustment). Applying the dialectical terminology, we can describe the repression of a memory (isolated amnesia) as the negation of remembering.[1] The treatment of such forgotten incidents requires the undoing of the negation—their return into the mental metabolism. Often, however, it will happen that the patient, rather than facing the memories in question, prefers to make a neurotic symptom (general forgetfulness) out of the forgotten facts. Instead of *undoing* the negation, he will develop a *negation* of the negation.

The man who represses a certain memory—originally aiming only at the denial of the existence of one specific fact—does not recognize the purpose of his amnesia, but interprets it as a sign of mental disfunction. He will complain about his bad memory, develop a habit of jotting things down, thereby weakening his ability to remember still further. He might take up a course of commercialized psychology, which persuades him that by learning senseless verses—so many a day—he will improve his memory. Actually he will only produce a neurotic layer which has no bearing on the original issue—he will create a negation of a negation.

We have come across a number of such double negations. We have, for instance, extensively dealt with the consumption of very spicy food as being the negation of a palatal frigidity which in turn is the negation of the desire to vomit. We have called this process (in accordance with the psycho-analytical terminology) resistance against a resistance.

A double negation, similar to that found in the mouth, sometimes exists in the anus. The result is constipation—manifest or masked.[2]

---

[1] The biological forgetting, the absorption of an incident by the organism, is different from forgetting by repression. In the first case, the "memory" is dissolved, in the second one both the memory and the repressing activity remain very much alive.

[2] By masked constipation I mean a constipation which is overcome not by a defaecation urge but by habit, for instance by going to the lavatory daily at exactly the same time

For the normal healthy defaecation, only three activities are essential: to go to the lavatory, to relax the sphincter and to feel the defaecation itself. Anything beyond these functions is unnecessary, pathological, and produces a great amount of complications and difficulties. Keep these three points in mind and learn to understand and to master them. Contrast the three healthy functions with the pathological procedure!

The main condition for a healthy defaecation is that you must limit yourself to the mere task of going to the place of defaecation, but only in the service of a defaecation *urge* and not in order to overcome your constipation. No conscious effort is required to go to the lavatory if you suffer from diarrhoea. On the contrary, your effort will then be directed to keeping the stool back until you are on the seat. The *urge* drives you to the proper place. How different is the attitude of the constipated! They don't feel any urge, but go to the lavatory driven by *commands*.

Realize that constipation is an unconscious reluctance to part with the faeces, and you have already won half the battle. Actually most people find this very difficult to accept. But if you "suffer" from constipation, a real cure is impossible without your taking the responsibility that *you* retain, that *you* don't let go.

In order to prove that I am wrong, you will tell me that you do everything possible not to be constipated, that you would not dream of keeping anything back, because this is detrimental to your health. All this, however, is justification, over-compensation in the service of the Super-Ego, dictated by duty, conscience, or what is supposed to be "good for your health," as your grandma and laxative manufacturers assure you. It would trouble your conscience if you would consciously allow yourself to be constipated. In spite of all your assurances the fact remains that in constipation you simply do not feel and therefore do not obey the urge, but follow introjected ideas about constipation.

Pluck up courage and wait for the urge to come. K. Landauer told me once of somebody who was constipated for four weeks. This, of course, is an extreme case, which I only mention to show that the danger of constipation is very much exaggerated in our time. What we want to achieve is self-regulation. One of the best points which W. Reich ever made is his demand that the regulation of our sex life by morality should be replaced by the rhythm of self-regulation. The sexual urge must disappear not by repression, but by gratification, till the renewed tension demands our attention again. In the same way "you" must not regulate your bowels. What is required is their self-regulation.

In the chapter on Body Concentration we were mainly interested in the muscular contractions. Contraction of the muscles is a repressing factor: we hold down, keep back such sensations, feelings or emotions, which we do not want to release. The basis of all "keeping back" is the withholding of the excretions, as the result of the training in cleanliness.

There originates the idea that self-control is identical with suppression. Psycho-analysis, according to its main interest in repressions, has decided on constipation as the basic resistance. I have mentioned already that Ferenczi realized so fully the importance of the contracting function of the sphincter ani, that he called the intensity of its contractions the mano-meter of resistance. A great amount of constipation, mental as well as physical, coincides with a rigid contraction of the sphincter, the anal closing muscle. Concentration exercises and regaining conscious control of the working of this muscle will assist in the cure of anal mal-functions and repressions.

In case you never get an urge, or suffer from one of the unpleasant results of chronic constipation—from piles—what steps are to be taken?

Piles are an excellent example of the result of the negation (forcing) of a negation (constipation). In the following pictures S represents the

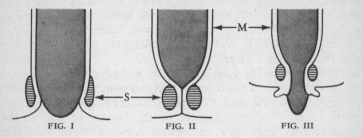

FIG. I   FIG. II   FIG. III

closing muscle, the sphincter, M the internal skin, the mucous membrane of the rectum.

In Figure I the sphincter is *relaxed* and the faeces are passing out without any undue resistance. In the next picture the sphincter is *permanently contracted* (constipation) and in Figure III the faeces are *forced* out against the contracted sphincter. The internal membrane is pushed out with them. The result must be piles or even a prolapse of the rectum.

Proper concentration exercises, which aim at controlling contraction and relaxation, are the only means to bring about an improvement of "psycho-genetic" piles. By attending to the following exercises, a number of cases have greatly improved, or have at least prevented a further deterioration, but the exercise is meant for every case of constipation, not only those who have already developed piles.

The first thing you have to remedy, whilst sitting on the seat, is avoid-ance of awareness of the defaecation activity, for instance reading or mind wandering or futuristic thinking. You must concentrate on what is going on at that very moment. Any looking ahead like "I want to get it over quickly"—"how long will it be to-day?"—"what amount am I going to produce?"—any anticipation of any kind whatsoever should be realized as such, and you should return to what you actually experience in your senso-motoric system. Realize that you are pressing or squeezing, and try to omit both. See what happens if you don't squeeze. Probably nothing —but a remarkable insight might dawn on you: the fact that you are just playing the fool, that you are pretending, that you just sit on the lavatory seat without any real urge or intention to defaecate.

In this case you had better get up and wait till a real genuine urge occurs. If you do not want to do this, concentrate on the resistance: find out how you produce the constipation, how you contract the sphincter muscle and how, by these means, you keep the content of your bowels back. Learn to feel the resisting muscle and to contract it deliberately. You will soon get tired and you will relax the sphincter muscle and dissolve the constipation in a natural manner. Try to isolate the tense muscle from its surroundings; a haphazard deliberate contraction of the whole bottom region does not establish conscious anal control. Once you have learned to isolate and to control the sphincter consciously, you can contract or relax it at will.

Should you, however, have developed a scotoma for the defaecation-sensations, then the above exercise will be difficult. The undoing of the scotoma and the relaxation exercises will more or less overlap each other.

In our discussions on Body Concentration we were mainly interested in the kinaesthetic sense, in the feel of the muscles, and we have rather neglected the possibility of complete anaesthesia. We were interested in what was actually there and not in the lack of it. The next step in our exercises, therefore, must be to find the blind spots, the gaps, the places which we avoid in the feel of ourselves. Again take stock of the whole of your body, and observe which parts you jump over or you do not feel. Can you feel, for instance, the expression on your face? What sensations have you in your mouth? How much of your pelvis region do you feel? Are you aware of the existence of your genitals? Of your anus?

You avoid all these "feels" because you do not want to feel. Find out *what* you want to avoid and *how* you manage to avoid the real feel. Do you let your attention wander too quickly? Do you imagine sensations like cotton wool or being frozen? Do you notice, once you try to hold your attention to a spot, that you run away into thinking, day-dreaming, sleeping or deprecation ("that's all bunk"), or do you remember suddenly another urgent duty? Unmask all these tricks as means of avoiding the contact of your "Ego" with other parts of yourself.[1]

[1] This concentration method is, with or without the help of an analyst, the very way to cure sexual frigidity. There is no case of sexual dissatisfaction with sufficient awareness of genital contact. In every case the attention is consumed by either some kind of fear, or thinking, or experimenting. This, in my opinion, is the actual basis of the castration complex. The castration memories are pure rationalizations. One can bring the feel of the penis into existence without digging up one single castration threat. The basis for this sexual frigidity is a negation: the genital

The anal sensations are much less intense than the genital ones. Although their disfunction does not create very conspicuous symptoms, it is yet responsible for a number of neurotic disturbances. The anal numbness is part of a vicious circle. The training in cleanliness, or lack of courage to go to the lavatory whenever you feel like it, induces you to avoid the feel of the urge. The decreased feel increases the danger of being surprised by the urge, chiefly in the state of excitement, therefore one completely locks the bowels by rigid control. In some cases the numbness is so complete that people have completely forgotten how an urge to defaecate feels. They invariably show signs of a paranoid character, although the anal link of the paranoic mechanism is more centred in the numbness during the defaecation process than in the lacking defaecation urge.

One condition for the cure of the paranoid nucleus is the proper feel of the defaecation process, of the contact between faeces and anus. Failing the proper contact, a pathological confluence—an inability to discriminate between inside and outside—will result. With the assistance of this new insight, cases which looked hopeless made an excellent recovery and achieved a cure of their disintegrated personality. I doubt whether this could have been achieved otherwise. In any case, their analysis took a considerably shorter time. In our concentration exercises, therefore, I stress the utmost importance of the anal concentration, which is not easy, as the numbness in many a person has attained such a degree that they do not feel anything at all in that region.

Once you have realized that you feel nothing, try again and again to penetrate the veil, the numbness, the cotton wool feeling, or whatever resistance you have created between your "mind" and "body." Once you manage to make mental contact, you proceed as in the other concentration exercises: watch for development and mainly for sensations like itches or heat, which want to come to the surface, and against which you will find yourself contracting again.

Next comes the most important point, namely, to feel the functioning of the defaecation, to feel the passing out of the faeces and their contact with the passage. Once this feel is established, the vicious circle of the paranoid metabolism is interrupted, the recognition of projections facilitated and this pathological place of confluence is fenced and censored.

The following speculation might also be of assistance: the anal numbness resembles the oral frigidity. Generally speaking, the numbness in defaecation corresponds to the disgust. Thus, whenever you find something to be wrong with the process of defaecation, make an attempt to get hold of the parallel phenomenon in the oral sphere. My investigations point

orgasmic sensation was at one time so strong that it became intolerable. Add to this a shyness in making the corresponding noises and movements, and you can easily realize the result: an urge to avoid those strong feelings.

to a strong relationship between the anal and oral attitudes.[1] Although I have not yet enough material to prove it, it does not seem unlikely that the projection is originally a vomiting process. This would account for the non-assimilation and the ejection of the material which cannot be utilized. Definitely clear is that the interchange of introjections and projections works like an avalanche, taking up more and more contact possibilities till all relationship between the individual and the world becomes empty and paranoic.

[1] This learning by the anus from the mouth confirms Freud's observations, but I don't see the necessity of involving the *libido* in this process.

XII

ABOUT BEING SELF-CONSCIOUS

People speak of a "subconscious mind," but this term is not recognized either in psycho-analysis or in gestalt psychology. We can, however, find one situation where the term "sub-conscious" may be permitted: when emotions and impulses urge to come to the fore, but are barred from their proper expression. In this case they are neither repressed nor expressed; at the same time there is too much self-awareness to allow their projection. *Self-awareness changes into self-consciousness.*

In these cases the proper self-expression becomes inhibited as soon as it is sensed that it might bring about a decisive change either in oneself or in one's environment. A conflict, for instance, must not come to a crisis: it must remain *hypo*critical. Unexpressed, but incapable of being repressed, the challenging impulse can neither disappear into the background nor dominate the foreground. It must find some medium, and so we have, under these pathological conditions, to accept the existence of a subconsciousness, of a middle-ground.

A middle-ground does not exist in the healthy mind. There can only be foreground figure coming out from and receding into the background. Sometimes, however, two figures tend to be present at the same time. We then speak of a conflict. To stand such a situation of conflict, such a double configuration, is incompatible with the inherent holistic tendency of the human mind. One figure will always tend to push the other aside, or else, a synthesis like a compromise or a neurotic symptom will bring about a kind of unification. Often the two figures will sit on a see-saw, a state of mind which we call indecisiveness and instability.

Under certain conditions, however, an emotion will strive hard, but unsuccessfully, to come into the foreground, and in such instances we might talk of a middle-ground, but we must remember that the middle-ground phenomenon is a pathological occurrence. The inhibiting instance is partly the censor (according to Freud's meaning), but it is also and to a far greater extent the *projected* censor—the worrying about what people will say. The censor is a retroflecting, disparaging, critical attitude in ourselves which, in the projection, is experienced "as if" we were scrutinized by others and in the limelight. If, for instance, we hide the expression of annoyance, or love, or envy, or any other powerful emotion of which we are ashamed or afraid or which we are too embarrassed to reveal, then we experience self-consciousness and its motoric equivalent —awkwardness.

Recently a man consulted me exclusively about his self-consciousness. He found it surprising that, contrary to his expectations, he was not self-conscious with his superiors, but only with his subordinates, and particularly his typist. Unable or unwilling to express the annoyance she aroused in him, he felt awkward, ill at ease and self-conscious in her presence. Not his annoyance but the expression of it was repressed, and he felt immediate relief after I had urged him to address her in phantasy as he would like to in actuality, to let himself go. Having a good command over his imagination, he gave full vent to his vituperation, expressing freely all his accumulated anger and annoyance, shifting it from middle-ground to the foreground, where it belonged. Not that in this case phantasy action alone was sufficient; he told me later that he had changed his typist. The phantasy explosion had given him sufficient confidence to enable him not only to dress down but dismiss the supercilious employee.

The term "self-conscious" is not a bad one. It indicates a retroflection, the fact that one's attention is directed towards one's self and not towards the object of one's irritation or potential interest. It suggests an inward-bound instead of an outward-bound emotion. It is the consciousness of one's own condemned or despised features and behaviour.

Often self-consciousness forms a nucleus around which a number of character features develop. Under its influence some people become brazen, impudent, offhanded, cynical, rough or profane. Others develop in the opposite direction and become servile, unctuous (Uriah Heep) or awkward to such an extent that they knock things over, venting their aggression by spilling or breaking things ("by accident," "I couldn't help it"). Avoidance of the object of one's discomfiture often manifests itself in the inability to look the hated or loved person in the eye, and the self-conscious individual, fearing his attitude might give him away, trains himself to overcome it by developing a rigid stare.

In every fit of self-consciousness there is some suppressed (not repressed) action or emotion—something unsaid or undone. Very frequently the inability to say a clear-cut "No!" to demands which one would like to refuse is the basis of self-consciousness. The grudge against the person who makes these demands leaves us with a feeling of weakness and impotency that produces an atmosphere of tension and self-consciousness. The inability to say "No!" represents the usual fear of bringing about a change in the world, in this case the fear of foregoing the benevolence of our environment. The difference between projection and self-consciousness in this instance is that in projection the "No!" vanishes into thin air, as soon as it ought to become foreground figure, and reappears as a feeling that something is denied to you. In self-consciousness, the

"No!" remains in the middle-ground, it wants to become obtrusive but you want to keep it in obscurity.

It is important to avoid confusing self-consciousness with self-awareness. Unfortunately there is no word conveying the meaning of self-awareness that does not also suggest that in self-awareness, too, retroflection takes place. This, however, is not the case. Self-awareness means—at least I mean by self-awareness—that subjective state of primary feeling *that* one exists, as well as the feel of *how* one exists, a state which psycho-analysis calls "primary narcissism." The term, "intuition," in the sense of Bergson would be appropriate, but this word is generally used as indicating a mental act. Following a widespread scientific custom of composing terms from the Latin or Greek language, I would suggest "autaesthetic" to express "being aware of one's being and doing," but—apart from the danger of being confused with "self-consciousness"—I consider the expression "self-awareness" as being quite capable of conveying what I mean.

When, for instance, you are so fully absorbed in dancing that you feel the oneness of mind, body, soul, music and rhythm, then you realize the pleasure of self-awareness, of the "feel" of yourself. But there might be a disturbance which prevents you from catching the rhythm of the music, or your mind and body might not be in step, or your partner might not harmonize with you. If in such cases you feel like venting your disappointment, but you do not, then you lose self-awareness, and become self-conscious.

In self-awareness, even the greatest thrill brings not only satisfaction, but peace of mind which in self-consciousness never exists, because in self-consciousness there is always something unexpressed, an incompleteness which can only be overcome by breaking the tension through expression. Often it will be enough to do this in phantasy, but on occasion self-consciousness can only be disposed of by conveying in actuality your feelings to the person concerned. In any event the phantasy-action will be successful only if you can imagine your opponent plastically, four-dimensionally, so that you get the feeling of having wrought a change in him. Actually, the change will take place in yourself; you will lose, through the power of expression, your self-consciousness, and you will gain—and this is so much more important—confidence, a new ability to deal with difficult situations, and recognition of your environment.

People with high-flying ambitions, who want to be admired, to be the centre of attraction, often suffer from an intense form of self-consciousness. They have to be contrasted with people who are also in need of admiration, but are only too ready to exhibit anything that might gratify their narcissistic needs. They might display precious jewels, or their well-dressed children, they might exhibit cleverness or facetiousness, narrate smutty or not-so-smutty stories, they might do anything to impress others, to squeeze admiration out of their friends. Should this narcissistic need however, be strongly present, without the "means whereby" at hand, or should an uncertainty prevail about producing the desired reaction, then the outcome must be self-consciousness. There are very few young girls who do not dream of being the belle of the ball, but who, being uncertain of achieving their goal, will be "all arms and legs." Compare their awkwardness with the bearing of the sophisticated woman who is sure that she can collect as many knights as she wants.

Generally speaking, people with ungratified narcissistic wishes will develop self-consciousness, whenever there is a chance that they might become the centre of attraction, the figure against the background of their environment. Whenever they stand out against the mass, for example, when they enter a room full of people, when they have to rise to make a speech, when they have to leave the company to go to the lavatory, they feel self-conscious, expecting all eyes to be on them. The moment they forget their narcissistic wishes or are concentrated fully on their objects instead of on themselves, their self-consciousness disappears. In brief, one way to cure *self*-consciousness is to change it into *object*-consciousness.

A similar self-consciousness is experienced by many people if they feel they are being watched whilst they are working, e.g. when playing the piano, typing or writing. They are perfectly aware of the change in their attitude, of their lack of concentration, confusion and general discomfiture. They often maintain—wrongly—that they suffer from an inferiority complex. The fact that they lose all their unpleasant feelings, as soon as their work, and not they themselves, is the foreground figure, should be sufficient proof that they suffer not from an inferiority complex, but from self-consciousness. If they are concentrated on the impression they are making, the concentration on their work is lost and mistakes and incoherence must result.

The best knowledge about self-consciousness can be gained by a thorough understanding of the figure-background phenomenon. One can go so far as to maintain that self-consciousness is the disturber of the figure-background phenomenon of the "personality." It is the individual personality that wants to stand out against the background of the environment; if, for instance, a pupil is suddenly asked to step forward he will enjoy exhibiting himself if he has no inhibitions. He might even glow with pride and he will slip naturally into the foreground of the picture. If, however, his unexpressed desire for admiration shrinks from this enforced publicity, he will blush with shame, want to disappear and become background again. Finding himself suddenly where he has always wanted to be, he will become conscious of himself and display this self-consciousness in gaucherie. Such an attitude may become permanent. The timid character, the person who always plays second fiddle, the conscientious employee who always does things so perfectly and inconspicuously that he blends into the background, the producer of a play, the psycho-analyst who sits *behind* a patient to escape observation—they are all bent on avoiding the limelight, and they all condemn any coming to the fore as exhibitionism. Exhibitionism, however, is the self-conscious form of expression, brought about by pushing aside feelings of shame, fear and embarrassment.

The curative steps to be taken are obvious: you have not only to become fully aware, what emotion, interest or urge you are concealing, but you must also express it by words, art, or action.

Self-consciousness and day-dreaming often go hand in hand, as the day-dreamer is full of unexpressed material. The higher his imagination soars, the greater is the shock he suffers when, in reality, a situation is approached which contains the chance of realizing his suppressed wishes. Owing to his pre-occupation with the phantasy-dummy he cannot apply his motoric-expressive system within the real situation, but remains self-conscious and paralysed between his wishes and inhibitions.

The value of the field conception becomes particularly evident in the therapeutic approach to self-consciousness. As one can induce electricity in a coil of wire by putting it into an electro-magnetic field, so one can induce self-consciousness in its specific danger-field, and intensify or diminish it with varying distance. The two poles of this danger-field are the sufferer's self-awareness, and his projected criticism (inhibition).

By eliminating one of the two poles self-consciousness will disappear. In order to free oneself from the unbearable conflict, this is often done by drinking liquor, by recklessness, impudence or other means whereby an emotional frigidity is produced.[1] This method of overcoming self-consciousness is the "wrong" one. If self-consciousness is the negation of spontaneity, then drinking, brazenness and so on are the negation of the negation. The "right" method, however, cancels the negation by undoing the retroflections and assimilating the projections; in the case of self-consciousness this means: you have to change the wish to be admired, the fear of being stared at, and the feeling of being the centre of interest, into the activities of being enthusiastic, of observing and of concentrating one's interest on to an object.

[1] The inability to deal with one's self-consciousness is a frequent inducement to become a drug or alcohol addict. I know of two patients in a deplorable state of progressive alcoholism, who could not stand any company in a sober state and who could give up drinking only after their self-consciousness was cured.

XIII

THE MEANING OF INSOMNIA

It has been more and more realized that the very unpleasant phenomenon "insomnia" cannot be cured by drugs, relaxation, silence, dark curtains or the counting of sheep. Admittedly in the single incident these "remedies" frequently induce a kind of unconsciousness resembling sleep, yet contrary to the purpose of sleep: to give rest and freshness. Occasional nights of sleeplessness should not be called insomnia and should under no condition be treated as a neurotic symptom. I would like the term "Insomnia" reserved for a state, where the majority of nights are considerably disturbed, and "Chronic Insomnia" where for a lengthy period rarely a night is slept through. Only real insomnia should be remedied. As all the above-mentioned prescriptions are never able to cure insomnia, I propose to approach the question of insomnia from a different angle altogether.

If the organism is invaded by bacteriae, you will find their enemies, the leucocytes, in the blood increased; if somebody has incorporated too much alcohol, he might vomit. Would you regard the increased leucocytes or the vomiting as phenomena of illness and would you try to suppress them? You rather would, I am sure, look for the meaning, which in both cases is unambiguously: organismic self-defence. *Insomnia in most cases is not an illness, but a sympton of a long-range health policy of the organism in the service of holism.* All dopes, be they medicine or a night-cap or reading before falling asleep, are means of suppression, contrary to the needs of the organism.

A statement to the effect that sleeplessness is not a pathological but a curative symptom, arouses in most people the same bewilderment which we experienced once upon a time, when we learnt that the earth but not the sun is moving. Before, however, I am in a position to prove that my apparently paradoxical statement is correct, I have to say a few words about rest. You will agree with me that the aim of sleep is rest, and that drugs produce a paralysis rather than rest. The search for a drug which leaves the patient without headaches and dizziness is a clear indication of this. The striving for rest is but one expression of the often mentioned general tendency of our organism to restore its balance by eliminating a disturbing influence, or by concluding an unfinished situation. How long are you interested in a cross-word puzzle? Exactly up to that moment when you have finished the problem and the solved puzzle becomes an uninteresting piece of paper to be thrown away or, at best, to be collected for the war effort.

A commercial traveller, a happy-go-lucky fellow, visited a small town. The proprietor of the hotel begged him to make as little noise as possible, because his neighbour was very nervous. He promised, but he came home slightly intoxicated, happy and singing. He started to undress and threw a shoe against the wall. Suddenly he got a fright, remembered his promise and went quietly to bed. Just when he was dozing off, he heard an angry voice from the next room: "When the devil is the other shoe coming?"

We often go to bed with incomplete, with unfinished situations, and there are hundreds of possibilities in which it is more important for the organism to finish a situation, than to sleep. In most cases we are not aware of this organismic need. We only feel that something is disturbing our sleep, and we vent our rage against the disturber. We misdirect our annoyance from the unfinished situation to the barking dog or the noise of the traffic, or the hard pillow, which we hold responsible, or rather which we take as scapegoats. The actual traffic noise is not a bit worse than on those nights in which we are ready for sleep.

As I have said before, there are innumerable possibilities of unfinished situations. The disturber might be a mosquito, and the situation will not be finished until you have killed the insect and disposed of the fear of being bitten; or maybe somebody has offended you and your mind is full of revenge phantasies. An examination, an important interview may await you the next day, and you rather anticipate difficult situations than give yourself a rest. An ungratified sexual urge, a spell of hunger, a feeling of guilt, a wish for reconciliation, a desire to get out of an ugly situation, all such unfinished situations will upset your sleep.

An old proverb says: "A good conscience is a soft pillow." You remember the classical example of insomnia: Lady Macbeth. She tries to persuade herself that the murder situation is finished: "I tell you yet again, Banquo's buried, he cannot come out of his grave. What's done, cannot be undone." But the lady's auto-suggestions are not successful: "What, will these hands never be clean? All the perfumes of Arabia will not sweeten this little hand."

Some time ago I had to treat an officer with a very strict conscience. Every day this man had to deal with a number of problems, and his ambition made him tackle too many different items on the same day. The unfinished problems went with him to bed, with the result that he got insufficient rest and started the next day with fatigue. The fatigue decreased his ability to tackle the next day's problems and a vicious circle started, with the result that every few months he suffered a nervous breakdown that kept him from his work altogether. Once he had grasped the importance of limiting the number of problems and of finishing situations *before* going to bed, he improved rapidly.

The objections to this approach will be: firstly, sleeplessness is very unpleasant and the organism needs rest; thus we cannot afford to waste our precious night-time. Secondly, that my theory applies only to the psychological aspect.

To deal first with the latter objection. I maintain that the physical cause of sleeplessness (illness, pain) falls in the same category as the psychological (e.g. worry). An illness is always an unfinished situation; it is only finished with cure or death. In emergency cases, however, when pain connected with an illness is the disturber, such disturber can be temporarily eliminated by a pain-drowning drug. (No drug kills pain.) The first objection—the unpleasantness of insomnia—will soon be disposed of by a proper approach. Once the patient has grasped its meaning he will become able to recondition himself to direct his energies into the proper biological channels and to turn the unpleasantness of insomnia into a gratifying and productive experience.

If we want to cure insomnia, we have to face a paradoxical situation: we have to give up the will to sleep. Sleep takes place when the Ego is melting; volition is an Ego function and as long as you say: "I want to sleep!" your Ego is functioning and sleep cannot take place. It is a most difficult task to realize that although consciously we are perfectly convinced that we desire sleep and are unhappy if we cannot obtain it, the organism does not want to sleep, as problems have to be attended to, which are more important than sleep.

If, in addition to your wish to sleep, you get annoyed with your inability to sleep, then a very unwholesome situation must arise; the subdued excitement will interfere even more with your sleep; with the undischarged annoyance you have created an additional unfinished situation. If by violent tossing and turning in bed you would at least allow the discharge and expression of excitement! But no! You force yourself to lie still intensely watching (another conscious activity) for the first signs of drowsiness, and in the meantime the excitement keeps on boiling, with the result that you burn up more energy than you would do if you got up and did a spot of work. *Often the attempt to sleep wears people out more than the lack of sleep itself.*

The second step is, instead of getting annoyed with the disturber (be it the barking dog or the thoughts and pictures which invariably will be part and parcel of unfinished situations), to become interested. Do not resist them, but give them all your attention. Listen to the noises around you, or look at the pictures in your mind, and you will soon experience the feeling of drowsiness which is the forerunner of sleep.

Often some forgotten memory, or the solution of a problem, will jump into your mind and will leave you with the feeling of satisfaction and the reward of restful sleep.

Not every situation can be finished, either that very night or ever, yet the realization of this fact helps considerably even in the case of insoluble problems. Then there is always the possibility that the situation may be finished by resigning oneself to the inevitable—to the fact that nothing can be done about it.

The other day I read the definition that insomnia is sleeplessness plus worries. This is correct for the obsessional character, but insomnia affects other types as well. It occurs very frequently in neurasthenia. You all know that worries keep you awake and that a worrier seldom obtains restful sleep. This is no small wonder, as the worrier is characterized by his general inability to finish situations, to take action.

It is a mistaken idea to assume that closing one's eyes induces sleep. Just the opposite is the case. Shutting the eyes does not induce sleep, but sleep induces the closing of the eyes. This is sometimes so intense during a boring lecture, especially on a hot day or late in the evening, that it is hardly possible to keep one's eyes open. People who complain about insomnia will then often be the first to fall asleep.

The dream is a compromise between sleep and the incomplete situation. One finds, for instance, that a person who wets his bed, always completes his urge to urinate by the dream of being in a lavatory. In this case, at least, I am convinced you will not defend sleep at any price. On the contrary, the obstacle in the cure of bed-wetting is the child's reluctance to interrupt its sleep. With a bit more insomnia, much suffering could be spared for both parents and child.

XIV

STAMMERING

All people stammer. Of course, few will realize this, and often enough the stammering will be so slight as to pass unnoticed. Even the gushing society lady who spills her meaningless words and phrases all over the show, drowning one in a powerful stream of trivialities—even she might sometimes become stunned, flabbergasted, lost for an expression and might then begin to stutter. You all know the speaker who hesitates, searching for an expression, and fills the gaps of time with his "Er—er," or by stammering.

Stammering is another variation of the theme: inadequate self-expression. We find occasional stammering through embarrassment and self-consciousness. The same person who spoke fluently to you a few minutes ago in an animated conversation will stammer piteously when called upon to make a public speech. Therefore what will be said about the chronic stammerer will apply, to a lesser degree, to all those whose speech is impeded only in certain situations.

The chronic stammerer is characterized by his impatience, undeveloped sense of time and by his inhibited aggression. His words do not flow in a properly timed sequence; he has his mind and mouth crowded with a heap of words all waiting to come out at once. This is the exact counterfeit of his greediness, of his desire to swallow everything at once. In every stammerer one finds, as the remainder of this greediness, a tendency to inhale whilst speaking, thus betraying his inclination to swallow again even his own words. The stammerer will always use his teeth insufficiently; his aggression, deprived of its natural function, will search for queer outlets. Often the stammerer can produce a difficult word after he had a short outburst of violent aggression. He might, for instance, hit one hand hard with the other or violently grind his teeth, or stamp with his foot. This sort of aggression has the same brand of impatience which is the main characteristic of his stammering. The picture changes completely, however, when he flies into a violent temper. As soon as he is ready to give vent to his aggression, he suddenly finds he has the means at his disposal, and he shouts and swears fluently without a trace of stammering.

There is another condition where he can, likewise, be free of stammering: when his language does not express any emotion, or when the motor of excitement is completely absent, he can correctly perform the task of reproducing words which either do not mean anything to him, or else are not the expression of his real self. He might master the technique of word production to perfection, for example, in elocution or singing, as long as he is concentrated on the technical side of speaking and not on the content. But as soon as he has to express himself, he will get impatient again and the more excited he gets, the worse his stammering will become —except for those few occasions on which he allows himself to explode.

The treatment of stammering which disregards the reorganization of aggression and impatience can, in the best of cases, only result in producing a robot uttering words, but never a personality capable of expressing himself and his emotions. Thus for the cure of stammering it is absolutely necessary first to adjust the aggression and to attend to the exercises of the chapter "Concentration on Eating," especially the one referring to the emptying of the mouth after every bite.

The elocutional aspect, however, must not be neglected. There the stammerer must, in the beginning, be satisfied with producing sentences in an artificial technique, before he attempts to express his "Self." He also must learn—and this is most important—to distinguish between "training situation" and "real situation." The overlooking of this distinction has wrecked the attempts of many a pupil. He must be disappointed over and over again, as long as he does not appreciate the importance of the "situation." Disappointment leads to despondency and throwing overboard all those things already achieved. The stammerer will save himself from disappointment, if he does not expect too much. In the beginning a proper speaking can only be obtained in the "training" situation and he must not expect improvement in any "real" situation until he has overcome his hanging-on attitude. Otherwise he can only transfer the "training" situation to the "real" situation by desensitizing his personality—by losing his "soul," by becoming a mummy.

To avoid such danger, he must prevent his excitement from turning into anxiety. In an earlier chapter we have seen that anxiety is excitement with insufficient supply of oxygen. The stammerer always gets into difficulties with his breathing. He is not aware of the mix-up between his inhaling and exhaling, he is not aware of proper economical breathing. It sounds silly and banal to state that the real stammerer is not aware of the fact that one speaks whilst exhaling, that he must become "breathing conscious." Apart from the specific treatment of anxiety, described in the next chapter, I advise the stammerer to do the following graduated exercises:

(1) Inhale and exhale without any interference or action but be aware and distinguish between intake and outlet. There must be no strain or exaggeration. Simply lie down and concentrate on the "feel"

of your breathing. Resist any inclination to change anything. Continue till—without interfering or mind wandering—you can remain breathing conscious for a couple of minutes.

(2) Inhale normally and exhale with the sound of "M-N-S" till this becomes natural. The exhaling should be a kind of collapse, similar to sighing or moaning.

(3) Take any sentence you like and inhale after each syllable like this:
   "The (inhale) rose (inhale) that (inhale) lives (inhale) its/little/hour/is/praised/be/yond/the/sculp/tured/flower."

(4) Repeat this exercise in your phantasy whenever you have an opportunity. The main thing is to inhale between each syllable. If you can do this for five minutes you have taken the most important step towards proper breathing and conquering impatience.

(5) Only after you have fully mastered the previous exercise do the same exercises (3 and 4) with complete words instead of syllables.

(6) The next exercise requires a little thinking. Cut all your sentences into small, grammatically correct groups. For instance:
   "It is easier (inhale) to pretend (inhale) to be (inhale) what you are not (inhale) than to hide (inhale) what you really are (inhale) but he (inhale) that can accomplish both (inhale) has little to learn (inhale) in hypocrisy."

(7) Talk to people in your phantasy, applying the preceding technique. Do this at first silently, then with a whispering, soundless voice. After that add more and more sound to your speaking.

(8) Learn to streamline your voice. Train yourself to speak every word with a crescendo and decrescendo. You cannot overestimate the importance of this exercise. Tackle those words which provide the greatest difficulties, for instance those which begin with a "P." Take a deep breath, relax your mouth and throat muscles, and speak the "P" as softly as possible, but accentuate—with a crescendo—the following vowel.

(9) Transfer tentatively the training situation to the real one, take a friend who has patience and is willing to assist you, ask him to stop you every time you fall back into incorrect breathing.

(10) Search in your phantasy for situations of excitement, embarrassment or self-consciousness, and apply exercise (7) again.

(11) Train yourself in not-speaking. Develop the art of listening. Rather swallow other people's words than your own. Above all, remember: any recurrence of stammering must be a danger signal to you, warning you to stop and relax. Remember, there are few situations in life where it is absolutely compulsory to say something.

(12) After you have learnt to keep silent and to listen, prepare to attain the art of internal silence. Paradoxical as it sounds, you will learn

proper talking by proper silence. The exercises on body concentration are likewise of great importance; find out which muscles you contract (jaw, throat, or diaphragm), not only when you keep silent (chronic contraction), but also in the speaking situation itself. The aim is to learn how stammering is produced. Once a fully conscious control of the production of stammering is obtained in every detail, speaking without stammering is easily learned. How few stammerers, however, will be willing to stammer consciously, to give up their hostility towards it and cease fighting against it. How few will be willing to take full responsibility for their stammering!

(13) Once this responsibility is accepted the sense of the stammering will often reveal itself. The purpose may be to gain time, in order to hide the primary self-consciousness, or, as in the following case of my experience, to conceal hidden sadistic pleasure.

The analysis of a young stammerer revealed that he had an elder brother who stammered badly. Our patient suffered agony when he had to listen to him. As he was a very impatient character his suspense, his tension when listening was more intense than in other people. Later on, he introjected the brother's stammering and this became the "means whereby" to torture people around him, just as he had experienced torture through his brother's stammering. At the same time he could plead innocence by pushing the responsibility on to a physical disability.

If you are a stutterer, what do you achieve with this symptom of yours?

XV

THE ANXIETY STATE

Among the many symptoms of inhibited expression the anxiety attack deserves a special discussion. No other symptom demonstrates the need for adequate discharge of bottled-up energy as convincingly as does the anxiety attack, and even more so the anxiety neurosis (habitual anxiety reaction).

It is comparatively easy to understand the dynamics of anxiety and to regain control of the specific muscular contractions, provided two points are kept in mind. Firstly, the excitement which underlies the anxiety attack must be given free range. Fortunately, if you dislike making an exhibition of yourself, you can achieve a sufficient discharge on your own. But you must not mind to be insane for half an hour, if you are one of those people who regard every emotional outburst as the very symptom of insanity. Although it is a great relief to have a good cry in the arms of a beloved, you can cry alone in your own room. You might pull faces in front of a mirror or, becoming stark raving mad, punch a pillow till you are exhausted. As a second step you have to transform the chest armour into a living part of the whole organism: you have to reconstruct your breathing.

Whilst Freudism has examined the implications of the sex instinct, Adler those of the inferiority feeling, Horney of the need for affection, Reich of the muscular resistance, and myself those of the hunger instinct, the psycho-analysis of breathing has still to be done. Shallowness and sighing in depression, and chronic yawning in boredom are nearly as well known as the fight for breath in the anxiety state. I have shown that this fight for breath is the result of a conflict between the organismic need for oxygen and the rigidity of the chest. The muscles which tend to expand the chest are unconsciously counteracted by those which narrow the chest. By giving in to this narrowing we can relieve the anxiety attack already at a time before the complete conscious control has been obtained. We have only to abstain from the over-compensation, from "taking a deep breath." This deep breathing—the "big chest"—is a misunderstood ideal, a fetish of our society. The following analogy will illustrate what I mean: if you want to wash your hands and you find the basin half filled with dirty water, you would not pour clean water into the dirty, but you would first empty the basin completely of its dirty contents. Exactly the same fastidiousness should apply to breathing.

In the state of excitement or anxiety the oxygen metabolism is increased, therefore the residual air (the not exhaled rest) contains more CO_2 (carbon dioxide) than normally. This bad air has first to be eliminated before the (oxygen containing) fresh air can make sufficient contact with the alveolae of the lungs. Increased inhalation therefore is useless. The conclusion is evident: exhale first as thoroughly as possible. The following inhaling will come without an effort; it will be the deeply welcomed relief for which you were longing.

A frequent complication of anxiety is the projection of both the chest's narrowness and the organism's oxygen-hunger. This complication is called "claustrophobia." The oxygen hunger is experienced as desire for open air, the armour of the chest as the inability to remain in confined spaces. One of my patients, an air mechanic, whenever he got excited could not even stay in an aeroplane hangar, although there could be no lack of oxygen supply.

Orthodox psycho-analysis interprets confined spaces as symbols of the womb or vagina. Such an interpretation is correct in certain cases, but contributes little to the cure of claustrophobia. There one has:

(1) to interpret the projection of the armour;
(2) to realize the specific contraction of the chest muscles (armour);
(3) to dissolve the rigidity of the armour (providing an adequate oxygen supply);
(4) to express the bottled-up excitement.

XVI

DR. JEKYLL AND MR. HYDE

If you have succeeded in reading through all the exercises described in this book, you must feel confused and undecided what to do. There seems such a tremendous task lying ahead of you that you might not dare to tackle it at all.

But don't be discouraged! Every one of the exercises can be taken as a starting point, and every one gives you a chance to achieve concentration. When you are able to concentrate throughout one exercise, the others will provide no difficulty.

By calling the technique outlined in this book concentration-therapy, I mean to convey two facts:

(1) Concentration is the most effective "means whereby" neurotic and paranoid disturbance can be cured. The "endgain" is a negative one: destruction of a disturbance.

(2) Concentration is also an "endgain" in itself. It is a positive attitude which is coupled with the feeling of health and well-being. It is the symptom par excellence of a sound holism.

The art of concentration supplies you with an important tool for the development of your personality; but tools, if not applied as such, cease to be tools. Likewise a tool which is not adequate to its task is not a tool at all.[1] Therefore it is necessary to recognize the importance, structure and application of concentration. As we have dealt sufficiently with its importance and structure, I have only to say a few words about the application. As we are concerned with remedying shortcomings of the personality, we have to focus our concentration on the "means whereby" the psychological disturbances are produced.

In Russia, if a weak link in the rebuilding of the nation has become apparent, the whole country—the officials and the population, the newspapers and the radio, the scientists and the workers—concentrate on the elimination of the bottleneck. There, in mutual identification, everybody's interest is invested in mastering the common enemy. The weak point is thus annihilated, not by repression or destruction, nor by idealistic demands, but by analysis and reorganization. In warfare, too, concen-

[1] A pair of household scissors used for cutting a piece of paper is a tool. If you use it for cutting a piece of steel, it becomes a ridicule.

tration plays a decisive part; this has been recognized by strategists of all time. The amount of concentration required is, of course, relative: the weaker the resistance, the less troops and supplies have to be concentrated on the attack.

The human organism effects similarly varying degrees of concentration. Little conscious effort is required to concentrate on weak spots—like a painful illness or obsessional thoughts; they even *attract* attention. On the other hand, there are the powerful "holoids" which have to be brought out of the darkness of their autonomous existence into the limelight of consciousness.

These "holoids" are sub-divisions of the human personality and are characterized by a very stubborn conservative tendency—a tendency which we take for granted and justify as "force of habit," "character," "constitution," etc. The "holoids" do not change of their own accord, and they cannot be reorganized without conscious concentration. Without this reorganization, no reconstruction of the personality can be achieved.

The organismic "holoids" are known under different names: behaviouristic reactions, character features, complexes, "means whereby." This last expression (by F. M. Alexander) is especially useful, as it conveys the meaning of a tool. In *Constructive Conscious Control of the Individual*, Alexander brings clearly home the need for sensory appreciation, for the awareness of the "means whereby," for their analysis and change which are indispensable for the desired change of the "endgain." In his disapproval of psycho-analysis, however, Alexander oversteps the mark when he condemns the treatment of psychological "holoids," e.g. obsessions and complexes. The fact remains that Freud and Alexander independently discovered the need for detailed analysis and complete consciousness of the "holoids."

Both methods concentrate on the "means whereby"—on the details of the procedure. The endgain or purpose is suppressed or forgotten. With Alexander's method this is an intrinsic part, in Freudism a by-product of the concentration on the actual procedure of analysis. This one-sided orientation is ultimately as little successful as previously the one-sided concentration on the endgain, e.g. on the change of habits by resolution, or suggestion, or on the change of character features by punishment.

In psycho-analysis one often makes the following observation: as long as the patient is interested exclusively in his cure and talks about nothing else, he makes very little headway. The situation changes only if he becomes interested in the process of being analysed and if he forgets the "endgain," the cure. But in spite of the apparent concentration on the analytical procedure and in spite of continuous minor improvements, the analysis goes on endlessly without achieving a fundamental change. In the complete concentration of his interest in the *treatment* the patient has forgotten—repressed—his wish to be *cured*. By permanently searching for *causes*, the *purpose* of the treatment is obliterated: the psycho-analysis becomes a mere dummy-activity.

Alexander, while correctly stressing the decisive importance of re-conditioning the "means whereby," mis-applies the term "forgetting." What he means is not forgetting, but a temporary pushing aside of the "endgain," the cultivation of the ability to postpone (Freud's "sense of reality"). The golfer, who only concentrates on the "means whereby"— e.g. on how to hold his club or how to turn his wrist—if he forgets entirely the *aim* of his endeavours, will either lose interest and stop playing golf altogether, or become involved in a purely obsessional and meaningless dummy-activity.

If you are studying music, of course you will not become a musician by merely striving for the "endgain": to be a great artist; at best you will remain a talented amateur. On the other hand, if you concentrate purely on the "means whereby"—the technique—and you forget entirely about the "endgain"—the appreciation, reproduction and, perhaps, even composition of music—your practising will become mechanical and meaningless. In the best case you might become a "virtuoso," but not an artist.

The "endgain" must not be forgotten. It must remain in the field of consciousness. It must stay in the background, but guarding and planning the different "means whereby," which are temporarily in the foreground. Under no condition must the "means whereby" become isolated and lose their sense as means to an end.

When once upon a time you learned to write, you had only to attend to the "means whereby," to the reproduction of letters. The planning, the attention to the "endgain," was the teacher's task. But when you are grown up you have not always a teacher at your disposal, and if you intend making use of the exercises of this book you have to keep the inter-dependency of aim and technique in your mind. You have to find out "how" you react in detail (the structure of the "means whereby"); to realize these details you must feel them (sensory appreciation). If during this process you "forget" the endgain, you will condition yourself to a flight of ideas or actions. Such forgetting of aims (aimless talking or doing) is a symptom of insanity. Now you will appreciate that the difference between "forgetting the endgain" and "keeping it in the background" is not a quibbling over words, but entails a decisive difference of meaning.

The "endgain" is originally identical with the biological figure-back-ground formation (see Part I, Chapters III and IV). The organism uses the tools—the "means whereby" at its disposal, and if they have become inadequate develops new ones. The baby's striving for the endgain— food—entails simple "means whereby": crying and the hanging-on bite.

The adult, to secure his sustenance, has to deal with innumerable "means whereby," of which the earning of his livelihood is but one.

In most cases the "endgain" and the "means whereby" it is obtained, have been welded into one psycho-physical unit. As long as this unit is working satisfactorily, the organism does not experience the need for revising a process which feels familiar or "right." But such satisfactory working can be deceptive; I have given many examples of this. If you cannot fall asleep, your means whereby to induce sleep are drugs or the determination to sleep, whilst actually the insomnia itself is a "means whereby" for the "endgain": conclusion of unfinished situations.

We realize that a house cannot be built without the material required; we understand that the organism in its striving for gratification develops the instruments whereby the satisfaction can be achieved; in all these cases we accept easily that the "means whereby" and the "endgain" are parts of one whole. But to this rule there is at least one exception where the "means whereby" are either neglected or applied in an anti-biological manner: idealism, which is an attitude apparently concentrated entirely on the endgain. I say apparently, because as soon as one examines more closely the individual cases of idealism, one finds the ideals themselves to be the means whereby the need for affection, appreciation and admiration is being gratified. Even if the bearer of high ideals maintains that he is striving for perfection for its own sake, he is usually mistaken; he wants to be in God's good books, or he gratifies his vanity by picturing himself as perfect.

He is incapable of accepting himself as he is, because he has lost the "feel of himself" and with that the drive for biological endgains. Having lost the awareness of his biological being he must invent a "meaning of life" to justify his existence. These invented aims, called ideals—unconnected with his biological reality—float in the air, and any endeavour to realize them will leave him with a feeling of inferiority, impotency and even despair. Those biological aims which either are not yet or cannot be repressed are, at the same time, experienced as interfering with his ideals and are fought to the point of exhaustion. Result: nervous breakdowns and impulsive explosions.

Parents, by upholding impossible standards of behaviour, turn the life of their children into hell. They make the fundamental mistake of striving for perfection instead of for development. With their idealistic, ambitious attitude they achieve the opposite of their intentions; they arrest the development, spread confusion and promote inferiority feelings.

There is a famous book which shows the catastrophic results of idealism clearly enough, if you only understand it correctly: the story of Dr. Jekyll and Mr. Hyde. Dr. Jekyll represents an ideal, not a human being. He is an unselfish benefactor of mankind, loyal in spite of frustrations, and chaste in the face of strong instincts. To materialize his ideal he uses the

EGO, HUNGER AND AGGRESSION

"means whereby" of repression; he represses his animalistic existence; he hides in Mr. Hyde the jackal (Jekyll). The human being has been differentiated into the opposites "angel" and "devil," the one praised and welcome, the other detested and repulsed; but the one can as little exist without the other as can light without its shadow.

Isolationist, wishful thinking does not like such truth. Yet idealism and religion—by trying to achieve the impossible, to produce Dr. Jekylls from human organisms—simultaneously create their opposites: millions of Mr. Hydes. Without accepting their biological "reality," "idealistic" Dr. Jekyll and "materialistic" Mr. Hyde will go on existing till mankind has finally destroyed itself.

An *individual* might be cured of opium addiction, he might even be cured of his mental opium, of idealism. However, will *mankind* ever realize that an ideal is only a beautiful mirage, but incapable to provide the real camel with the real water for the real march through the real desert?

Index of Names

273

ABOUT THE AUTHOR

F. S. PERLS, M.D., Ph.D., was born in 1893 in Berlin and left Germany when Hitler came to power. He founded the South African Institute for Psychoanalysis in Johannesburg. After the death of Jan Smuts and the advent of apartheid in South Africa, Perls emigrated to the United States. He is now living in Big Sur, California, where he is an associate at the Esalen Institute, which its founders describe as a "center to explore trends in behavioral sciences, religion and philosophy which emphasize the potentialities of human existence."

Dr. Perls is the founder of the gestalt school of psychotherapy and is also the author, with Paul Goodman and Ralph Heferline, of *Gestalt Therapy*.

VINTAGE WORKS OF SCIENCE
AND PSYCHOLOGY

A free catalogue of VINTAGE BOOKS *will be sent at your request. Write to* Vintage Books, 457 Madison Avenue, New York, New York 10022.

VINTAGE POLITICAL SCIENCE
AND SOCIAL CRITICISM

A free catalogue of VINTAGE BOOKS *will be sent at your request. Write*
to Vintage Books, 457 Madison Avenue, New York, New York 10022.

VINTAGE HISTORY AND CRITICISM OF LITERATURE, MUSIC, AND ART

A free catalogue of VINTAGE BOOKS *will be sent at your request. Write to* Vintage Books, 457 Madison Avenue, New York, New York 10022.

VINTAGE BELLES-LETTRES

A free catalogue of VINTAGE BOOKS *will be sent at your request. Write to* Vintage Books, 457 Madison Avenue, New York, New York 10022.